America
Strikes
Back

America
Strikes
Back

STEVE BROWN

Chick Springs Publishing
Taylors, South Carolina

First published in the USA in 2001 by
Chick Springs Publishing
P.O. Box 1130, Taylors, SC 29687
e-mail: ChickSprgs@aol.com
web site: www.chicksprings.com

Library of Congress Control Number:
2001132998
Library of Congress Data Available

ISBN: 0-9670273-9-X

10   9   8   7   6   5   4   3   2   1

Author's Note

This is a work of fiction based on
extensive research about a momentous period in
our country's history. The conclusions drawn and
the particular areas covered were my decision
and no one else's. The veterans who were
kind enough to sign off on the story agree
this is how they remembered life
during the Second World War.

Acknowledgments

My thanks to the reading group: Missy Johnson, Ellen Smith, Kate Lehman, Elsie Finkelstein, Bill Jenkins, Dwight Watt, and, of course, Mary Ella.

Additional expertise was furnished by:

Robert S. Kronberger, National President, Pearl Harbor Survivors Association (USS West Virginia), and service on USS Enterprise at Wake Island, the Doolittle Raid, Battle of Midway, and landings at Guadalcanal.

Gene Keller, Sr., Pfc. C Co., 1st Pioneer Btn., First Marine Division and current Curator of the Guadalcanal Memorial Museum.

Vincent L. Anderson, US Marine aboard USS Lexington at Coral Sea and current historian, USS Lexington CV-2.

Doris M. Sterner, Capt., NC US Navy (Ret.) and author of *In and Out of Harm's Way*, the history of the Navy Nurse Corps.

Gordon W. Morgan, Past President, 1st Marine Division Association.

Gerry Schwartz, Professor of History, Western Carolina University.

Gregory Salmers, Librarian, Estevan, SK, SSR Webmaster.

C.P. (Pat) Weiland, Lt. Col., US Marine Corps (Ret.) and member of the Cactus Air Force.

Jack Brookshire, Staff Sgt., 1st Pioneer Battalion (combat engineers) serving on Guadalcanal.

Peter Roumelis, Sgt., HQ Co., 21st Marines, Third Division on Guadalcanal.

Ray F. Zuker, B-24 and B-17 pilot.

Thomas W. Reese, EMC, USN (Ret.).

Mark J. Brown, Lt. Col. USAF (Ret.).

George Nennstiel, 95th Squadron, 17th Bomber Group.

Wesley J. Rutledge, Jr., 1st Lt., Air Corps, Troop Commander.

C.B. Squire, volunteer ambulance driver, American Field Service, with the British in North Africa and Europe.

Former members of the South Saskatchewan Regiment:

W.M. (Bill) Sutherland, Pvt., 3 Platoon (Mortars), Support Coy, 2nd Canadian Infantry Division.

F.P. (Hank) Forness, Capt. (Ret.), 2nd Canadian Infantry Division

Paul Delorme, Pvt., 2nd Canadian Infantry Division.

Cast of Characters

In Europe:

McKenzie Rivers: Photojournalist
James Stuart: Major, armor, US Army
Antonio Petrocelli: Sergeant, armor, US Army
Sonya Molotov: Russian partisan
Anastasia or "Annie": Russian orphan
Wolfgang Topp: member of the *Ubootwaffe*
Harry Hopkins: Aide to President Franklin D. Roosevelt
Dwight D. Eisenhower: Supreme Commander, Allied Forces, Europe

In the Pacific:

Katie O'Kelly: Navy Nurse Corps
Nicky Lamm: Lieutenant, Army Air Corps
Vivian Riley: Nurse, US Army
Mason Monroe: Lt. Commander, Pilot, US Navy
Cleve Woodruff: Rifleman, First Marine Division
Harvey Meadors: Rifleman, First Marine Division
Frank Jack Fletcher: Admiral, US carrier task force
Alexander Archer Vandegrift: Major General, Commander, First Marine Division
Richmond Kelly Turner: Admiral, Commander, Amphibious Forces in the Pacific
Ernest J. King: Admiral, Commander in Chief, US Fleet and Chief of Naval Operations
Douglas MacArthur: General, Southwest Pacific Commander

The Japanese:

Mitsuo Fuchida: Commander of air groups, First Air Fleet
Chuichi Nagumo: Admiral, Commander of the Japanese carrier strike force
Isoroku Yamamoto: Admiral, Commander in Chief of the Japanese Combined Fleet

This book is dedicated to those who survived,
and those who did not survive, the Bataan Death March.

"Do you want to live forever?"
~U.S. Marine Dan Daly
at Belleau Wood

PROLOGUE

When "Bull" Halsey, commander of the USS *Enterprise*, sailed into Pearl Harbor and saw the damage inflicted by the Japanese on the American fleet, he snarled, "Before we're through with them, the Japanese language will only be spoken in hell." Halsey carried that attitude with him when he met with his new superior, Chester Nimitz, the successor to Kimmel and the new commander of the Pacific Fleet.

Nimitz had an outlet for Halsey's rage. "President Roosevelt wants to lift the country's morale and hit Tokyo. King and Arnold are aboard." He meant the Commander of the US Fleet and Chief of the Army Air Corps, respectively. "The president thinks such an attack will strike a psychological blow to the Japanese."

"Sounds good to me," said Halsey, "but no land-based bomber can reach Japan."

"Bill, we're going to use B-25 Mitchell medium bombers and launch them from an aircraft carrier. Jimmy

Doolittle has volunteered to lead the raid. We've had practice drills off the *Hornet*. Her decks are wide enough to house the Mitchells and she can steam at nearly twenty-five knots. Are you willing to take them out?"

"Yes, sir, I am."

"Good! Then it's all yours."

Halsey conferred with Doolittle and they agreed that whatever carrier was used, the ship should try to get within four hundred miles of Japan before launching the Mitchells. Running interference for the *Hornet* would be another carrier, *Enterprise*, with some destroyers and cruisers making up the remainder of the task force.

"You know, Jimmy, you won't be able to return to the *Hornet*," Halsey said.

Doolittle nodded grimly. A daredevil pilot with a doctorate from MIT, Doolittle was accustomed to overcoming obstacles: recruiting men without being able to tell them about the mission, and handling the skeptics who didn't understand that with a decent wind across the deck, a Mitchell could take off from an abbreviated runway. The real problem had been finding and training personnel who could yank a B-25 off a carrier at near stalling speed, against all instincts and training.

The Japanese believed their island invincible, and history reinforced this illusion. In the fifteenth century, Japan had been saved from invasion when the Chinese fleet was destroyed by a gigantic monsoon. From that moment on the Japanese believed they were protected by a "divine wind" called the *kamikaze*.

But Admiral Yamamoto, who hatched the plan to destroy the American fleet at Pearl Harbor, left nothing to chance. He established a line of picket boats as far as seven hundred miles out. Yamamoto guaranteed no plane would ever bomb the Japanese home islands.

Four months after the attack on Pearl, a lookout on a picket boat sighted planes approaching his position. The sailor went inside to wake his skipper.

"Planes above, sir."

His captain wasn't interested. No enemy could be this close to Tokyo, so he remained in his bunk.

An hour later, the lookout returned. "Two of our beautiful aircraft carriers coming in, sir."

The skipper leaped out of bed and hustled topside. Through binoculars snatched from the hands of the lookout, he watched the approaching ships.

The color drained from his face. "Yes. They're quite beautiful. But they're not ours." He went below and shot himself.

That had been the second boat to sight the task force, so Admiral Halsey assumed the element of surprise had been lost. The Mitchells would have to launch now and fly a hundred fifty miles farther than previously planned. Halsey flashed the following to the *Hornet:*

LAUNCH PLANES

Then:

TO COL. DOOLITTLE AND GALLANT COMMAND
GOOD LUCK AND GOD BLESS

The *Hornet* was rolling heavily, water breaking over the carrier ramps. As she turned into the wind, Jimmy Doolittle shook hands with the *Hornet's* captain, grabbed his bag, and ran for his plane. The klaxon sounded and Captain Marc Mitscher's voice came over the PA system with an order not often heard on naval vessels.

"Now hear this: Army pilots. Man your planes!"

Pilots jammed belongings into bags, bags into planes, and hopped in after them. Sailors removed engine covers and unfastened lines holding the Mitchells to the deck; a naval "donkey" pushed and pulled the B-25s into position. Gasoline tanks were topped off; then the Mitchells were rocked back and forth to get the bubbles out so more fuel could be added. Sailors passed extra cans of gas through rear hatches.

During all this preflight activity, Doolittle warmed up his engine. His plane would be the first to take off. Now he gave the thumbs-up to the deck officer. As the chocks were pulled from under the wheels, the launching officer waved his checkered flag in circles, the signal for Doolittle to push the throttles forward to the stops. Nice timing, or Jimmy Doolittle was every bit the aviator the army said he was.

The deck had dipped. Now it began to rise with another swell. Following lines painted on the deck to keep the Mitchells from hitting the carrier island, Doolittle took off—with feet to spare and every man on the *Hornet* willing the plane into the air. The rest of the squadron followed, racing down the deck far too fast, then pulling the Mitchells up to hang by their noses for a very long moment before righting their aircraft and roaring away.

In Tokyo, the Japanese were completing yet another air-raid drill when the first American planes roared over the city at treetop level, then climbed into the sky to avoid the blast from their own five-hundred-pound bombs. Many of the bombs dropped that day had messages scribbled on the side, such as: "I don't want to set the world on fire, just Tokyo."

The Americans sped away unmolested, and as they did, noticed people in the crowded lunchtime streets waving to them. Even Prime Minister Tojo, up for a midday flight, met the Mitchells as they flew toward the Home Islands, as did several patrol planes, which failed to report the intrusion. The Americans were also fortunate in that the silver barrage balloons, protecting the city from just such an attack, had been lowered for the air-raid drill.

Minutes later, the remaining bombers appeared and were met by heavy but inaccurate antiaircraft fire. Because the Mitchells were striking eight different points, the Japanese were completely confused. Only a handful of Zeros rose to intercept them and they shot down no one. The Mitchells themselves inflicted little damage—unless you credit the Doolittle raid for four Japanese divisions being recalled for the defense of the Home Islands.

Of the sixteen planes, thirteen reached China, and with their fuel exhausted, they either crash-landed or were abandoned in flight. It was nighttime and the

Chinese either were not expecting them or thought the planes were Japanese, and for that reason extinguished the ground landing lights. A Mitchell reached the USSR with serious fuel problems, where the crew was interned by the astonished Russians. Two crews were captured by the Japanese in China, found guilty, and sentenced to death. Five of these Americans were condemned to life imprisonment, one died in captivity. Three others were shot, as it was deemed their bombing run had killed schoolchildren.

In all, seventy-one of the eighty American airmen survived the raid. Doolittle returned to Washington to be awarded the Medal of Honor by the president. The Japanese occupiers, convinced the Chinese had played an active role in the attack, executed over a quarter million Chinese, more than had been slaughtered by the Japanese army during the Rape of Nanking.

A cheerful FDR met the press corps to announce the raid. When asked where the planes had come from, the president smiled and said, "Shangri-la," referring to the mythical Tibetan land in the best-selling novel by James Hilton.

ONE

Nicky Lamm looked down the trench at his fellow soldiers, or rather skeletons. Shreds of khaki that had once been uniforms hung on them. No one was dressing very well these days on the "Rock" called Corregidor, the fortress island guarding the entrance to Manila Bay in the Philippines.

To Nicky this was the Bataan Peninsula all over again. On Bataan, the defenders had reached the point where the men hardly moved. A glance at a fellow soldier showed your own reflection: bloodshot eyes in burned-out sockets, and a pale, shrunken face mounted on a skeletal body. And the goddamn Japs taunted them from across no-man's-land with loudspeakers, saying *their* relief unit had arrived and there were hundreds of tanks and thousands of infantry-men forming up for a final push.

First, Nip aircraft would bomb hell out of them, and then Jap helmets would appear over fallen timbers, sunlight glinting off their bayonets, and finally camouflaged bodies would rush out of the rain forest and across no-man's-land. Hundreds of sweaty, dirt-smeared Japanese would charge, cursing, growling like animals, and tossing huge firecrackers. On and on they would come.

Nicky Lamm had celebrated the arrival of 1942 as part of a column extending for miles from the Philippine capital to the peninsula of Bataan. Sometimes the line slowed, but with the Japanese pressing from the rear, the grinding and clanking of military and civilian vehicles never completely stopped, unless strafed by Zeros. Then everyone but the wounded took to the rain forest. If the Japanese had blown a couple of bridges, the refugees would have been trapped and slaughtered along the road. The Japanese general, however, had more important things on his mind, such as his triumphant entrance into the city of Manila.

Settling in on Bataan, the Americans and their Filipino allies, along with thousands of civilians, found their new home overrun by monkeys, snakes, and wild pigs, and so infested with mosquitoes it was almost unlivable. Pythons and coral snakes roamed the peninsula with impunity, but no one could shoot them without giving away his position. The air was hot and humid and filled with dust. At night, a breeze off the Pacific found its way over the mountains. Both Americans and Japanese welcomed the relief.

The overwhelming numbers of Japanese had forced Douglas MacArthur to pull his forces onto the peninsula, set up a line of defense, and pray he could hold on until Washington sent relief. The plan should have worked, but though supply depots were full of ammo, there wasn't enough food or medicine. Now, with more than a hundred thousand Filipino soldiers, refugees, and Americans holed up on the peninsula, MacArthur cut rations in half. Several months later, they were cut again.

When Nicky heard the Americans on Bataan were to surrender, he leaned back in his trench and stared into the wild blue yonder. He was supposed to be up *there*, not mucking around in a hole with wet feet, clothing in tatters, and suffering from diseases he'd never heard of. Didn't he have more to offer his country than to end up as a prisoner for the duration of the war?

The sky was blue, broken only by the occasional drifting cloud, so close it seemed you could reach out and touch it. When Nicky reached for the freedom of the sky, a shot rang out from the other side of no-man's-land, and the bullet whistled by close enough for Nicky to feel the breeze at his wrist.

"Lamm, are you nuts?" His fellow soldier wore his steel pot with a "V" scratched on it. The "V" wasn't for victory, but for victim.

Nicky jerked down his hand.

Was he losing his mind? If so, what else did he have to lose? Certainly the opportunity to soar through the sky was slowly slipping away.

He'd heard reports of boats sneaking over to the island fortress of Corregidor where MacArthur and his staff were hiding out. Perhaps he could catch a ride.

Perhaps on Corregidor the Americans could hold out until their relief unit arrived.

In Manila, General Masaharu Homma had an entirely different opinion of MacArthur's effective double-retrograde movement that had allowed the Americans and their allies to slip away to Bataan. The battle for the Philippines was to have been fought on the streets of Manila, not on the slopes of Bataan. True, the conquest of the islands was in sight, but the army might never regain the momentum needed to seize Australia.

MacArthur's plight was the subject of an exercise that George Marshall, army chief of staff, gave Dwight D. Eisenhower at their first meeting. For years, generals had fought over this rising star, using Ike for planning and preparing but never executing those strategies. There was something else: Eisenhower had served with MacArthur in the Philippines.

By December of 1941, Dwight David Eisenhower had become completely bald, but was trim and fit from the Louisiana Maneuvers. He wore a first star on his shoulder, spoke with authority, and ticked off points using his fingers. At that meeting with Marshall, the chief of staff fixed Ike with his cold blue stare and outlined the state of affairs in the Far East, then asked, "What should our general line of action be?"

Eisenhower asked for a couple of hours to consider the question. Very quickly he was shown into an office where he hunted and pecked on a borrowed typewriter. Ike returned to report that the Philippines were lost and it would be best to fall back to Australia, that the navy, devastated by the disaster at Pearl Harbor, would not risk the Japanese gauntlet to resupply MacArthur.

Marshall swallowed hard before saying, "Do your best to save them."

Then he ordered the chief of the army air corps to ship pursuit planes to the Philippines to beat off Japanese bomber attacks. The planes arrived, but without solenoids for the wing guns. Stuck to the side of the crates, the solenoids had been discarded by flight crews hustling to get the planes to the Philippines—where it was quickly learned the guns would not fire. Marshall also sent officers to the Far East and Australia to locate anyone who would run the Japanese blockade. They found no takers for the half a million dollars those officers toted from one port to another.

Over the wireless, the Americans on Corregidor heard the Emperor's birthday was coming up. Soon the Japs would be pounding the Rock as if there were no tomorrow. Unfortunately for the Americans, the twelve-inch guns on Corregidor were aimed out to sea to protect Manila, not to bombard anyone who had seized the harbor behind them. Worse, the Japs had a hot-air balloon hovering over a hilltop on Bataan. From there they could pound American positions with impunity, and that's just what they were doing. Hearing about the approaching birthday, Nicky knew what the army's gift to the Emperor would be: Corregidor, the place where he'd taken refuge to wait for the relief column that had never come.

Lamm picked up his Springfield rifle and left the bunker. He had the Springfield by accident, having snatched it off a dead Marine on his way to Bataan. Then, before he had a chance to trade it for the newer M-1, too many soldiers had wanted to trade *their* M-1s for the Springfield, manufactured in 1903. During the retreat to Bataan, Nicky learned when you pulled back the bolt and shoved it forward, a bullet always chambered in the Springfield. That couldn't always be said of the M-1. Proponents of the M-1 thought the cynics were being too tough on the new weapon. After all, every time you fired a Springfield, you had to manipulate the bolt, while the M-1 was self-loading and ejected its empty cartridge.

"Where you headed?" asked the guy Nicky had been playing cards with on the Rock. Cards were about the only diversion on Corregidor until the Japs began their shelling. On those occasions, every soldier knew the exact number of paces to his bunker on this so-called island fortress.

"Going to the hospital. Got to see if they have any quinine left."

His gaunt companion flashed a ghoulish smile. "Tell the truth, Lamm. You're going to see that nurse, and you're going to see her for more than quinine."

Nicky only grunted as he walked away.

Lamm found Vivian Riley treating another bag of bones in one of the many tunnels running through the Rock. Using obsolete equipment and prison labor, the US Army Corps of Engineers had drilled a tunnel wide enough for traffic to pass east to west. A wing in one of the lateral tunnels housed the hospital. Actually, more than one tunnel housed the sick and wounded, and all were filled to capacity.

The first time Nicky had been inside the Rock was to ask a radio operator to see what the RTO could learn about a young woman at Pearl Harbor. Nurse Riley had been amused that Lamm had wanted to know the status of a girl who, Riley later learned, had been hell-bent on committing suicide. Finally, word came through. Katie O'Kelly had been reinstated in the Navy Nurse Corps, and Nicky's friend, Mason Monroe, had been assigned carrier duty, giving the Nips whatever. Vivian Riley was the first person Nicky had confided in that he was thinking about leaving the Rock.

"You'd better have a boat," said Riley. "If you don't, the sharks will get you."

Vivian Riley was one of many young women from stateside military bases who had been seduced by tales of romance and adventure in the South Pacific. Shortly after arriving in the Philippines, she found those stories to be true. Despite being taller than most men and a little on the skinny side, very quickly Riley acquired four eager beaux. The night before the Japanese attack, she had gone with one of those suitors to see Gary Cooper play Sergeant York. Four months later, three were dead; the one she had gone to the movies with was listed as missing in action.

"Nicky, Nicky," said Riley, taking his face in her hands, "don't do this. Reinforcements are on the way." Riley had once looked like the Iowa farm girl she had been. Now any freckles stood in sharp contrast to her pale face and the dark circles under her eyes.

Lamm shrugged out of her embrace. "Our fleet is at the bottom of Pearl Harbor, the British fleet is in the same condition in the Java Sea, and the Australians are off fighting in Egypt. Where are these reinforcements coming from?"

"MacArthur said he'd return and I believe him." And Riley reiterated the dangers of crossing the ocean in an open boat, even if Lamm did slip past the Japanese or wasn't picked up by the locals and turned in.

"The Filipinos wouldn't do that."

"Hey," said Riley, with another laugh, "you're the one talking about someplace called Nanking, not me."

"Vivian, I asked you to go with me because I fought side by side on Bataan with a soldier who saw the Japs burn Chinese in Tientsin and rape their women."

"The Japanese are one of the oldest cultures in the world. I dare say we'll be in good hands." Riley looked out to sea. "If MacArthur doesn't return first."

And that's where their conversation usually ended. Still, Nicky would try one last time to convince Riley to leave. Nicky had arrived at Clark Field flush with money from his last temporary duty station. He would use that money to purchase a seat for himself and Riley to get off this rock.

As soon as Lamm entered the ward, Riley knew why he was there. American listening posts had picked up the sounds of mobilization across the bay. Lookouts could see little at night. With everyone on the Rock suffering from a lack of vitamin E, soldiers' ears had to do double duty.

Another nurse worked across the tunnel so Nicky lowered his voice. "It's time, Vivian. Any minute Japanese barges could be landing on Bottomside."

Riley didn't look at him. The tunnel reeked of rotting bodies and death.

"Vivian, please . . . ."

Riley placed a wet cloth on her patient's forehead.

To Nicky, the guy looked as if he wouldn't survive the night. Pale, skinny, eyes sunk back in his head, muscles shrunken from protein loss.

"Sorry," said Riley, after straightening up, "even if we surrender, our men will need nurses. If I go with you, there'll be one less nurse."

"I'll go," said a weary voice from behind him.

"Big Bertha," so nicknamed because of the size of the woman's chest, significantly reduced with rationing, had spoken. Bertha's olive-drab coveralls had holes worn in them and her once long black hair had been cropped short to avoid the time it took to pin it up.

"I'll do anything to get off this damn rock."

"Betty, I've warned you about using such language," said Riley, using the woman's real name. "Besides, you can't leave these men."

Betty shook her head. "When General Wainwright sent those twenty nurses out, I thought I could take it, but then another group left on that sub with all that gold and I'm asking myself: Why not me? Why I got to stay?"

"It's your duty."

"I'm sorry, Vivian, but I can't take it no more."

"Betty, this could get you court-martialed."

Tears began to run down the shorter woman's face. "Vivian, you don't know what it was like on Bataan. They ordered me to leave my patients on the operating tables, pick up whatever I could carry, and get on the boat." She wiped the tears away. "I'll have to live with the memory of those wounded boys calling for me not to leave, the doctors watching me go . . . . Then we get to the dock and the boat has already left. They came back for us. Just in time. The Japs blew that pier to bits when we were halfway to the Rock. You were there, Lieutenant. You remember what it was like."

Nicky remembered a hospital that looked more like a greenhouse than like any stateside facility. On Bataan you never cut the vines or trees that gave a hospital cover. Some patients had beds. They were the lucky ones. Rats hardly bothered a guy in a bed. Neither did the ants.

"You treated me . . . twice," admitted Lamm.

"I'm—I'm sorry," said the emaciated young woman whose chest had formerly been such a subject of admiration. "I—I don't remember . . . everyone."

Nicky did. Every time he'd been wounded, a nurse had been there for him. "Vivian, are you going to cause any trouble if Betty leaves with me tonight?"

Riley shook her head. She had heard rumors of the Japs shelling Santa Barbara, California. What did it matter where someone died? Or was interned for the duration of the war.

"He's my fiancé," said Betty, pointing at the soldier

Riley had been tending. The thin man's eyes watched them from where he lay on a filthy blanket on the rock floor. "He swam over from Bataan to be with me."

"Betty, you're putting Nicky at risk by increasing the size of the escape party."

"Can he make it to the beach?" asked Lamm simply.

The soldier with the pale face and sunken eyes sat up. "Just tell me where and when." He got to his hands and knees, and then stood.

"Pendergrass," said Riley, "you've been malingering."

The soldier stretched uneasily, using the rock wall to stand. "Accommodations are better here. And I could be closer to Betty."

"Nicky, you're nuts if you take these two along. They're not the sort who can be counted on."

Pendergrass snorted. "We counted on MacArthur and where did it get us?"

❊   ❊   ❊

On the other side of the world, American Major James Stuart had his own set of problems. The Russian partisans he and Sergeant Antonio Petrocelli were assigned to had been outmaneuvered. Usually German infantry would fall behind, unable to keep up with the advancing tanks. This time, however, German soldiers had been ferried north of the partisans by those same tanks and dropped off. Now, with the usual contingency of infantrymen falling behind their Panzers, the Russians were trapped between the two forces. Moreover, the partisans had no tank, air, or artillery support.

Worse, the leader of the partisans had been severely wounded. In subzero temperatures any serious wound meant death, at least amputation. So while the War Cabinet in Washington celebrated Doolittle's raid on Japan, Major James Stuart was pinned down in a demolished farmhouse with Russian Colonel Georgio Gorovets. The partisan leader lay on a straw-strewn earthen floor. Gorovets could still use his hands, but his legs had no movement.

"So this is the end for me, my American friend."

"Nonsense," said Stuart, who spoke fluent German and Russian, the reason Harry Hopkins, FDR's chief aide, had selected him for this job.

Would the Soviet Union hold or collapse? With the Allies being pushed back everywhere, Washington had to know. Washington even agreed that the American troops arriving in England could serve under British command if it was determined an immediate cross-channel invasion was the only way to keep the Russians in the War.

It might take that. Only a few months earlier, Goebbels, the Nazis' propaganda minister, had told foreign correspondents in Berlin that "the annihilation of Timoshenko's army (referring to the group responsible for the defense of central Russia and Moscow) has brought the war to a close."

The dark-haired and dark-eyed American major was insistent. "We can return you to the forest." Most of the partisans lived in the great forests of White Russia, and had set up de facto towns and governments there.

The partisan leader shook his head. "I am not worth

the risk because of the seriousness of my injuries."

Gorovets called for his second in command from those huddled in the rubble that had once been a farmhouse. A young man wearing a heavy gray-khaki uniform and snow-powdered felt boots hustled into the ruins. This sudden movement caused a flurry of bullets to slam into slabs of wood or zing off the collapsed stone walls. Ivan Kushnir carried a semiautomatic rifle, and his dark eyes took in this American, who always seemed to be in the company of his commanding officer.

The three men ignored the firing as Gorovets said, "Stuart, my good friend, you have seen people in Leningrad die from lack of food, you have seen the Russian army crushed by the initial thrust of the Nazi onslaught, but you must also tell your masters in Washington that you saw a spark of determination in the Russian people. The partisans are giving the Russian army time to regroup and reorganize."

"And showing them how to win," said the young rifle-carrier who had joined them.

Whenever anyone spoke, the speaker's breath could be seen in the air. The temperature stood at freezing, whether it was measured in Celsius or Fahrenheit.

"Even Stalin fears our autonomy," added Kushnir.

A mortar round fell north of the building, causing everyone to flinch.

Gorovets grasped the tall, slender American's arm. "Tell Washington not to give up on Russia as they did during the last war." The partisan leader released his hold on Stuart's arm. "As we did ourselves." He turned his attention to his subordinate. "Ivan, it now falls to you."

In Gorovets' hand was a pistol. He used it to gesture at the American Stuart. "I know you don't trust this man, but for the sake of our comrades' lives, consider his advice. He attended the German War College and understands the German military mind."

"Is that so?" asked Kushnir with obvious contempt. "Did he know the Germans would shoot those who surrendered? Shoot them through the stomach and bury them alive? Was he here when the Germans sent beaters through our villages to drive out the occupants to be slaughtered in the streets?" Kushnir's black eyes searched Stuart's face. "I doubt there is much this American can tell me."

Gorovets shook his head wearily. "Well, this is it for me, but if you are smart, you will not fight among yourselves." With that Gorovets put the pistol to his head and pulled the trigger.

For a moment Kushnir stared at the remains of his former leader, then spit in the snow. Very quickly the spittle iced over. "It is time to draw in the perimeter."

Stuart pulled a worn map from the pocket of his heavy white coat and laid it on the snow-covered ground that had formerly been the floor of the farmhouse. With a gloved finger he jabbed at the line representing a creek running behind what was left of the stone building. "The topography signifies a high bed." Stuart moved his finger along the frozen ground that ran east. "Here we could leave the bed and return to the forest without exposing ourselves."

"No," said Kushnir, shaking his head. "We cannot move toward the forest."

A second mortar round landed south of them. Their position was being bracketed.

"Ivan, the Germans already know that the partisans operate from that forest. With the same maneuver that trapped us, they could be moving in from the east to cut us off. The creek bed gives us the necessary cover to return to the forest."

Kushnir gestured to the rear of the former farmhouse and the expanse of white behind it. "No. We will move away from the forest, then turn back and hit their lines from the far side. There is no Panzer support. These men, like us, are caught in the open."

Kushnir concluded the conversation by ordering his men to move out. Hand signals were used and his order relayed to those huddled around the ruins. The partisans scrambled to their feet and moved out.

Antonio Petrocelli climbed out of a hole created by an artillery round. Staying low and following a snow-covered wall, the short but solidly built soldier with a dark complexion hustled into what was left of the stone house. Petrocelli had been with Stuart during the Louisiana Maneuvers, then assigned to the War Department before both men had been sent overseas to evaluate the Russian war effort.

Glancing at Gorovets' brain splattered across the snow, he asked, "What we doing, boss?" The American sergeant wore the same white uniform as James Stuart. A white sleeve covered his rifle, all of which blended in nicely with their snow-covered surroundings.

"Kushnir's unit is headed thataway."

The Italian-American looked in the direction of the

white terrain. German bullets whizzed over the wall as Petrocelli said, "Partisans operating in the open and without support. I hope you have another plan, sir."

Stuart watched the Russians move away. "Kushnir is using his aversion to reentering the forest to mask his lust for killing Germans."

"Well, I always did like these guys better when they were blowing rail lines." Petrocelli raised up enough to look through a broken window. The enemy was moving toward them, dark figures staying low, rifles at the ready, heads up.

Stuart ran his finger along the creek bed on the map. Petrocelli glanced at the rear of the building and nodded. In a crouch, he hurried through what had been the building's back door, across a small corral that had once held livestock, and slid down into the creek, coming to a stop on the ice. Stuart slipped the map back into his parka and followed him.

Approaching their position was a lone partisan, rifle held in both hands, a scarf covering most of the man's face. A patch of ice covered the material through which he breathed. Oh, well, thought Stuart, there's always someone who doesn't get the word.

Stuart stopped to tell the Russian that his unit was moving in another direction. He never got the chance. A mortar round hit the house and the explosion knocked the partisan into Stuart and James Stuart to the ground. Rock, wood, and shrapnel landed on top of them.

Petrocelli scrambled up the creek bank and pulled the partisan off his superior. "You okay, sir?"

Stuart nodded. "What . . . about him?"

Petrocelli touched the scarf covering the man's throat. "This guy hasn't seen any elephants. He's still with us."

After getting to his knees, Stuart took an arm of the partisan as Petrocelli slung the extra weapon over his shoulder. Hunched over, the two Americans pulled the unconscious Russian down the creek bank and onto the ice.

Two

The volcanic island called Corregidor has three levels: Topside, Middleside, and Bottomside. Its beaches are rather narrow and lined with palms, perfect for an assault. Topside held the cottage where MacArthur's family lived, and it was where the general stood on the terrace during aerial attacks and counted Japanese planes.

"The shell hasn't been made to kill MacArthur," he was often heard to say. MacArthur's wife, son, and nanny usually were elsewhere during the Japanese attacks.

This was just the sort of grandstanding that made Franklin Roosevelt want General Douglas MacArthur inside the administration's tent instead of outside. During the Depression, many Americans had called for "a man on horseback"—someone who could do in America what a Mussolini or a Hitler had done in Europe. There were two candidates for that job: Army Chief of Staff Douglas MacArthur and Governor Huey Long of Louisiana.

When the MacArthurs arrived on Corregidor, the military base had the appearance of a tropical university: flowerbeds and manicured lawns, palms and well-tended roads, all swept by sea breezes. Now, as Nicky Lamm prepared to depart under the cover of darkness (technically, desertion in the face of the enemy), little flora or fauna remained, only piles of rubble and dust kicked by the breeze off the ocean. The officer and non-com clubs had been destroyed, as had the library, the commissary, and the grade school for dependent children. The golf course was pockmarked with shells that had fallen wide of their intended mark, as was Kindley Landing Field.

The trolley car line had been knocked out, so Lamm and his party had to troop down to the beach. Soldiers stared through the evening darkness as the refugees passed by. No one challenged them. People left the Rock all the time. Occasionally, some made it ashore, where the Japanese would generally capture them. Few reached the guerrillas operating in the hills above Manila.

The boat would depart from the officers' beach at 7 P.M. and anyone who didn't have the money or wasn't on time would be left behind. From Bottomside's beach, the boat would navigate through the shark net at the point where the steel fence had taken an accommodating hit from a Japanese shore battery during one of the early morning shellings. Morning shellings were a favorite of the Japanese, when the mist was thick and the sun in the Americans' eyes. The dingy, powered by an outboard motor, was filled to capacity. Each of the eight passengers held a bible. All luggage had been jettisoned. What you could jam in your pockets and a bible were all you were allowed to bring along.

Among the civilians sat an American soldier, shoulders slumped, wearing a torn, burnt, and bloodied uniform. He carried no weapon. "I have to return to the Walled City and check on my family." Looking across the bay toward Manila, he added, "I'll surrender, but first I have to check on my family."

The engine sputtered to a start, money was passed to a young Filipino at the stern, and Nicky and Pendergrass shoved off, following the boat into the water. The two men clung to the side, women huddled in the center, and water lapped over the side from the load.

The Springfield was strapped across Lamm's back. Heavy as it was for a man who had lost more than thirty pounds, Nicky couldn't bring himself to leave the rifle behind. Besides, it could be another form of currency, along with its remaining rounds. Once he hooked up with the guerrillas, he'd strike out for the southern end of the archipelago. There he'd find a way to cross to Australia and fly again. The question was: Had he waited too long? Did the Japs control that end of the islands, too?

Betty glanced at faces she couldn't possibly see in the darkness. "It wasn't a hospital like we expected. No red brick, just long buildings with woven bamboo for walls, thatched grass for roofs. Most of the time it was just tents stretching into the jungle. Flies . . . the heat and dust . . . . We slept in triple-decker bamboo beds." She searched the darkness for a sympathetic face. "We gave up all the bunks to our boys." Suddenly her spirits lightened. "You know, you could make two beds out of one if you threw a blanket across the springs."

As they passed through the opening in the shark net, a shushing sound came from the stern.

"The wounded," Betty went on, "they never stopped coming. The fighting was fierce, and right over the hill behind the hospital. We would patch up the men and send them back over the hill . . . . They would come back over and over again until . . . they didn't return."

A woman put her arm around Betty.

Betty looked at her. "We thought the war would be over in a few months. Soon we'd be back in Manila, dancing the night away in our long dresses."

Lamm stared up at the woman he could not see. On Bataan there had been no shell shock because there had been no rear, no safe place to go. Now Betty felt she was heading for safety and she continued to ramble.

"There was always the sound of a saw cutting through bone, the plop of the limb falling into a bucket, and the swish-swish of the mop cleaning up the blood. Was it morning or night? We never knew. Bodies waited in line on stretchers and moved through the operating room like Henry Ford's assembly line."

"Betty, you have to shut up," said Pendergrass from the water, and he said it rather loudly.

Fifty yards away a Japanese patrol boat switched on its searchlight. The light scanned the darkness.

＊　　＊　　＊

Petrocelli and Stuart shuffled down the frozen creek bed, traction for their boots given by the latest snowfall covering everything. Ice crackled under their feet, signaling spring approaching. Heads up and rifles in one hand, they dragged the Russian partisan along. To the west of their position came the sound of small arms and mortar fire.

"Seems like Kushnir made the wrong decision."

"We're not out of the woods yet." Stuart inclined his head to the east. German soldiers moving on line were approaching at the double time.

"That tree, boss?"

Petrocelli was gesturing with the partisan's rifle at an uprooted tree that had fallen across the creek ahead of them. Stuart looked at the tree, and then examined the creek bed.

"Here. Now." Stuart knelt down and turned his back to his companion.

The chunky man also let go of the partisan, placed his rifle on the ice alongside him, and untied the white blanket from under Stuart's pack. Seconds later, Stuart had done the same for him. Then, on their knees and with the cold biting into their bones, they dragged the Russian over to an indentation in the creek wall. There, they sat down and pulled him into a sitting position between them, their backs to the approaching Germans. The partisan's head sagged on Petrocelli's shoulder. The man's scarf was dirty from cordite. He moaned.

"Not the heaviest Russian I've dragged down a frozen creek bed."

Stuart only smiled as he laid his weapon across his lap and pulled the white bedding over him, blending into the snow-covered bank. The material was the same sort of fabric favored by Finnish ski troops, and because of the color, it had caused several partisans to trip over the sleeping Americans during the night. Petrocelli and Stuart also wore snow-colored parkas, glasses to prevent snow blindness, and white sleeves over their rifles. This time, however, they weren't fitting the blanket around them for warmth, but using the extra cloth to cover the partisan, whose head lolled back and forth.

Suddenly, the Russian threw off the blanket and sat up. "What is this?" he asked in a high-pitched voice, blue eyes flashing.

When he looked at Stuart, Petrocelli slammed an elbow into the back of the man's head and the partisan fell into unconsciousness again.

"My God, Tony!" Stuart's voice was a hoarse shout.

They quickly re-covered themselves with their blankets and leaned into the bank, bringing the partisan along and holding him upright between them.

Moments later, the German point man reached the creek, scanned the open area in both directions and hurried across, using the fallen tree. On the other side of the creek, he crouched down and looked around. Satisfied, the soldier moved on. An officer and his radiotelephone operator followed, crossing on the fallen tree. A sergeant, bringing up the rear, ordered everyone moving on line to scramble down the bank, across the ice, and up the other side of the bank.

After seeing several of their companions slip on the ice and fumble up the far side of the bed, and an even heavier companion fall through the ice and soak himself to the waist, the remaining Germans opted for the tree and the quick movement to the far side. Their sergeant cursed. On the other side, the officer shook his head, then moved out with his radiotelephone operator.

After the last man crossed the creek, Stuart and Petrocelli remained still. As did the Russian, head resting on Petrocelli's shoulder. A couple of minutes passed before a solitary German arrived. The rear guard surveyed the frozen bed and quickly shuffled across the downed tree. Another minute passed with Petrocelli and Stuart remaining motionless.

"Now," Stuart said.

They threw off their covers and brought up their weapons, letting go of the Russian, who fell over and came to rest where Petrocelli had previously sat. In a crouch, Petrocelli faced east over the creek bed and Stuart took the west. Back to back, each man scanned more than a hundred and eighty degrees. Nothing moved on the snow but the lone figure of the rear guard. All was quiet. Even the partisan.

Stuart put down his rifle and shook out his blanket. He quickly rolled up the cloth, then wrapped the blanket with a piece of rope and handed it to Petrocelli, who tied the bundle across the lower portion of Stuart's pack. Stuart did the same for Petrocelli, neither man's attention on the task but the terrain surrounding them.

Finished, Stuart propped up the partisan, pulled down the scarf, and applied snow to his face.

"Is he worth the effort, sir?"

"It's not a man, Tony, but a woman."

Petrocelli gaped at the woman fighting to get away from the snow being rubbed on her face. She sat up and looked around. Cordite was smeared across her face. In wiping the snow away, the woman smeared even more of the black substance across her cheeks.

"What has happened?" she asked in Russian, standing and backing away. Under her feet, the ice crackled. The woman wore trousers, a thick jacket, gloves, and a hat that covered her ears and hid her hair. As she glanced around, her blue eyes flashed. "Where are we?"

Petrocelli was too embarrassed to speak, so Stuart explained, including the course of action the new partisan unit leader had chosen.

"Then I wish to thank you," said the woman, refitting the scarf across her face so only her blue eyes would show. She picked up her weapon from the ice. "Kushnir is the wrong choice for a leader. He would rather martyr himself than be effective."

✳   ✳   ✳

After winter's stalemate, the Germans had resumed their advance toward the Caucasus Mountains and their oily, black gold. In the Atlantic, merchant ships were being sunk faster than they could be replaced, as Admiral Ernest King, chief of naval operations, remained unconvinced of the merits of the convoy system. This alarmed the English. German U-boats, operating in packs, threatened to sever the lifeline between the grain fields of North America and the British Isles. And the Japanese, though bogged down in the Philippines, were planning to seize Port Moresby in New Guinea. From there they could attack Australia.

First, the Japanese would seize the Solomons and Port Moresby to gain mastery of the air over the Coral Sea, a primary resupply route from America to Australia. The second part of their plan was to lure the remainder of the American fleet into battle at Midway Island and destroy it. This done, a "ribbon defense" would be anchored from the northernmost islands of the Pacific, extending south all the way to New Caledonia, the Fijis, and Samoa. Australia would be cut off and defenseless, leaving Douglas MacArthur to rant and rave but able to do little after his amazing escape from the Philippines.

At Pearl Harbor, Katie O'Kelly, navy nurse and girlfriend of Nicky Lamm, was seeing Mason Monroe off on his new assignment. The American aviator's long exile was over. The navy needed every pilot, and former disciplinary problems were being tolerated to get as many experienced pilots in the air as possible. And Mason Monroe was ready to fly. With a vengeance.

O'Kelly was worried about Monroe. The young man had not been the same since the attack on Pearl. No one was quite the same, but what Katie saw in Mason's eyes was remoteness, a stare that seemed to go on for thousands of yards. Mason had always been hell-bent on drinking, partying, and whoring. Now, with his return to flight status, Mason's reassignment appeared to have given new impetus for the aviator to set off again on the road to self-destruction. This time, however, the stars and stripes would mask his course of self-destruction.

"I worry about you," O'Kelly said, taking Mason's arm as he prepared to board a launch that would take him to his new assignment. Monroe was slight of frame and short, as many naval pilots were.

"Nothing to worry about, kiddo. All I wanted was a chance to fly again."

"You should've asked Halsey to take you back." O'Kelly's family had a long tradition of naval service. Her great-grandfather had sailed with Perry when the commodore had opened up Japan and her grandfather had steamed into Manila Bay with Dewey and blown Spanish warships out of the water.

"I'll never serve under Halsey again," Monroe said with considerable bitterness. "Halsey doesn't give a damn for flyers he's canned."

O'Kelly's arm fell away. "I swear, Mason, all I hear from you is that sort of foolishness. I'm going to get that Dale Carnegie book and make you read it."

Monroe gestured at the launch, rapidly filling with sailors and airmen. "There's nothing wrong with me that's not wrong with the rest of these guys. All they want is a turn at the people who did this."

From where they stood, they could see the wreckage lining the harbor. Crews worked around the clock.

Amazingly, many of the battleships were close to repair, Ford Air Station was back in operation, and the sub pens were empty, the silent service surreptitiously checking the waters around Pearl.

Still, Chester Nimitz, commander of the Pacific Fleet, knew battleships would only slow down the aircraft carriers in their hit-and-run attacks, so the task force would go to sea without them.

When the nursing corps learned of Admiral Nimitz's decision, a collective shudder ran through the women. Most hadn't recovered from the day of infamy when the dead and wounded had overrun the hospitals, filled up the mess halls, and lined the tennis courts. It had been like the railway scene from *Gone With the Wind*.

O'Kelly tried to speak, but Monroe silenced her with a finger to her lips. "The person you have to worry about is your boyfriend in the Philippines."

✳   ✳   ✳

The searchlight flashed overhead. Everyone hunched down and remained silent, except for Betty, who continued to blab. A woman who had kept records for the United States government in Manila for more than twenty years formed her hand into a fist and socked Betty in the jaw. Betty collapsed against the woman and the boat fell silent. The searchlight was bright but well overhead.

"Oh, my Lord," gasped the soldier. "They're right on top of us." With a leap, he sprung over the side.

That caused more water to wash over the side, the women to cry out in surprise, and Nicky to let go of his side of the boat. When he did, the weight of the Spring-field and its extra rounds pulled him down into another darkness.

*   *   *

Stuart's meager party had found a tank. The battlefield was littered with them, Russian and German alike. They had the tank moving now and the woman was driving. Petrocelli shook his head. Russian partisans were something else, even their women, and that went for Sonya Molotov, the one traveling with them.

Petrocelli noticed most Russian regulars walked away from broken-down machinery. They didn't seem to have the skills American boys had from tinkering with their hot rods. For that reason many Russian T-34s remained on the battlefield, waiting for overworked mechanics to come along. The Germans appeared to be far better at this, performing maintenance on the move. Stuart had pointed out that the Russians had only one tank to speak of, while the Germans labored to service a complete line.

Using a collection of tools from the damaged tanks, Petrocelli tore the transmission apart, and they were moving again, even though they couldn't get the machine in any gear higher than second. Now all they had to do was talk their way through the German lines—in a Russian tank and with the woman talking nonstop. The woman was always talking, but not the usual female chatter. She appeared desperate to be able to communicate with Petrocelli in his own language.

Tanks can be hot as hell during summer; during a Russian winter they can be downright cozy, if you can stand the smell. James Stuart had taken one of the dead Germans—several lay around the battlefield where the Russian T-34s had been ripped through by German Panzers—and with the assistance of Sonya, he had slipped the dead officer's almost headless corpse inside to defrost. Stiff as a plank, the man was leaned against the driver's seat while Petrocelli worked on the engine.

"I can smell him, sir." A smear of grease crossed Petrocelli's forehead where he had wiped sweat away. Early on, the sergeant had removed his coat and gloves. "I think he's done." Blood and gray matter ran down the dead officer's almost nonexistent head onto his greatcoat.

Sonya stood guard, straddling the turret with a machine pistol she had taken off a dead German. The two men grabbed the defrosting German and thrust him out the hatch. Sonya grasped the headless man under the arms and dumped him over the side.

When Petrocelli tried to follow, the woman's blue eyes flashed again. *"Nyet!* You make tank go."

Before disappearing back into the tank, Petrocelli said, "I don't know about these Russian women, sir. They don't seem to want our help."

"Unless you fit into their future, and we don't." Perhaps, thought Stuart, that was something Washington had best be prepared for when this war ended, an opinion he shared with George Patton.

Stuart took the boots Sonya had removed from the corpse and worked them with his hands, making them pliable. By the time he was through, Sonya had the man's pants off and was loosening his jacket. During all this, the woman kept her eyes on their surroundings. The machine pistol lay in her lap.

Their tank sat in a grove of beech trees with few of the remaining trees at their full height. A frost covered their limbs and the beeches stood rigid in the cold. Still, it was decent cover, between two snow-covered hills. Once, a contingency of Germans had swept through, and work ceased until the Germans had moved on. Hatch locked, the three of them, and the corpse of the German officer, had hidden inside. The tank had been ignored since its cannon had been blown away. Finally, Petrocelli was ready to give it a go, and Stuart, dressed as a German officer, climbed inside.

Sonya demanded the controls. "Me drive." Then to Stuart in Russian, "Once my country regroups, Russia will need all the tank drivers they can find. I intend to be one of those drivers."

Petrocelli looked at Stuart. Stuart only shrugged and the two men hung on as the woman mowed down one beech tree after another, passed a sleigh with two dead horses, a motorized cart with its wheels missing, and bodies lying as dark shadows under new-fallen snow. Petrocelli climbed into the commander's chair, where he fed a fresh belt into one of the two machine guns. Despite the missing cannon, the operational tracks and machine guns had made this tank an easy choice.

Following Stuart's directions, Sonya drove through

the snow-covered countryside, and then past a rutted-out crossroads with a wooden stake and makeshift wooden arrow. On the arrow was scrawled "Moscow."

There was no way to avoid the German lines, so Stuart timed their arrival to coincide with first light. After he successfully talked his way through the sentries, the T-34 passed infantry wagons with horses hobbled nearby, machine guns pulled by Russian tractors, antitank guns and gasoline drums towed by Caterpillar tractors, a variety of trucks, baggage wagons, armored cars, and soldiers at their mess or toilet. Germans, in their bulky white outfits and felt-padded boots, many wearing blankets over their shoulders, stared as the tank rolled by. An officer hustled over, buttoning up his pants.

"Stop," he ordered. Several soldiers followed with submachine guns. Newspapers fell from inside the soldiers' coats, having been jammed inside for additional warmth. "What is this?" he asked his fellow officer whose head and shoulders stuck out of the tank.

Stuart yawned behind a gloved fist, then said in perfect German, "As you know our Panzers have to be in close proximity to a T-34 to destroy it. For that reason, the general staff has determined that, inoperable cannon or not"—Stuart gestured at the busted barrel of the tank—"the armor of our enemy, rather its machine guns and functional tracks, can be used to break through when we make our thrust toward the Bolshevik capital."

"I have heard of no such offensive."

"More T-34s should arrive within the hour." To the men around the tank, Stuart said, "Listen to me, soldiers. The Russian army has very few troops between Moscow and our victorious troops. In a few days we are going to drive toward their capital. I have been ordered to place as much firepower and armor forward as possible." Looking at the lieutenant standing on the ground below him, Stuart asked, "Now where do you wish to have the two extra machine guns mounted?"

A position was quickly pointed out and the T-34 moved between an artillery piece on one side and an antitank unit on the other. Stuart spent the next few minutes giving instructions to Sonya so that the tank's tracks would have a decent start across the ice. Those who had followed the tank to its new position drifted away. Breakfast and toilets had been interrupted.

Seeing them go, Petrocelli stuck his helmeted head out of the hatch. "Is this your plan, sir? To join the German army?"

"Tony, if you'd been able to get this thing into third gear we wouldn't be in such a predicament."

"Is that a slur on the motor pool, sir?"

"If you please, Major," cut in Sonya from inside the tank, "we need to leave rather quickly. I have seen what German soldiers do with Russian women they capture."

"Sonya, can you operate a machine gun?"

"Certainly."

"Then prepare to do so." In English, he said, "Petrocelli, take the wheel. We are about to—"

"Stuart, is that you?" asked a blond man from behind the tank. He wore a captain's insignia and spoke in German. "What are you doing driving a Russian tank and wearing a German uniform?"

Stuart faced the man. "I might ask you a similar question," he replied in German. "I've seen no Panzers with this unit, Karl."

"A minor misunderstanding between my commander and myself." The blond man grinned and, switching to English, said, "I never thought I would see you again, James. You are aware that we shall have to shoot you?"

Stuart thrust his hand into the greatcoat of the dead German officer, pulled out a Mauser, and pointed the weapon at his friend. "I would not like to kill you, Karl. We shared many a pleasant evening in Berlin."

"Nor would I care to be shot. People who are shot in this weather usually die." He went on to curse the Russian winter.

Stuart glanced around. The other soldiers had lost interest in them. There was breakfast to be eaten, toilets to be finished, and more tanks with spiked cannon on the way, which meant this unit was about to move out. At such times soldiers didn't pay much attention to the banter between two old friends. They wanted to get their gear, stomach, and bowels in order.

"Your German, James, it is still flawless."

"And your English sounds as if I'm speaking to someone in the House of Lords. Did you marry that girl in Berlin?" Stuart slid down from the turret to the ground to stand alongside his friend. "What was her name?"

"Emily Heitz now. We have a son and another on the way. Due any day now, I would imagine." Heitz smiled again. "We are slightly out of touch on the front."

"Would you allow me to pass? I have someone waiting for me in Moscow."

The German officer chuckled. "It will break many hearts in Berlin, especially those who have not lost theirs to the Führer. Sorry, James, but I cannot let you cross over." He glanced toward the tree line on the far side of the frozen lake. "Why not stay with us? I can certainly make your last hours comfortable."

Stuart carelessly examined the Mauser. "I really did like that girl Emily."

"And she is going to be surprised you and I met again. I never would have thought . . . ." Heitz reached for the weapon. "Come on, James. All you are doing is prolonging the inevitable."

Without looking behind him, Stuart shouted, "Petrocelli, start your engine!"

"Don't do this." Heitz glanced at the tank as the engine turned over. "It is more honorable to be shot by a German firing squad than be blown to pieces in a Russian tank."

"Actually, I prefer neither." Stuart hit his friend alongside the head with the Mauser, and then grabbed the unconscious officer and lowered him to the ground. To a soldier who appeared from behind a tree buttoning his fly, he asked, "Could you assist me?" The pistol had been returned to Stuart's pocket. "He hit his head when he tried to climb onto the tank. You know how the captain is, always wanting to drive everything."

"That is why he was sent to the Russian Front. He is much too reckless. I'll see he's taken care of."

As the soldier called for a stretcher, Stuart remounted

the tank. Inside, Sonya was on the radio, using a partisan frequency and telling them they were headed for their position. Her Russian comrades didn't believe her and said so.

The woman became indignant. "A single T-34 is approaching your position with a spiked cannon and machine guns facing the wrong direction? Have you taken leave of your senses?"

When the woman received a muddled reply, she told them she would come back from the grave to haunt them if they fired on her. She broke the connection, and then gripped Petrocelli's shoulder.

"I drive," she said in broken English. "You fire weapon."

Petrocelli shook his head.

"But I know minefields."

That got Petrocelli out of the driver's seat, and only after he was seated behind the machine gun did he realize there were few landmines on any frozen lake.

That woman!

At warning cries from the front lines, Germans gave up their morning toilet or breakfast and hustled to their positions. Artillery pieces were loaded, but their sights were set for the partisan positions in the tree line, over two hundred meters away. Mortars and howitzers had similar problems. It was left to the .50 calibers to stop the T-34 from crossing the icy no-man's-land. When they fired, Petrocelli returned fire. Germans ducked into their bunkers.

Throwing off the soldier who was helping him, Karl Heitz staggered back to the edge of the lake. Stuart's tank was moving slowly. It wasn't the ice, thought Heitz, it was something else, perhaps the transmission. The former Panzer commander snatched a knapsack of grenades, jumped into a truck with chains on its wheels, and set off in pursuit. Two soldiers leaped onto the running boards, hooked arms around the mirror mounts, steadied their rifles, and fired at the tank as they crossed the ice. Inside the tank, Stuart ordered Petrocelli to shoot out the truck's tires.

"Shoot out the tires? What do you think this is, a Tom Mix movie?"

"Just shoot out the tires. That's an order."

Petrocelli tilted the barrel and fired at the frozen lake, bringing down the arc until the bullets sprayed the tires. The soldiers on the running boards ducked. One ducked too low and was shot off. He fell to the ice and rolled away.

"Sorry, sir. He got in the way."

"Just keep trying for the tires."

"Sweet Jesus," muttered Petrocelli, "if that's what it means to be an officer and a gentleman, then I want no part of it."

In the truck, Heitz felt one of his tires blow, and at the same time saw the second soldier fall off the running board. Heitz cursed, then released the flaps holding the tarp overhead. By the time the roof was flapping in the wind, his remaining front tire had also been shot out.

What did it matter? The rims would slide across the ice and the rear wheels would give the truck all the traction it needed. Heitz stood up, foot on the gas, a hand on the wheel; the other hand held a grenade. He was less than twenty-five yards from his target when he sent the first grenade stick soaring toward the tank. The grenade hit the turret, fell off, and exploded seconds before Heitz reached the same spot.

Hmm. Have to do better, and he flung the next grenade ahead of the fleeing tank so that the tank would run over it. Run over it the tank did. The grenade exploded under the right track and the track shook loose of its mount. Still the T-34 continued forward, but parallel to the tree line, and finally in a circle.

Sonya cried out, "I can't control it!"

She didn't have to tell Stuart and Petrocelli. They were no longer facing the truck but the Russian lines.

When Heitz tossed his next grenade, he lost his footing and the grenade went flying just ahead of the truck. When the cab passed under the grenade, the stick weapon landed behind him, wedged between the seats. The German fumbled for the grenade for a second, then threw open the door and leaped out, hitting the ice hard and having the wind knocked out of him.

Sonya was already out of the tank, running for the tree line, waving her hands over her head, and shouting to be allowed to pass. Petrocelli slid off the turret and fell to the snow-covered ice in the same manner as Heitz. When he got his breath, he was shocked to see the German truck skidding toward him. Instead of scrambling to his feet, Petrocelli rolled over and over, and prayed that the tank with its broken track wouldn't follow him.

The truck and tank collided—at the same time the

grenade in the truck went off. As Petrocelli got to his hands and knees, he saw the German truck and the Russian tank locked in a fiery embrace. The busted turret of the T-34 had penetrated the windshield of the truck and flames from the truck were spreading to the T-34.

Stuart was nowhere to be seen, but Sonya was motioning to Petrocelli from the tree line where several Russians stood, submachine guns at the ready. Both Russian and German soldiers appeared to be holding fire, and Petrocelli didn't understand why until he saw Karl Heitz dragging James Stuart toward the German lines. Stuart's head sagged and his arms hung limp at his sides. Since he still wore the uniform of the German army, it was a wonder Sonya had been able to keep the Russians from shooting both of them.

Petrocelli headed across the ice on the far side of the burning wreckage. As he shuffled along, he felt the ground move. The explosion had caused the ice to fracture, and as Petrocelli made the far corner of the burning wreck, cracks ran in all directions.

Heitz stopped and stared at a crack running between his feet. When he did, Petrocelli came out from behind the fiery tank and truck and launched himself at both men. All three went sprawling. When they stopped sliding, each man came up on his hands and knees and viewed his opponent.

"James Stuart is going with me," said Heitz in English. "We are old friends."

"Sorry, but he has a date with a gal in Moscow."

Behind Petrocelli, the tank and truck slipped through

the ice, and the resultant crack ran under the unconscious Stuart, who lay several yards away.

The German smiled as he stood. "Then it appears
this is just between you and me, Yank."

"You got a gun or something?" asked Petrocelli, still
kneeling on the ice.

Heitz patted his jacket. "It doesn't appear I do." The
German slapped his hands together and glanced at
the soldiers staring at them from opposite sides of the
ice. His hands became fists, upraised and in front of
his chest. "We'll do this by the Marquis of Queensberry
rules; to the winner goes Stuart."

The ice widened under Stuart and the American's
shoulder slipped into the crack, followed by an arm.

"We don't have time for that." Petrocelli slipped a
knife from his boot and, straightening up, whipped the
blade toward the German.

The knife hit Heitz in the chest, and the German
officer staggered back and sat down on the ice. He
reached for the blade, but with his heavy clothing, it
was a moment before he could remove it. By then,
Petrocelli had Stuart by the collar and was dragging
him toward the Russian side of the lake.

THREE

Wolfgang Topp stood with his companions on a pier overlooking submarines manufactured by Krupp Ironworks. Slight and blond and not yet nineteen, Topp was a former member of the National Labor Service who had built roads throughout Greater Germany before being drafted.

A morning mist floated over the harbor, and the sky was turning purple. Most of the huge lights were still on as the final fitting was done to the boats that lay like enormous metal cigars with noses where someone had been a bit careless with the clipper. Instead of the blunt nose of a cigar, the submarine noses came quickly to a point. Lines held the underwater boats to their moorings, piers running longer than the length of each boat.

Shipyard workers moved with a lively step, and Wolfgang wondered if the workers were as excited as he and his companions at the launching of these new crafts. Guards were everywhere, submachine guns hanging around their necks. The guards had watched Wolfgang's unit troop down the pier, where they had been left to stare at the row of underwater boats. Behind the subs stood the hangars—looking like incomplete aircraft hangars, from the bottom up, that is. In those roofless hangars, the underwater boats began as circular tubes, and slowly but surely were transformed into submarines.

One of the men beside Wolfgang slapped him across his narrow back. "That is our ship!" said the suntanned man wearing a blue uniform. He was pointing at the sub moored nearest them.

"It is not a ship. It is a boat. Ships are much larger. Remember your training."

His companion laughed. "That is my ship, and I, for one, cannot wait to put my hands on her. I want to meet the British in the North Atlantic."

A raspy voice behind them said, "You will have a good deal of time to get to know your new girlfriend." Both young men turned as their petty officer added, "I doubt she would want such clumsy hands on her, much less risking her metal skin in the North Atlantic."

Wolfgang thought back to his selection for underwater duty. At morning formation, his former sergeant had said, "I need five volunteers." Pointing at the men standing at parade rest in front of him, he said, "You, you, you, you, and you." Wolfgang was "you" number four. The five young men grumbled as they packed their bags, more from a loss of routine than anything, then left their barracks, boarded a truck, and reported for service in the *Ubootwaffe*.

Wolfgang expected training for the U-boat force to mean boats, but there had been none of that for almost ninety days. There had been, however, a good deal of sports and teamwork, in the mud and snow. More of the same severe and demanding training any infantryman might be subject to, along with the additional harassment of going without decent food, water, and air.

Air. The lifeblood of any submariner. Not that it was fresh air. In the *Ubootwaffe*, you operated in cramped conditions with nothing to breathe other than stale air and the smell of the men around you.

He looked down the line of strangers who had bonded into a unit. Whether they came from the farm or the city (Wolfgang was from a small town in the Black Forest), those remaining were the ones who could work in close quarters and work as a team. Many who had begun their training were no longer here. It had taken Wolfgang some time to understand why particular candidates had been dismissed—those who had endless questions about what in the world their training had to do with submarines.

Sometimes their petty officer would not allow them to pee for hours, sometimes all day. What that had to do with being a member of *Ubootwaffe*, Wolfgang had no idea. Claustrophobia had washed out many. That was something no man could hide, the look of terror when a sailor was in an enclosed space, alone or with others. Wolfgang and his fellows were awakened in the middle of the night, run and exercised past the point of exhaustion, then seated in rows, cheek to jowl, and lectured. Many of the talks were about the value of teamwork, sacrifice, and the simple fact that if you were a member of the *Ubootwaffe*, you were part of a team that would bring England to its knees.

✳   ✳   ✳

In the Japanese Imperial General Headquarters there was disagreement over the course of the war. The army wanted to finish off China and consolidate Japan's gains, but the navy wanted to draw the Americans out at Midway Island and finish them there. The navy said it had the capacity to cut the American supply lines that ran through the Coral Sea to Australia, not to mention that Midway could be a jumping-off point for attacks on Hawaii and the American West Coast. This was another result of the Doolittle raid. If the Empire of Japan did not go on the offensive against the Americans, said spokesmen for the Imperial Navy, the Japanese fleet would spend most of its time defending the Home Islands.

The navy thought it was invincible and, in fact, was infected by "victory disease." Instead of sustaining twenty-five percent casualties, as expected at Pearl Harbor, they had lost only ten percent, and instead of taking six months, they had overrun the Pacific in four. Their largest loss had been a single destroyer. How could anything go wrong? Except if the Midway Island/Coral Sea plan was adopted, it would violate a cardinal rule of naval warfare: never disperse your forces. Unfortunately, the Americans were reading the Japanese mail and knew what the Japanese were up to. Any feint, like the one planned for the Aleutian Islands, would not fool the Americans.

It was finally decided that Admiral Chuichi Nagumo, the hero of the attack on Pearl Harbor, would be dispatched to sink what was left of the British Royal Navy between the Japanese Home Islands and India. His task force did so with more Pearl Harbor-like raids led by Commander Mitsuo Fuchida's First Air Fleet. Another task force would begin the business of extending a "ribbon defense" across the Pacific from island to island, ending in the Coral Sea.

Attacking Australia might be a bit much—the army flatly refused to participate—but cutting the island continent off from the rest of the world could be done by seizing Port Moresby in New Guinea, an island second in size only to Greenland and very near Australia. That, the army would support. A fortunate by-product of this plan was that it brought an island rich in phosphate into Japan's Greater Southeast Asia Co-Prosperity Sphere—phosphate that would soon be flowing into the Home Islands and increasing crop yields.

What was bothering the commanders of the Japanese army was Douglas MacArthur. No Allied general was held in higher esteem than the one who had escaped from Corregidor. Sooner or later, Douglas MacArthur, a genuine hero of the Great War and the former chief of staff of the American army, would lead a counterattack, and it would come against the Home Islands.

The Allied command was likewise torn. With the Japanese sweep through the Pacific, even Winston Churchill, prime minister of England, understood the need for the United States to shift two divisions to the Pacific Theater. This gave Admiral Ernest King, in charge of operations in the Pacific, the opportunity to press his case that Europe should not be America's top priority. In this, King had the support of the American people. A recently conducted poll revealed sixty-five percent of Americans wanted some sort of strike at Japan.

Instead, Washington told King that Hawaii and Australia were to be held, and a drive north from the New Hebrides would begin sometime in the future. This, however, wasn't something you could tell the "Hero of Corregidor." Upon arriving in Melbourne, Douglas MacArthur learned the army he expected to lead against the Japanese didn't exist and he was expected to share command with the navy. This set the "Hero of Corregidor" off on another tirade against the navy, which he had never forgiven for abandoning him in the Philippines. Adding fuel to the fire was MacArthur's chief of staff, Richard Sutherland, who never hesitated to say, "It's that damn George Marshall and his boy"— meaning Ike—"cutting your throat again."

A map had been put together at Admiral Nimitz's headquarters in Pearl. The movement of the enemy was marked in orange on tracing paper pinned to a sheet of plywood resting on two sawhorses. Another result of the Doolittle raid when the Combined Fleet had been ordered to the sea to track down and destroy the Americans who had insulted the Home Islands. American code breakers had a field day with all the radio traffic, and they were able to fill in the blanks of many Japanese naval codes. This was what was meant by the Americans being able to "read" the Japanese' mail.

In April of 1942, radio traffic focusing on the stronghold of Rabaul (five airfields and a major harbor complex) on the island of New Britain increased far out of proportion to other transmissions. Cross-checked by Hawaii and Washington, not to mention old-fashioned spies, coast watchers, and the numerous American and Australian planes scouring the area, the information alerted the Americans when the Japanese task force sailed for New Guinea to seize Port Moresby. Because of this, the Australians manning a sea base on the island of Tulagi were immediately evacuated.

Told by his intelligence officers that Hawaii wasn't in immediate danger, Chester Nimitz, commander of the Pacific Fleet, sent his battleships to the West Coast to save oil. Nimitz also gave Admiral Frank Jack Fletcher, a sailor familiar with the Coral Sea, the uneviable assignment of stopping the Japanese. Joining aircraft carrier *Yorktown* would be the *Lexington* and two Australian and six American cruisers.

Unknown to Frank Jack Fletcher, Ernest King, chief of naval operations, was on a campaign to rid Pearl of timid and pessimistic officers, and Ernest King had focused his attention on a sailor who had won the Medal of Honor at Vera Cruz. Always erring on the side of

caution, Admiral Fletcher took any opportunity to refuel his ships so they could be ready to sail at top speed.

Following the attack on Pearl Harbor, the Marines
were hit on Wake Island. The Marines threw the Japanese back into the sea. Then, while Frank Jack
Fletcher's carrier was away taking on fuel, the Japanese returned, overrunning Wake. The defeated Marines were shipped to Shanghai, and along the way,
two of them were beheaded for the amusement of the
ship's crew.

Tulagi, the seaplane base recently evacuated by the
Australians, is, along with Guadalcanal, part of the
Solomon Islands, and the Solomons lie southwest of
Hawaii, almost at Australia. Flushed with success and
believing their own propaganda that the Americans
would do little to oppose them, the Japanese covering
force abandoned its landing party at Tulagi only hours
after it had secured a beachhead. The landing party's
air support had been grounded by rain, but what was
there to worry about?

On the *Yorktown*, Fletcher received a report from
MacArthur's headquarters in Melbourne. Army planes
based in Australia had sighted two transports debark-
ing Japanese troops at Tulagi. This was "just the kind
of report they'd been waiting for" so the *Yorktown*
steamed north at twenty-seven knots. This had to be
the beginning of the invasion of Port Moresby, and if
the Japanese controled Moresby, they could bomb Australia into submission and cut off the Australians' lifeline to the States.

"Where are we?" asked a pilot who had taken a seat across the linen-covered table from Mason Monroe. Very quickly a black mess steward in a white jacket was at his side, pouring coffee in a china mug.

"A hundred miles southwest of some island called 'Guadalcanal,'" said Mason Monroe after the steward had taken the other pilot's breakfast order.

The other pilot shook his head. "When I was training in Pensacola nobody told me I'd be flying by maps ripped from old *National Geographics*. Have any idea why the Japs haven't discovered us? They're supposed to have all kinds of seaplane scouts out here."

"There's a belt of clouds overhead."

The two men were finishing their coffee when the flyer asked, "So how'd you make it off the *Arizona?*"

"I wasn't aboard when she was hit."

"Lucky for you."

"Yeah." Monroe drank quickly from his coffee.

"They had quite a few aviators on the *Arizona?*"

"Far as I know, I was the only one."

"And your duties were?"

Monroe put down his cup and pushed back from the table. "You've got a lot of questions, bub."

The flyer shrugged. "I drew the short straw."

Monroe scanned the room. Across the wardroom a table of flyers stared at him. The men in his air group.

"What'd you expect?" asked the man seated across from him. "Guys want to know who they're flying with."

Monroe got to his feet, taking his tray with him. "Maybe they'll get a chance to learn today." He left the wardroom without looking at the men in his air group again.

As the *Yorktown* approached the launch point, the edge of a cold front enveloped the group. Pilots went to their planes under an overcast sky, occasional squalls, and winds gusting from twenty-five to thirty-five knots. The front would cover the carrier's planes until they were twenty miles off Tulagi.

Just before sunrise, the attack was launched without fighter support: twelve Devastator torpedo planes and twenty-eight Dauntless dive bombers. The fighter aircraft would fly in rotation from an eighteen-plane group providing air cover over Fletcher's task force. Each squadron flew to the target and attacked independently, as was the practice of the time. Diving from ten thousand feet, the Americans broke through the clouds and into the moist weather below.

"Damn!" said more than one pilot and bombardier, wiping his windshield or bomb scope clear. "I can't see anything."

"Then follow my tracers!" shouted Mason Monroe. "Shoot at what I shoot at." Monroe wiped clear his windshield and dove for the bay where the seaplanes were moored.

The torpedo planes and bombers made their first pass, then on subsequent runs opened up with their machine guns and chewed up the newly established base, slicing through one man who threw up his hands and ran no more. Monroe was over the seaplanes now, holding down the trigger even as he rose into the air.

Out of the corner of his eye he thought he saw a de-stroyer. He'd have to make a return and release his—

Planes at ten and two and firing at him! Mason reached for the trigger, but the planes with American markings were gone. Mason soared straight up, through the clouds, with the G forces telling him he was getting the hell out of there. Soon his windshield was no longer foggy but wet as the temperature dropped. In the soli-tude of his cockpit Mason trembled. He had given back some for his former shipmates who had died aboard the *Arizona*.

Over the radio came shouts of glee from other pilots as they re-formed their group. Several shouted "Re-member Pearl Harbor!"

"I saw a destroyer," announced Monroe.

"Me too," came the voice of another flyer.

"Forget the recon planes," ordered the air group com-mander. "Concentrate on the destroyer."

Several affirmatives came over the radio, and then the group broke through the clouds and windshields and bombsights fogged up again, causing more trouble in locating their target. Their target, however, didn't have trouble finding them, and the antiaircraft fire became intense once the Americans appeared out of the clouds.

Damn, thought Monroe, we should've hit the de-stroyer first. He dove for the ship and raked the decks with machine gun fire, his finger again remaining on the trigger long after he had passed over his target. Have to come around and try again. Didn't have the right angle to release the torpedo.

When Monroe came around, he faced the ship's bow. That was no target. And still the flak came at him, chewing holes in his right wing. Monroe broke off his attack and flew away, out to sea. Returning to the bay, he tried to clear his windshield.

Damn fog! The destroyer was coming up fast so Mason dropped his torpedo, exhausted the rounds of his machine guns, and returned to the *Yorktown* for the celebration.

At his headquarters in Pearl Harbor, Chester Nimitz would later remark that perhaps more target practice should be the order of the day. In the raid, more than a hundred bombs and torpedoes had been dropped and plenty of ammunition expended, resulting in the destruction of one Japanese destroyer, three minesweepers, four landing barges, five seaplanes, and a patrol boat. That was not what the American pilots reported. They thought they'd sunk several light carriers and repulsed the Japanese's main force.

The following day, the *Yorktown* shot down a Japanese seaplane in the midst of radioing back the Americans' position. Unfortunately for the Japanese, their forces operating in the Coral Sea did not receive this message. Meanwhile, Admiral Fletcher, hearing of an attack on Port Moresby, set a course for New Guinea. The Americans knew nothing of the Japanese strike force approaching from the eastern entrance of the Coral Sea—right behind them. The Japanese had sailed halfway across the Coral Sea and seen nothing. Disgusted, their commander turned south—cutting across the path of both American carriers as they refueled! Fortunately for the Americans, the Japanese sent out no air patrols.

Nor did American search planes locate any Japanese. When American planes flew over the strike force, the Japanese were hidden under an overcast. Then, incredibly, the Japanese failed to receive another communiqué pinpointing the exact location of the *Lexington* and the *Yorktown,* refueling under clear skies and only seventy miles away.

The Japanese weren't the only ones to botch intelligence reports. A light aircraft carrier accompanied the Japanese headed for Port Moresby; information MacArthur's headquarters failed to pass along to Admiral Fletcher, and at a time when Fletcher was splitting his forces. Admiral Crace, the commander of a mixed Australian and American force, was ordered to find and destroy the Japanese invasion force. If he did, Crace was sure to run across that light aircraft carrier MacArthur's headquarters had failed to report.

The Japanese who had entered the Coral Sea from the east gave up trying to find the Americans and headed for Port Moresby. The only action they saw was when American Flying Fortresses dropped twelve bombs on them. All the bombs fell wide of their mark and the strike force's fighters drove off the Americans. That was the same day General Wainwright surrendered all American forces in the Philippines. In the southern part of the Filipino archipelago, American officers encouraged their men to take to the hills and resist while they surrendered, per instructions from General Wainright.

Finally, some American ships were sighted by Japanese scout planes. Excited pilots from the strike force reported a carrier and a cruiser with no support. When the Japanese planes flew in for the attack, they recognized the oiler and destroyer for what they were and flew off, searching for the American carriers. An hour later, they had found nothing, but they remembered where there were two targets of opportunity.

The *Neosho* and the *Sims* had been broken off from Fletcher's task force and sent sailing to safety. Now, as targets of opportunity, the *Neosho* and the *Sims* worked hard to avoid the high-level bombers and a group of horizontal bombers. They had less luck with Japanese dive bombers, who sunk the destroyer *Sims*, then went after the oiler *Neosho*. The Japanese scored seven direct hits, along with a gasoline fire ignited from a damaged Japanese plane that crashed on deck.

The *Neosho's* captain ordered all hands to *make preparations* to abandon ship. Boats went over the side, along with anxious sailors who had watched the *Sims* sink. Many sailors were hauled back on board, some drowned in the confusion, and many of the rafts drifted away. For several days, the *Neosho* was adrift because of an incorrect location reported during the heat of battle. When the damaged ship was finally located, there was no time to search for survivors as the seriously wounded needed to be ferried to hospitals in Australia

Like the Japanese, Admiral Fletcher also wasted a

sortie. His raid was against two carriers and four heavy cruisers that turned out to be two light cruisers and a couple of gunboats. The downside was that Japanese scouts sighted the *Yorktown*. Fortunately for the *Yorktown*, the strike force did not hear the scout's signals because it was busy sinking the *Sims* and the *Neosho*.

Then, a scout from the *Yorktown* discovered the Japanese carriers. Both the *Yorktown* and the *Lexington* launched planes. The *Lexington's* air group attacked the aircraft carrier *Shoho*, but all the Americans were able to do was blow a few planes over the side and into the water. *Shoho* was safe—until it turned into the wind to launch its planes. That's when the *Lexington's* dive bombers and torpedo-carrying aircraft turned the ship into a blazing inferno. The excited voice of Lieutenant Commander R. E. Dixon came through on the squawk boxes on both the *Lexington* and the *Yorktown:* "Scratch one flattop. Dixon to carrier, scratch one flattop."

Those in the radio rooms quickly spread the good news, one wag saying, "Thank you, Billy Mitchell."

The ships commanded by Admiral Crace of Australia drew the attention of Japanese land-based aircraft. The planes, however, were repulsed. While Crace's men were celebrating their success, American Flying Fortresses attacked them. The Flying Fortresses were driven off, and Admiral Crace reported this to his superiors. He was told there were plans in the works to improve the Americans' recognition of naval vessels.

Flushed with the success of destroying the *Sims* and the *Neosho*, the Japanese strike force launched their planes against the *Lexington* and the *Yorktown*. In the dusk they couldn't find either ship, and returning home ran into a group of American fighters. In the ensuing dogfights, nine Japanese planes were shot down at the cost of only one American plane. Breaking off the attack, the Japanese mistakenly flew toward the *Lexington*. Not having radar, the Japanese blinked their lights and the Americans blinked back. When the Japanese planes closed, the Americans opened fire. Despite the American advantage, only one enemy plane was shot down.

The following morning candy bars were passed out on American ships, extra rice cakes on Japanese, and then both countries' planes took to the air before first light, sure of the location of their enemy. The two attacking forces actually passed each other on the way to attack the other's aircraft carrier.

All over the world, navies believed the airplane was simply a scout to seek out the enemy for battleships to destroy. That was not true for Japan or the United States. If the army was the queen of battle on land, the carrier-based aircraft was the queen of the unlimited expanses of water. Here in one of the most beautiful oceans in the world, a place that never knew winter, naval flyers from both countries would prove that carrier-based aircraft were the queens of the sea.

The *Lexington* was turning circles when crew members heard over radios that Japanese scout planes had discovered their position. At the same time an American scout located the Japanese strike force, which included the aircraft carriers *Zuikaku* and *Shokaku*. Fletcher put Admiral Fitch, commander of the *Lexington*, in charge of tactics because Fitch was the more experienced air commander. Before the Americans could close with the *Zuikaku*, the carrier disappeared into a squall, so everything the Americans had was thrown at the *Shokaku*.

Only two American bombs hit the carrier, one on the *Shokaku's* starboard bow. Fuel that had caught on fire damaged the flight deck, so the enemy carrier could only recover planes, not launch them. When the *Zuikaku* emerged from the squall, her crew saw the *Shokaku* in flames. The wounded carrier's planes were transferred to the *Zuikaku*, and the strike force commander released the *Shokaku*, as he thought both American carriers had been put out of commission.

He was pretty close to correct. Torpedo planes came in from both sides of the *Lexington*—called the anvil approach—and released their loads. One of the attacking planes was blown apart and the bodies of the crew were seen hurtling through the air. The *Lexington's* captain tried to maneuver between the torpedoes, but the forty-thousand-ton ship was slow to respond. Of the eleven torpedoes fired, two hit home. Dive bombers followed, and one of their bombs exploded in a ready-ammunition locker. Another hit the smokestack. The ship's siren jammed and shrieked throughout a battle lasting only thirteen minutes.

The *Yorktown* was more fortunate. It had a tighter turning radius and avoided all torpedoes. After that, it became a matter of dodging steel eggs from overhead. Only one hit; an eighteen-hundred-pound bomb penetrated to the fourth deck, killing or seriously injuring more than sixty. Fires were quickly brought under control and the remaining Japanese attacks fought off.

Returning to their carriers, Japanese pilots reported they had sent to the bottom American aircraft carrier *Saratoga* and either the *Enterprise* or the *Yorktown*. The Japanese retired much too soon. Lady *Lex* was steaming away at twenty-five knots and still recovering her planes.

The *Lexington* might be listing, her boiler rooms might be flooded, and the plane elevators inoperative, but the crew was hard at work. Several fires burned throughout, and the damage-control personnel, which included members of the engineering division, the ship fitters, and the electricians, worked from one end of the ship to the other to bring the fires under control. Topside, Lady *Lex* was landing and launching aircraft. Only one returning plane went over the side. Still, when the deck became crowded, the excess planes had to be recovered by the *Yorktown*.

Fighter control was still trying to bring in the stragglers, and without radar. One of those stragglers was Bill Ault, the leader of the dive-bombing group. Ault could not locate Lady *Lex*, and without radar she could not assist him. In his last broadcast, Ault said, "So long, people. We got a thousand-pound hit on the flattop!" He was never heard from again.

The damage-control officer reported that everything was under control. Minutes later, the *Lexington* was rocked from bow to stern by an explosion of gasoline vapors ignited by a generator left running below. More explosions followed, as the paint on bulkheads melted and allowed the fire to continue its movement throughout the ship despite watertight doors and sealed hatches. Black smoke choked those who tried to work below, but it was the breakdown of the communications system that made everyone realize Lady *Lex* was finished. A sailor came to the bridge to report that the temperature near the bomb storage area had reached 140 degrees.

That was enough. The *Lexington* ran up three flags that signaled "I am abandoning ship." Destroyers came alongside and the sick and wounded were disembarked in whaleboats. Knowing the flight deck would soon be too hot to stand on, or would catch fire because it was made of wood and sealed with tar, Admiral Fitch told the captain it was time to disembark the men. The damage control personnel were ordered topside after securing the engines and boilers.

The ship slowed to a stop. All hands prepared to abandon ship, including the captain's dog. Doughnut rafts were tossed overboard and the Marines and sailors, after setting their shoes in a neat row, descended hand over hand on ropes to launches or dropped into the gentle swells of the Coral Sea.

One of the sailors did a swan dive off the bow into the warm water, another took a fire axe to the stores, liberating the ship's ice cream, and there was plenty of time for the *Lexington*'s ship doctors to minister to the injured before sending them over the side. Men who had gone over the side and floated in their gray kapok life jackets, watched red flames shoot into the twilight sky as bombs and planes exploded on the deck of the listing ship.

At 7:45 P.M., with the sky lit by fires from the dying lady, Admiral Fletcher ordered the *coup de grace*. Two torpedoes were used, and the Lady *Lex* disappeared from sight with three thundering explosions felt by many on the accompanying ships. Appearing to have ended in a tie, the battle of the Coral Sea was over, but the U-boat training of Wolfgang Topp had just begun.

FOUR

McKenzie Rivers opened the door to her hotel room in Moscow and saw James Stuart standing there. She threw herself into his arms. After a long kiss Stuart stepped into the room and Antonio Petrocelli followed him.

"Where's Annie?" asked the enlisted man.

"Asleep, I hope."

"I'll just take a peek."

As Petrocelli disappeared into the bedroom, Rivers gripped Stuart again. She was a slender woman with black hair to her shoulders. She wore Levis and a shirt from the days when she had first met Stuart during the Louisiana Maneuvers. Her hair, however, was longer than he remembered, and her body was much thinner.

"Oh, James, I'm so glad to see you." She clung to him, and then began giggling.

Stuart held Rivers at arm's length. Tears began to run down her cheeks. She giggled again.

"McKenzie, are you all right?"

The woman pointed at the coffee table across the room. A yellow sheet of paper lay on the table. The furniture was oak, large and overstuffed. Velvet curtains hung from cornices at huge double windows. The curtains were open, allowing in the gloomy light of winter.

Puzzled, Stuart took Rivers by the arm and walked her over to the sofa and sat her there. He picked up the telegram. As he read it, Rivers burst into what could only be described as joyous laughter. Petrocelli returned to the parlor and asked what was going on.

Stuart held out the telegram to the enlisted man. "We're to leave for Archangel immediately."

Tears streamed down Rivers' face as she nodded and slapped the cushions with hands made into fists. "We're going home! We're finally going home."

Petrocelli glanced at the telegram, and then at the woman on the sofa.

"Could you give us a moment, Tony?" asked Stuart.

"No problem," said Petrocelli, dropping the yellow paper to the table and adjusting the white parka he had never taken off. "I have to make arrangements to take Annie with us when we leave."

Rivers shook her head. "You can't . . . take her." She began laughing again.

"McKenzie, please . . ." started Stuart.

From the door, Petrocelli said, "I damn well will even if I have to smuggle her out of this damned country." The soldier slammed the door behind him.

Stuart went to the liquor cabinet and poured a glassful of vodka. When he returned to the sofa, Rivers took the glass, gulped down the contents, and shuddered.

"McKenzie, what's wrong?" Stuart took off his white parka and dropped it over a straight-backed chair. Matching scarf and gloves soon followed. Underneath was a wool uniform pants and shirt with the rank of American major, branch of service: armor. "Why did you taunt Tony about not being able to take Anastasia to the States?"

Rivers fumbled with the empty glass, trying to make it to the coffee table. The glass fell to the floor and rolled away. When Stuart bent down to retrieve it, McKenzie clutched his arm, bringing him down beside her on the sofa.

"Please hold me."

When he did, Stuart realized the woman had a significantly smaller chest. Still, there was something hard there, a crucifix, or what?

"James, I want to go home," Rivers said with pleading eyes. "I don't want to see any more people die."

Stuart took out a handkerchief and wiped the tears away. Rivers kept the handkerchief to touch up her face, a face much thinner than the last time Stuart had seen her. When had that been? Only a few weeks ago.

Rivers went on. "I don't want to see any more people dragging their relatives outside the city, using ropes, sleds, whatever they can find, then sit beside their dead mother, father, brother, or sister." Her arm gestured carelessly as she fell back into the sofa. "Or child. I don't want to watch them sit there, not out of devotion, but because they don't have the energy to return to where they can get warm."

The nervous woman glanced at the window. Below the dirty panes gurgled a steam radiator. "I don't want to be reminded that there's any army in the world that would starve a whole city to death." Again Rivers shuddered. "I shouldn't've come here. I thought . . . I was being so smart . . . I didn't know I was going to be trapped in a city the Nazis would try to level . . . the bombs dropped . . . the thousands of shells . . . ." She put her hands to her ears to shut out an imagined noise. Tears streamed down her cheeks. "All that noise . . . ."

After dabbing more tears away, she said, "It was worse than horrible. Russians singing in unison and linking arms to keep anyone from hanging back, and then walking into the mouth of the German war machine and being slaughtered." She shuddered. "The worst was when the women of the Communist Youth League, some only girls, picked up weapons and tried to lead the breakout . . . ."

All Stuart could do was hold her, and from time to time, feed her more liquor. Finally, the woman sat up, dabbed at her eyes, and straightened her shoulders.

She cleared her throat. "I got my interview with Joe Stalin."

"Good for you."

"No," she said, shaking her head. "I made an absolute fool of myself. The table was covered with food. His generals were there. Margaret Bourke-White—who's never been to the front but had all those photos published in *Life*." Rivers tried to force a smile. "Everyone had a gay old time. No one was starving in that majestic, marble room, no one close to death, and no one looking grim as they prepared to lead another charge out of a doomed city."

She looked into her lap. "I—I threw up." Rivers cleared her throat. "Stalin was so solicitous. He thought I might be sick, maybe even pregnant." She raised her head. "But it was all that food . . . and I didn't eat a bite." She gripped Stuart's arms again. "Please take me away from this place."

When Petrocelli returned to the hotel, he found Rivers asleep in the bed where he had left Annie. In Leningrad, Anastasia's mother had pressed the girl into the arms of the American sergeant and begged him to take care of her, then staggered off to die. Since a younger brother had died from hypothermia, Petrocelli readily took the girl in.

When Petrocelli came through the bedroom door, Annie rushed into his arms. "Sergeant Tony," exclaimed the little girl in English as spoken on the streets of New York City, "I've missed you." The girl wore a new yellow dress, her dark hair had been curled, and on her feet were a pair of sturdy brown shoes.

"And I've missed you," said Petrocelli, whipping the child up and swinging her around before setting her on her feet again. He stooped down in front of her as James Stuart watched with considerable concern from the far side of the bed next to where Rivers lay.

The girl's cheeks were rosy, her eyes bright; nothing like when they'd last seen her; clothing dirty and in tatters; thin beyond belief, with hands and lips cracked and bleeding from the cold. The change was remarkable, and in only a few weeks.

"Annie, you look great." With his cold weather clothing removed, the enlisted man's wool uniform and the three chevrons on the upper arm denoting the rank of buck sergeant could be seen.

The girl pointed at the woman sleeping in the bed. "Miss Rivers made me eat and eat and eat."

Stuart pulled down the covers. Rivers was sleeping in one of Stuart's shirts, and Stuart pulled the shirttail up over Rivers' underpants without exposing her breasts.

Petrocelli gaped at her. "My God, Jim, you can see her ribs!"

"She made me eat," said Annie, nodding and smiling. "Every time I woke up Miss Rivers made me eat."

"It's 'Mrs. Rivers,'" corrected Stuart, covering the sleeping woman, then tucking the sheet around her. "Her husband was shot down while flying with the Canadians."

"McKenzie had food in this burg?" asked Petrocelli, openly perplexed.

The little girl nodded. "Lots of it."

Stuart leaned over, loosened a chain around Rivers' neck, and kissed the woman on the forehead. Straightening up, he saw Petrocelli and Annie watching him. He cleared his throat and gestured across the room. "Over here."

They followed him to a wardrobe where he unlocked the doors with the skeleton key that had hung around Rivers' neck. Inside the heavy wooden piece were rows of breads, canned foods, and bottles of wine; fresh vegetables, stacks of canned milk, and miscellaneous items such as cheese, sausage, and hard candy. There was even a small tin of caviar.

Stuart closed the doors and locked the wardrobe. "From the land of plenty to the land of nothing. Worse than nothing." He stooped down in front of the girl. "Mrs. Rivers has taken good care of you, hasn't she?"

"Oh, yes," said Annie, beaming. She stuck out her stomach. "I am quite fat now."

"Since Mrs. Rivers watched over you, would you watch over her? Sergeant Tony and I need to talk."

In the parlor, both men lit cigarettes and sat on the sofa. After a drag off his smoke, Petrocelli asked, "Is McKenzie going to be okay, sir?"

"She was just dehydrated. Once I got some wine in her, her color returned. McKenzie comes from a privileged background. She never missed a meal, even during the Depression."

"But her father publishes a newspaper reporting everything horrible that's happening in the world."

"The head knew, but the heart had to learn." Stuart leaned over and tapped his cigarette into an ashtray on the oak coffee table. "What did you learn at the embassy?"

A frown appeared on the enlisted man's face. "Russia doesn't have enough damn food to feed their own and still they won't let Annie go. I don't know what'll happen if Moscow is taken. Will Moscow be taken, Jim?"

"If I were Hitler, I'd drive for the city, cut the rail lines, effectively cutting the country in half—"

"That's enough," said Petrocelli, holding up his hand. "I remember you saying the Japs would have to hit Pearl Harbor to have any chance of controlling the Pacific. I don't need to hear any more to know I have to get Annie out of Moscow."

"You really think you should take this girl away from her own country?"

"If Moscow falls, that's it for the Reds. That's why we were sent here, wasn't it? Someone will debrief you when we get home."

"And if I don't make it, someone will debrief you."

Petrocelli bit his lip. "How long before McKenzie's well enough to leave?"

"A couple of days."

"Cripes, the Germans are just down the road."

The door opened and Annie's head appeared. "Major Stuart, Mrs. Rivers is still asleep. May I come be with you and Sergeant Tony?"

When Stuart nodded, the girl closed the door carefully, and then ran across the room and leaped into Petrocelli's lap. Stuart saw the look of pleasure on his subordinate's face as he snubbed out his cigarette and embraced the eight-year-old. Both men were listening to Annie's description of the huge sled and horses that had brought them across frozen Lake Ladoga when a knock at the door sounded.

"Now who could that be?" Stuart snubbed out his cigarette and got to his feet.

"The Big Bad Wolf," said the little girl, scrambling out of Petrocelli's lap. "I've got to hide." She ran over to a wooden chest against the wall, opened it, and took out a stack of blankets. "Please help me."

Both soldiers glanced at the door, and then went to the chest.

"Take this, please," said Annie, not sounding at all youthful.

When Petrocelli took the blankets, the girl crawled inside the chest and drew up her legs. "Cover me."

Another knock and a voice said, "Please open the door, Major Stuart."

"Will you be okay, Annie?" asked Petrocelli.

"Hurry, Sergeant Tony. They've been here before looking for me."

✳   ✳   ✳

Nicky Lamm woke with the sun in his eyes. A voice asked if he was hungry. Who was doing the asking? Nicky could see the figure of a slim woman outlined against the sun. Maybe he was back on the Rock, but then the ground moved and without the benefit of an explosion. Around him came laughter and someone plunging into water. He was on a boat. Now he remembered. The Filipinos had pulled him out of the bay. After drinking some soup, he'd passed out.

"How long have I slept?"

"Four days."

"And the others?"

"You've been very ill. You should drink something. You have not eaten but once since arriving."

"Arriving where?"

"At my parents' boat."

"You . . . you speak very good English."

"At one time I worked for your army, Lieutenant Lamm."

"You know my name?"

"And Katie O'Kelly's. I have heard that name more than any woman would care to hear."

"I'm . . . I'm sorry." Nicky teared up.

"Don't worry, Lieutenant Lamm. I won't try to seduce you away from your girlfriend."

✳　　✳　　✳

Two men wearing heavy coats with gloves and musquash caps stood at the door of the hotel room. Their cheeks were rosy and their greatcoats could not hide their girth. Malenkov, the older of the two, asked in very good English, "Comrade Major, you have returned."

"Within the hour."

"From the front?" asked his companion. Boris Yegorov was shorter than Rodion Malenkov, and his dark, black eyebrows ran together whether he was frowning or not.

"May we come in?" asked the senior Malenkov.

"Of course. Rude of me to keep you standing in the hall." Stuart stepped back and held open the door. Petrocelli, who had taken a seat on the chest, lit up a cigarette.

Stuart gestured at the enlisted man. "I believe you know Sergeant Petrocelli."

"Usually your driver," said Malenkov, "but there is

little to drive in Moscow these days." A twinkle played in Malenkov's eyes when he added, "It has come to our attention that you are very well-acquainted with T-34s."

Stuart and Malenkov crossed the room and sat on the sofa while Boris Yegorov took up a position between the sofa and the bedroom door. From there, he glared across the room at the American sergeant sitting on the chest.

Stuart eyed the younger agent but spoke to Malenkov. "You cannot tell me the KGB doesn't have proper transport."

Malenkov removed his hat, gloves, and scarf and dropped them on the coffee table. The telegram no longer lay there.

"Not as well as we should." The KGB agent opened his coat to better let the warmth in from the radiators. "I have heard reports of spies crossing Lake Ladoga to escape the siege at Leningrad."

"Cowards," said Yegorov from where he stood near the bedroom door. The younger man had not removed any of his cold-weather gear.

"Boris," said Petrocelli from where he sat on the chest, "if Russians were seen sneaking out of Leningrad, I'm sure they were all political officers."

Yegorov's eyes narrowed but he said nothing.

"Now," continued Malenkov from where he sat beside Stuart, "I hear spies have slipped through the German lines and are in Moscow. Would you have any idea where these spies might go next?"

"If these are good spies—" started Stuart.

"And brave ones," interrupted Petrocelli.

Stuart glanced at Petrocelli. "If these spies have been in Leningrad, White Russia, and Moscow, it's only logical they would report to their masters what they have seen."

"And what would these spies have seen in Leningrad?" There was no twinkle in Malenkov's eyes now. "Would you care to speculate?"

"A city the Germans intended on starving and bombing into submission, but the people hold on—because of that ice bridge across the aforementioned lake."

"And in White Russia these spies would have seen?"

"Partisans with the will to win."

"And on this side of the lines?"

"An army stymied by the shock of the Nazi attack and lacking a sense of focus."

The junior KGB officer stepped away from the bedroom door. "There can be no doubting the spirit of the Russian soldier. We will soon launch a counteroffensive and drive the Nazis from our homeland."

"Boris," said Petrocelli, dropping the cigarette to the hardwood floor where he snubbed it out, "I have never doubted the courage of the Russian soldier; it's those who spy on them that worry me."

Yegorov started across the room, but Malenkov stopped him with, "Boris, these are our comrades. We may have our differences, but we are still comrades." He returned his attention to Stuart. "So, the Russian army with the proper leadership . . . ?"

"Will do exactly as Boris said: push the Nazis from your country."

"And these spies will tell their masters in Washington . . . ?"

"That your army will continue to be pushed back, more generals will be replaced, and more cities will fall, but nothing can sap the Russian spirit."

"Very well." Malenkov stood, taking his gloves, scarf, and hat with him. He shook Stuart's hand and crossed the room to shake Petrocelli's. "Sergeant, could you tell me the purpose of today's visit to the American embassy?"

"It's the only way I can communicate with my mother in the States. The phone service in this country is god-awful, so I write her whenever I'm in town."

Yegorov snorted as he followed Malenkov to the door. "A mama's boy."

"Actually my sister's ill," said the American, getting to his feet and evaluating Boris as any fighter would an opponent.

"This is a good thing that you do," said Malenkov, nodding, "to remain in contact with your mother." Then to Stuart, "So you leave for the port of Archangel when?"

Stuart produced the telegram and showed it to the Russian. "As soon as we are able."

"Good."

Stuart put away the telegram. "But I may have a problem."

"And that is?"

"Mrs. Rivers has become rather attached to the girl."

Yegorov shook his head. "My country may need the support of your country, but we do not care to have our children raised by capitalists."

"She's a frigging orphan, Boris," said Petrocelli.

"And the state will raise her."

"A child raised in an orphanage instead of a real family?"

"The Soviet nursery system has been turning out children for decades."

"Yes, Boris, people like you."

Yegorov bristled but said nothing.

"Comrade Yegorov is correct," said the older man. "It is best for the child to be raised by the state than by a soldier."

"So if Petrocelli was married?" asked Stuart.

"Who would want him?" asked Yegorov with a sneer.

"Oh, I don't know," said the Italian-American. "That Russian dame I met in the partisans seemed to have a thing for me."

Malenkov waved this off. "Comrade Sergeant, we did not come here to discuss your wedding plans."

"Would you discuss mine?" asked Stuart.

"Yours?" Malenkov faced the man who favored the American actor Robert Montgomery. "You have plans to marry?"

"Mrs. Rivers. If she will have me."

All three men stared at him. From the chest came a giggle. No one seemed to notice.

"How long will it take to have someone marry us and set up the adoption?"

"Major Stuart," demanded the younger KGB agent, "you expect the Russian government to do your bidding?"

"Not at all, but I do expect you to remember what Comrade Stalin told you the day you were assigned to us."

"Something about making sure we had everything we needed to accomplish our mission," said Petrocelli with a grin. "I always thought that included field duty for you, Boris, but evidently—"

"And this marriage would ensure—" began Malenkov.

"And adoption."

"And this marriage and adoption would ensure that your report reaches the ears of the American president?"

"Rodion, you cannot consider this," said Yegorov.

"If it takes one Russian child to secure a second front, then—"

"I will be no part of this." Yegorov reached for the door. "This is a slight against my country, and as for a second front, everyone knows the Americans are as afraid of the Nazis as the English are. Otherwise, why are the British fighting Italians in North Africa?" Yegorov left, slamming the door behind him.

"Will he be a problem?" asked Stuart.

"Only for me. When do you wish to have the ceremony performed?"

"Tomorrow at noon. I have some matters to tie up."

"I'll say," muttered Petrocelli, glancing at the bedroom door.

Malenkov buttoned his coat. "It is true what they say about you Americans. You are an impetuous lot."

"Well, Comrade, I can only say: Watch what we set our hat for."

"Your country had best set its hat for that second front. Comrade Stalin is becoming rather anxious." Malenkov glanced at the window behind Stuart. It was still overcast outside. "I'm not sure I'm not a bit anxious myself." Returning his attention to Stuart, he added, "You did yourself no favors by deserting the regular army and joining the partisans."

"The regular army was in retreat," stated Petrocelli. "We wanted to be—"

"Where we could find something positive to report to the president," cut in Stuart.

Malenkov nodded. "If there is anything else you should need, all you need to do is ask."

"Send over an aide that you trust."

"For the ride to the station. Of course. Consider it done."

"No," said Stuart, gesturing at the bedroom door. "There will be a great deal of food left behind when Mrs. Rivers leaves."

Malenkov smiled. "Then I will make sure I do not send Boris." Before leaving the room, the KGB agent glanced at the low wooden chest against the wall. "By the way, Comrade Major, who is the Big Bad Wolf?"

"That," said Stuart, opening the door for the Russian, "changes from time to time."

※　　※　　※

A few days after Nicky Lamm arrived in Manila, a Filipino came to see him. The woman caring for Lamm almost sent the young man away because Lamm had broken down when General Wainwright was forced by the Japanese to read the terms of surrender over nationwide radio. Jonathan Wainwright had personally executed MacArthur's double-retrograde (retreat) that had allowed thousands of Americans and Filipinos to escape to Bataan.

The young Filipino had a question for Lamm. "I understand you insist on leaving our country."

Lamm smiled at Terray del Mundo, who had nursed him back to health. "As soon as the good doctor releases me."

"You are aware that American soldiers have taken to the jungle and are organizing a resistance against the Japanese?"

Lamm nodded.

"We would like for you to join us."

"If that's true, why didn't you send an American so I'd know this was legit?"

"Nicky!" said the slender, dark-skinned woman. "Don't be rude."

Lamm lay in a bed filled with cushions. The Filipino had to hunch down beside the bed to speak to him.

"You won't find many of your kind in Manila. The Japanese say your fellow countrymen have been given sufficient opportunity to surrender and now must be considered part of the resistance. Colonel Claude Thorpe sent me—do you know him?"

"He was detached from Bataan by MacArthur to establish a resistance movement."

"His unit is encamped above Fort Stotsenberg."

"I can fly bombers, fighters, torpedo planes, scout planes—you name it and I've flown it. I'm not about to waste that training for the opportunity to run through the jungle and take potshots at Japs."

"Nicky," said Terray del Mundo, "if I'd known you were going to be so rude, I would have never pulled you out of Manila Bay."

"Lieutenant Lamm," said the resistance fighter, "if you choose not to become a guerrilla that is your decision. It's strictly voluntary. Anyone can turn himself in to the Japanese and enter one of the camps. Americans do it every day."

Lamm shook his head. "I'm heading to Mindanao. That's where MacArthur took off from."

"My God, Nicky, how do you propose to do that?"

Lamm inclined his head toward the partisan. "I figure your friend has a way to get me down there."

"Is this true?" asked del Mundo. "Do you have a safe passage for Nicky to Australia so he can fly again?"

"To reach Australia, I don't know. But we do have a secure route to the south."

"And that's why you're here, isn't it? You have a message for MacArthur."

"Only if you can bear to carry it, Lieutenant."

An increase in radio traffic by the Japanese convinced American intelligence that the Japanese were about to move on Midway. Ernest King disagreed. He believed the target was to be the islands in the South Pacific, whereas the Army Air Corps thought the attack would come in California. Douglas MacArthur knew it would be Australia, and each commander asked for more men and equipment. The chief of staff of the army sent them nothing. George Marshall was worried about Russia, as collapse of the Soviet Union would eliminate any possibility of an Allied invasion of Europe. Hitler would simply move his freed-up German divisions from the Russian Front to the shoreline of France.

To confirm that the Japanese thrust would be at Midway, a cryptanalyst in Honolulu instructed the commander of the island to send a message in the clear that Midway was running low on fresh water. A day later, Japanese radio traffic included a signal that their primary target was apparently running short of fresh water. Now Chester Nimitz, the commander of the Pacific Fleet, knew where to marshal his meager forces, but how close did he dare move toward the Japanese? And when?

Sweat poured off Nicky's body and drenched his worn and tattered uniform as he struggled through the hills outside Manila. His legs ached, and he had just begun his trek. A bowl of rice and a piece of chicken, a feast on Bataan, weren't enough to keep him on his feet.

"I'm not up to this," he said, clinging to a palm tree.

The young Filipino had stopped along the trail to wait for him. From each side of the trail, the jungle bore down on them, creating a dark, moist, and noisy tunnel as frogs, cicadas, and other insects chimed in. "Colonel Thorpe says the shock of the Japanese attack is a good thing. It will separate those who can fight from those who will turn themselves in for internment."

Nicky released his hold on the tree and straightened up. With a towel given to him by del Mundo, he wiped the sweat from his face, his neck, and then slapped at a mosquito.

The Filipino fished a pack of Camels from his shirt pocket. "Cigarette?" He extended the pack.

Nicky took a cigarette, then the light. "You're not

worried about me, are you? You're wondering if you've bet on a winner, the United States—right?"

The partisan let out a smoke-filled breath. "For years I have watched your countrymen leave their duties early in the day for a swim or a game of golf or tennis."

He gestured at the jungle surrounding them. Monkeys chattered from the jungle roof and parrots called out to each other. Insects chirped and the aroma of orchids filled the air. Orchids of all colors grew from trees, bushes, and from the ground. "The wives of your officers say to live in the Philippines is to live in paradise. They love the smells, the colors, and the sound of the surf striking the beach." The guerrilla took another drag off his cigarette and let it out. "But mainly the cheap labor."

"You believe the United States will free your country in 1946 as promised?"

"If you can defeat the Japanese—yes. But you Americans don't understand the Japanese mind and that is why I have been ordered to return you to Bataan."

Another guerrilla stood several paces off the dirt road that ran from where the American defense had collapsed on Bataan to San Fernando, the location of the internment camp. This Filipino also smoked an American cigarette and wore a clean uniform. His hair was neatly trimmed and his Springfield rifle greased and oiled.

Nicky still wore the clothing from his escape. There had been no way Terray del Mundo could request an American uniform without drawing attention to herself. And Nicky refused to wear civilian clothing and be taken for a spy.

"This is the one they sent?" asked the other Filipino, regarding Lamm.

Nicky was bent over, clutching another palm tree, trying to catch his breath.

"Lieutenant Lamm escaped from Bataan and Corregidor, and swam across Manila Bay." Manila Bay was thirty miles from Corregidor.

The Filipino reevaluated the American. "And how did he do that?"

"I don't think that's important," said Lamm's guide. "Lieutenant Lamm is determined to reach Davao and cross from there to Australia as General MacArthur did." Turning to the American, he added, "Corporal Roxas will be your guide for the remainder of your trip."

Nicky straightened up, still clutching the tree. "You're leaving?"

"Yes. I have seen as much of the road to San Fernando that I care to see." With that his guide turned his back on Lamm and disappeared into the jungle.

"Ready, sir?" asked Roxas.

Lamm let go of the palm. "As ready as I'll ever be."

"With all due respect, sir, that may not be enough."

Again Nicky had to use a tree to stand. He was suffering the dry heaves from what he'd just seen along the road leading to the internment camp. The ragged skeletons of his comrades had been left to rot where they had collapsed. Their bones littered both sides of the road. Starving, sick, and fatigued men had been herded down a dusty road by Japanese using bayonets. Nicky wondered if he would've made it.

"But why?" he asked Roxas.

"Japanese soldiers are drilled in the discipline of Bushido."

"Come again?"

"It's part of the Samurai code that demands you save the last bullet for yourself. You disgrace not only yourself but your family by being taken prisoner. If this happens your name is removed from the town or city of your birth."

"That's nuts."

Pointing at the skeletal remains of a corpse, his new guide said, "When these men were taken prisoner, they became nothing, less than human."

Nicky shook his head. "That's sick."

"Lieutenant Lamm, that is the way of the Japanese, and I would caution you, on your trip south, that you not forget it."

"And save the last bullet for myself," Nicky said wryly.

"It might comfort you to know that because Bataan held out so long, General Homma was returned to Japan in disgrace."

"Good," Nicky said, releasing the tree and standing on his own. It was one thing to bayonet a body, sever its limbs, or cut off its penis and stuff it in the mouth of the victim, but American soldiers had been ordered to bury the dead—and dying—in trenches along this dirt road. A guerrilla unit, of which Corporal Roxas had been a member, excavated a grave after noticing hands thrust from the dirt. Inside were men who had been clawing to free themselves from the earth.

"And the Filipino constabulary?" asked Nicky.

Roxas glanced down the road in the direction of San Fernando. "Two of each three dead are my people."

Nicky stared down the road. There were troops approaching in trucks. Japs.

Seeing the trucks, Roxas said, "We have to leave."

"No." Nicky staggered into the middle of the road in the direction of the convoy. "I want to kill some Japs before I leave."

Roxas came after him. The truck and jeep were less than a mile away. Dust kicked up by the convoy billowed around the vehicles.

"Lieutenant Lamm, you cannot do this."

"I—I can do something," said Nicky, stumbling in the direction of the convoy.

"I won't permit it."

Nicky glanced over his shoulder. "You won't let me kill a few Japanese?"

"No!" said the smaller man, throwing a punch with his whole body that connected with the American's jaw. "I won't let this road be forgotten."

Lamm collapsed in the dirt as Roxas glanced at the convoy now less than three-quarters of a mile away. Slinging his rifle over his shoulder, Roxas put his hands under the arms of the unconscious American and dragged him off the road and into the jungle.

✳   ✳   ✳

The door to the train's compartment swung open

and Annie burst in. She leaped into Stuart's lap. "I'm back, Papa."

"And where have you been, young lady?"

Petrocelli slid the compartment door shut behind them. "Terrorizing everyone on the train. Annie seems to think her papers give her the right to go anywhere and do anything she wants."

The girl pulled on Stuart's uniform blouse. "Come with me, Papa, or I won't be allowed to ride in the engine."

"Well," said Stuart, lifting the girl off him, "we will have to see what we can do about that."

In the seat across from him, McKenzie Rivers openly shivered. Stuart pulled the blanket around his wife's shoulders, kissed her on the forehead, and left the compartment with his daughter. After he was gone, his wife continued to stare out the foggy window at the miles and miles of snow, drifts piled up against the roadbed.

"This is how you're spending your honeymoon?" asked Petrocelli, taking a seat across from her. "You and the major can have separate accommodations. Annie could bunk with me."

"I feel better around everyone."

The enlisted man smiled. "Never thought I'd see the day when McKenzie Rivers didn't want to be alone with James Stuart."

McKenzie looked at him. "Before that ceremony in Moscow, Stuart never spoke of marriage. What I want to know is: Did Stuart marry me because he loves me or from some misguided sense of duty all Virginians have?" She glanced at the compartment door that her new husband and new daughter had disappeared through. "As he has toward Annie." McKenzie shook her head. "No, Tony, I don't care to be alone with James Stuart, not until I learn whether he truly loves me or not."

FIVE

Admiral Yamamoto, the commander of the Japanese combined fleet, had opposed war against the United States. Yamamoto had attended the Washington Naval Conference in the Twenties and served as a naval attaché in Washington. Yamamoto knew firsthand of America's industrial potential, which stood in sharp contrast with Japan's meager resources in both steel and oil.

Nevertheless, being the good sailor, he went about planning a strike to destroy the Americans' Pacific Fleet at Pearl Harbor, followed by driving the Americans from the Pacific, and then negotiating a peace in return for Japanese access to resources that would make it possible to forge more steel and refine more oil. That would be the *only* way to win this war.

So while the naval high command took kudos from an admiring public over the destruction wrought at Pearl Harbor, along with the fall of Malaysia and the

Philippines, Yamamoto warned that unless they finished the American fleet by the end of 1942, there would be trouble ahead. The Americans would begin cranking out more warships, planes, trucks, tankers—anything to aid their war effort.

Japan must force the United States to sue for peace, and Yamamoto would do this by luring the American fleet into a trap at Midway Island, the outermost link of the Hawaiian chain. That was to be coordinated with an attack on the Aleutian Islands, a ploy the Japanese navy was famous for: ships popping up here and there and smashing the enemy from an unexpected direction. If Japan gained control of Midway, from there it could seize Hawaii and force the Americans back to Seattle, Los Angeles, and San Francisco. The Americans would have to sue for peace, thus making the Pacific Ocean a Japanese lake.

The Midway task force was under the command of Chuichi Nagumo, the hero of Pearl Harbor. Trailing Nagumo was Yamamoto, with transports carrying troops for an amphibious landing. Even if the Americans didn't go for the Aleutian Island bait, Yamamoto still had more than enough ships to overwhelm the paltry resources of the Americans, totaling as few as twenty-five ships.

Just how did this superior number of the proper ships come about? During the Washington Naval Conference of 1921, the Americans and the British forced the Japanese to restrict the number of capital ships they would be able to build. Restricted so, the Japanese read the tea leaves of the future and determined that sea battles would be decided by who had the most aircraft carriers, not who had the largest fleet. By 1941, the Japanese had the best-trained carrier fleet in the world—just as German Panzer divisions were superior to other forces on the continent of Europe.

As an additional precaution, Yamamoto, as he had done around the Home Islands, set up a submarine picket line between Pearl Harbor and Midway. When the invasion of Midway began, Nagumo's four carriers, alerted by the picket line, would sail on an intercept course and finish off the Americans. To insure that the American fleet was at Pearl, Yamamoto ordered flying boats to rendezvous with submarines and refuel so they could fly on to Oahu for reconnaissance. Unfortunately, when the submarines arrived at the rendezvous point, they found Americans at the refueling point so Yamamoto canceled plans for the look-see at Pearl.

The admiral wasn't overly concerned. It wasn't merely his and Nagumo's fleet closing on Midway, but several transports and minesweepers from the southwest, along with a heavy cruiser from the occupied island of Guam. Perhaps Admiral Yamamoto would have been more concerned if he had known that the submarine picket line arrived on station several days later than expected. Japan had never lost a battle when the element of surprise was on its side, and now that edge was gone.

The attack on the Aleutians came first. Japanese ships were able to slip behind American lines and inflict damage on various ports and facilities. Then more good news. When the Americans discovered the strike force on its way to Midway, and B-17s flew out to bomb it, none of the Japanese ships were hit. This was a good sign, thought Yamamoto. The enemy was terribly inept.

Admiral Nagumo was having the same good fortune. After surviving a treacherous fog that threatened to cause collisions among his ships, the strike force sailed toward Midway under cloudy skies, similar to those that had hidden him six months earlier when he attacked Pearl Harbor. Nagumo also had the wind with him, which would aid in launching and recovering planes. That was not all. Staggering to the bridge was Commander Minoru Genda, air operational officer, who was suffering from a high fever. To see the architect of the attack on Pearl Harbor standing on the bridge alongside Admiral Nagumo raised the morale of every member of the staff.

The sound of planes being readied for takeoff brought another hero of Pearl Harbor topside. Recovering from an attack of appendicitis, Mitsuo Fuchida slipped out of sick bay. That was the easy part. With all the water-tight doors shut, Fuchida had to climb ladders leading through holes the size of manhole covers to reach the flight control center. Several times, in his weakened state, Fuchida had to stop and rest. Still, he arrived at the flight control center, in uniform, as the first wave finished warming up their engines. Fuchida immediately became concerned that the one-search-plane tactic was being used to search the waters up to three hundred miles around Midway.

The weakness of the one-search-plane versus the two-search-plane tactic is that the single plane, taking off before daylight so as to fly to the farthest reaches of its search and report back, flies over miles of ocean in the dark. A second plane, launched after daylight, compensates for the first plane's missing all the ocean that had been flown over during the hours of darkness.

Fuchida also noticed that two carriers were late in launching their scouts. One of these planes had engine trouble. When the problem recurred flying through some rather nasty weather, the scout cut short its flight and returned to its carrier. That plane's task: To overfly the center of the search pattern.

A little more than a half hour before sunrise, the order came over loudspeakers: "Aviators, assemble!"

Pilots rushed to the briefing room for last-minute instructions, then ran for their planes as the flight control officer barked orders.

"All hands to launching stations."

Then, "Start engines!"

Followed by, "Captain, head full into the wind, and increase speed for a relative velocity of fourteen knots."

White flames from exhaust pipes lit up the flight deck, as did spotlights. The sound was deafening. From the flight deck came the report that all planes were ready.

"Commence launch."

Once again, as in the attack on Pearl Harbor, the green signal lamp was swung and the attack planes roared off. And, once again, the crew of the *Akagi* waved caps and cheered their planes into the air. In the flight control center, Mitsuo Fuchida felt pangs of regret. Still, that did not prevent him from praying for the safe return of his fellow warriors.

The flight deck remained relatively quiet for only a few minutes, then the loudspeaker barked again, bells clanged, and elevators raised the second wave of attack aircraft to the deck. Maintenance crews wheeled torpedoes from ammunition rooms and secured them to the planes. By dawn, the flight deck was full of more planes ready to attack.

From the pilots of the first wave came word that they were under air attack and from antiaircraft guns. The Americans had known they were coming!

Still, the first wave of Japanese bombers destroyed hangars and fuel dumps while their fighter escorts went after the American aircraft. About this same time, an American PBY, a long-range flying boat, overflew the strike force. Everyone on board braced for the impending attack.

Four American planes were spotted winging their way in the strike force's direction. Three of them were shot down, and the other flew off with Zeros on its tail.

Another six American planes came in. Antiaircraft fire was ineffective and it took the Zeros to knock half of the attackers into the water.

The American planes released their torpedoes, which moved so slowly they were easily outmaneuvered. Two of the American planes veered off, but one continued toward the *Akagi's* bridge. Officers and enlisted men hit the deck as the plane just missed the bridge and crashed into the sea.

America Strikes Back

Over the radio came reports of American Marines in the skies over Midway leading the Japanese aircraft into antiaircraft fire, which appeared quite heavy, or, when all else failed, reports said the Americans were crashing their slow-moving Buffalos into the faster Zeros.

The leader of the air attack on Midway suggested a second strike. The Americans seconded the motion when they attacked Nagumo's fleet once again.

With no reports of American ships in the area—presumably they were responding to the attack on the Aleutians—and no signals from the submarine picket line, Nagumo ordered the torpedoes on his ninety-three waiting aircraft be swapped for incendiary and fragmentation bombs. It would take about an hour to change the planes' armament from torpedoes to bombs, so down the flight elevators went the planes and their flying crews, where they joined maintenance men to complete the task.

While this was happening, American bombers attacked the *Hiryu* and the *Soryu*. Down came the bombs, up went the waterspouts, and the Japanese carriers continued toward Midway unmolested. Next was a glide-bombing attack by the Americans. Most of those planes were splashed.

Then a warning from a destroyer in the strike force to Admiral Nagumo: Over one hundred American planes headed in your direction! The destroyer opened up on these planes, and then promptly stopped.

Oops. It was the strike force's first wave returning from Midway. Hastily, decks were cleared and the planes swooped out of the air. Soon, all carriers were recovering planes. Thirty minutes into the hour that it would take to change from ship-killing ordnance, or torpedoes, to bombs necessary to destroy facilities on Midway, Admiral Nagumo was informed of enemy ships sighted to the north of the strike force's position.

"American ships in these waters?"

"'Ten ships. 'Apparently enemy' is the report, sir."

How could this be? The submarine picket line had radioed no such warning, nor had Yamamoto's staff. Even the general staff in Tokyo had informed Nagumo that the American fleet was operating around the Solomons, well south of the strike force.

"Ascertain ship types and maintain contact," was Nagumo's order, and his staff went to work plotting the enemy's possible position. If this were true, the Americans were only two hundred miles away—which meant if there were carriers among those ships that weren't supposed to be there, the Americans were within striking distance of his own force!

"What is the status of the rearming?" asked Nagumo of the torpedoes-for-bombs swap; in other words, ordnance for facilities on Midway Island that could do little damage to American ships.

"Half complete," came the reply from below deck.

The admiral thought for a long moment, then said, "Cease rearming our torpedo bombers with bombs."

Members of the admiral's staff bit their lips. They were still looking at each other when another report came in from the scout. "Enemy ships changing course."

"But what type ships?" demanded more than one member of the admiral's staff. That order was relayed to the scout with considerable heat.

Scout: "Enemy ships are five cruisers and five destroyers."

Visible relief swept through the bridge. "Just as we thought," said a staff officer. "There are no American carriers in these waters. We can finish Midway and then deal with the American ships."

Minutes later, the scout dashed those hopes. "Enemy force accompanied by what appears to be aircraft carrier bringing up the rear."

Nagumo's staff was stunned into silence. An optimist offered, "The report said 'what appears to be.'"

"If there is a carrier among the American task force," said another, "why have their planes not been spotted?"

An argument among the staff broke out while Nagumo considered his options.

Then another message from the scout. "Two additional enemy ships, apparently cruisers, sighted."

"There must be a carrier among a fleet that size."

"We must attack," said someone.

By now, Nagumo knew that the *Akagi*'s and the *Kaga*'s torpedo bombers had already been armed with bombs and their Zeros were fighting off the attacks of the shore-based aircraft from Midway. Thirty-six dive bombers on the *Hiryu* and the *Soryu* were their only defense against the American carrier.

"Send the bombers after the American carrier," suggested a member of the staff.

"And what will be their support?" Nagumo gestured

toward the remains of the American planes sinking into the sea. "You see what happened to the Americans."

From the flight control center: "Sir, our planes are returning from Midway, many low on fuel."

A member of the staff said, "We must launch our bombers against the Americans and clear our decks."

"They could be lowered into the ship," suggested another.

Nagumo made his decision. "Recover the Midway strike force."

"Sir, we don't have time—"

"Clear the deck for recovery!"

"Yes, sir."

The weary maintenance crews began once again to lower the torpedo bombers into the bowels of the ship. There, they received orders to switch back from bombs to torpedoes. Bewildered crews could only shake their heads. A flight officer laughed. "Here we go again."

While the returning planes landed, the work of rearming the torpedo bombers on the hangar deck below proceeded furiously. Bombs were piled beside planes to get them out of the way, and those attack planes with torpedoes were ordered not to change to fragmentary and incendiary bombs intended for Midway.

Glancing at the sky, Nagumo asked, "Would someone shoot down that American PBY?"

"We have tried, sir, but each time our Zeros go after it, the Americans disappear in the clouds."

"Well, tell them to try again."

Orders were signaled to all ships: Once the recovery was finished, they would turn north, engage the enemy task force, and destroy it. The course change would also make it more difficult for the Americans flying out of Midway to interfere with the strike force's operations. The four Japanese carriers sailed in a box formation and were being screened by a good number of battleships, cruisers, and destroyers. Now those screening ships reported enemy planes approaching the strike force's position. Intercepting Japanese fighters took off to meet the enemy . . . whose numbers grew and grew in size.

"There has to be an American carrier out there," said someone on the admiral's staff.

Nagumo rushed to the window overlooking the flight deck. "Speed preparations for immediate takeoff!"

Minutes later, fifteen American torpedo bombers arrived and ran into fifty Zeros. The American planes were all splashed.

From a lookout: "Enemy torpedo bombers coming in low." Another lookout shouted that he had sighted enemy torpedo bombers approaching the port side. Evidently the American commander did not share Nagumo's concerns regarding bombers flying without fighter support.

Most of these American planes were shot down. Seven limped away with Zeros on their tails. None of the Americans' torpedoes hit the *Hiryu* or the *Akagi.* Japanese fighters, out of fuel and ammo, returned to their ships.

Flyers were clapped on the shoulder, congratulated, reloaded, refueled, and sent aloft again. Status reports stated that not one single ship in the strike force had been hit. The American flyers, however, were not the soft and cowardly people reported in newspapers back home; they were brave aviators who were simply not very skillful.

Could there be a luckier man alive, wondered Nagumo as he stood on the bridge, to best the Americans at Pearl Harbor, then finish the task at Midway?

Preparations for a counter-strike had continued on all four carriers throughout the Americans' recent torpedo attacks. Planes were hoisted from below deck and arranged on the flight deck, engines warming up. But with all the twisting and turning to avoid the inept American flyers, the carriers had to come about into the wind.

"Launch when ready," ordered Nagumo.

"Five minutes, sir," reported the flight control officer, "and all planes will be away."

The carriers began to turn into the wind. Visibility was good, clouds at three thousand meters, though there was a good bit of smoke from fighting off the American attacks. The air officer gave little thought to the fact that the smoke marked his position. He flapped his white flag, and the first Zero fighter gathered speed and whizzed off deck. At that same instant, a lookout shouted, "Hell divers!"

Everyone on the bridge rushed to windows and peered into the sky. There they saw three American dive bombers, not using dive flaps—meaning the Americans were coming in at a high rate of speed to drop their load—racing toward the deck of the *Akagi*. Machine guns swung around and fired at the attacking

Americans, then several black objects were drifting toward the *Akagi*. Those on the flight deck gaped and then ran for cover.

One . . . two . . . three bombs hit the *Akagi*. By the time the Japanese could get to their feet, the dive bombers were gone, unmolested, because their Zeros were too close to the water after returning from chasing the American torpedo bombers out of the area.

Nagumo stared at the flight deck. Craters had appeared among the water hoses and high-octane fuel hoses, bomb trolleys, and the bodies of pilots and their ground crews. Deck plates reeled upward in grotesque configurations. Everywhere he looked, planes stood with fiery tails pointing at the sky or broken in half or were nothing more than smoldering shells. Screams and pleas from the wounded floated up to the bridge. Then the smoke became so thick it was impossible to see the deck . . . until several huge fireballs from the torpedo storage blew out the hangar. The amidships elevator was twisted like molten glass and collapsed into the hangar. More explosions chased everyone off the flight deck. On the bridge, the staff felt the tremors.

Below deck, smoke billowed through passageways, forcing sailors topside. As the fire spread among the wing-to-wing planes, torpedoes began to explode. With the deck heating up and ordnance beginning to explode, the fires could not be brought under control. The captain ordered all magazines flooded to prevent more explosions.

Then came the report: "The helm is not responding."

Reports were coming in from the *Kaga*. Their sister

carrier had been hit four times, one bomb destroying the bridge; the worst was a hit on a fuel truck. The *Kaga* was an inferno, with members of the crew leaping overboard. Almost a thousand sailors would go down with that ship.

During the confusion, an American sub fired three torpedoes at the carrier. Two missed and one bounced off harmlessly. Once the nose broke away, sailors clung to the torpedo's aft section until picked up by destroyers rushing over to drop depth charges. The American submarine didn't reappear so the destroyers began rescue operations.

"Sir," said Nagumo's chief of staff, giving a curt bow, "you must transfer your flag to the *Nagara.*"

Nagumo could only stare at the damage on the flight deck.

"Sir," insisted the officer, "most of the fleet is still intact. You must command them."

"I cannot leave *Akagi.*"

Then came reports that American dive bombers had caught the *Soryu* turning into the wind to launch her planes. *Soryu* took three American bombs in less than three minutes, causing monstrous gasoline fires and walls of smoke that engulfed the carrier's stern. *Soryu's* captain, sword in hand to prevent anyone from removing him from his ship, sang the national anthem as the *Soryu* sank beneath him.

"Admiral," said the captain of the *Akagi,* "I will take care of the ship. Please shift your flag to the *Nagara* and resume command of the strike force."

"Sir," reported the flag secretary, after returning to

the bridge, "the only means of escape is by rope from the forward window of the bridge, then onto the outboard passage to the anchor deck. *Nagara's* launch will come alongside and you can reach it by rope ladder."

Nagumo nodded, then said good-bye to the ship's captain and climbed through the window with the assistance of his staff. The remainder of his staff quickly followed.

Mitsuo Fuchida was one of the last to go over the side. He was about to drop to the deck when an explosion sent him sprawling. Trying to get to his feet, he realized that both of his ankles had been broken. Fuchida was transferred to the *Nagara* with the rest of the wounded.

As Admiral Nagumo watched from his new flagship, he saw the American dive bombers returning to an American carrier that wasn't supposed to be out there, and this time the Americans were returning without the loss of a single plane. Where was the *Hiryu?* It was not possible that all four carriers could have sustained such damage.

The staff of the *Hiryu* informed Nagumo that not only had the *Hiryu* not been attacked, it had not even been detected. At that very moment their planes were attacking an American carrier they thought to be the *Yorktown*. Pilots reported they had put three holes in the American ship. Yet it was hard to see for all the smoke.

There was news from the Japanese flight direction officer. He had noticed that fewer Japanese planes were returning, and the returning pilots reported that the

Americans appeared to have developed a new type of defense against the faster Zeros. If an American plane came under attack, another plane would swing in and counterattack.

These same pilots also confirmed there were fires aboard the *Yorktown* and damage had been done to the flight deck. Very quickly, planes were reloaded, refueled, and on their way. But once on station, the *Hiryu's* planes reported the *Yorktown* was up and running, making almost twenty knots.

Sink her! came the order from Nagumo.

Bombers immediately put two torpedoes into the American carrier, this despite American cruisers lobbing shells into the water to throw up a protective shield of erupting water around the *Yorktown*. Japanese pilots shot defiant fists into the air as they flew through this screen of water to attack.

Minutes later, they reported the *Yorktown* dead in the water and listing so hard to port that the carrier might turn turtle. Americans could be seen abandoning ship. Any sense of triumph on the *Hiryu* ended as Americans, flying out of the setting sun, made their own bombing runs.

Where were all these planes coming from? And how were the Americans able to keep so many aircraft in the air? They couldn't be from Midway. Japan controlled the sky there. Was another American carrier out there? That couldn't be. The plan was for any other American carriers to be on their way to the Aleutian Islands.

Evidently the Americans didn't understand their role

in the Japanese plan. Four direct hits and the *Hiryu* became another floating inferno. The crew abandoned ship, all but its admiral and his flag captain, who shared a pitcher of water with their staff and went down with their ship. With this in mind, the navigation officer of the *Akagi* returned to his ship. There he found the captain of the dying aircraft carrier lashed to an anchor. It took some doing, but finally he was able to talk his captain out of going down with his ship.

After an order to withdraw was issued, Yamamoto relieved the hero of Pearl Harbor and put Vice Admiral Kondo in charge. Kondo was ordered to make a night bombardment of Midway. Then that mission was scrubbed and the Japanese retired for the night.

At midnight, "Midway operation canceled" was flashed to the remaining ships. The troop transports, primed to take Midway, retired to Saipan. The following morning, in dense fog and rain, the *Mikuma* and *Mogami* ran into each other trying to avoid an American sub. Both ships limped off for repairs. With rough seas and rotten visibility, Yamamoto stood down the remainder of the day.

The next day brought more bad news. American search planes had located the damaged *Mogami* and *Mikuma*. The *Mikuma* was on its way to the bottom, its crew abandoning ship. The *Mogami* was so badly damaged, it would take almost two years to repair. Then some good news: A submarine had sighted and finished off the *Yorktown*, along with the destroyer *Hammann*.

Yamamoto's retirement to the west was a last-ditch

attempt to draw the Americans within range of Japanese aircraft at Wake Island. The Americans refused to take the bait, and Yamamoto was left to reflect on the fact that not only had his country lost four carriers and a cruiser, but also over two hundred aircraft and their irreplaceable pilots.

The worst of it was knowing that the Americans who had opposed him had done so with an inferior force. There was no way the Americans could have suffered as he had. Yamamoto took to his cabin and didn't come out during the return voyage.

When the ships returned to the Home Islands, the enlisted men who had participated in the battles of Coral Sea and Midway were shipped off to the farthermost points of the Empire and the officers sworn to secrecy. Even Prime Minister Tojo wasn't told of the disasters for more than a month. Then, when the Japanese high command was informed that a massive shipbuilding operation was underway in the United States, they dismissed this as so much Allied propaganda. It was not possible that American "Liberty Ships" could be built in a matter of weeks.

SIX

An underground newspaper in the Warsaw ghetto reported news of the death camp killings inside German-occupied Poland. A young Jew said he had escaped from Chelmno, where gassings were taking place. He had been detailed to bury Jews and others killed in vans while they were en route from the railway station to the burial site. The young man reported that whenever he opened the doors of one of the vans, everyone inside was dead.

Deborah Geller heard this at the paper where she worked, and the news was more than she could bear. She was a thin woman with a haggard look whose elderly father had volunteered for work outside the ghetto. Had her father been a victim of one of those vans?

Geller, who had been romantically involved with an American spy by the name of James Stuart, thumped a fist on the desk where she was composing an editorial. "Where are the Americans? When are they coming?"

Her coworkers glanced in her direction, shrugged, and returned to their work.

Something had to be done, thought Geller, and she went to work composing a different type of editorial. It was important that this information be made public. Each day that her people faced starvation they might be tempted to volunteer for work outside the ghetto.

Or could this gassing be another rumor? Rumor had it that the Americans had struck at Japan; another rumor held that more than a thousand planes had bombed Germany in one single night; yet another claimed that the American president had given Germany until May 15 to surrender. Well, May 15 had come and gone and still the Nazis occupied Warsaw and made life a hell on earth for any Jew. Perhaps those who had been sent to the camps were better off. Who was to say?

Outside Moscow, the German army launched an offensive against Russians who had formed provisional governments in defiance of being made part of Greater Germany. Now, over twenty thousand Germans were chasing an unknown number of partisans through Russian forests. So far, the Germans had killed only a thousand.

Sonya Molotov was not counted among the dead. At that moment, "that woman" was browbeating some poor officer into giving her a chance to be a member of a tank crew. All the officer would agree to was that she could join a maintenance crew as many other women were doing.

Near the Baltic Sea, a twelve-ton rocket with a one-ton warhead was tested. Many of the German senior staff had traveled from Berlin to watch the launch. The launch was successful, but the rocket crashed to earth less than a mile away. Everyone was disappointed. Still, research was stepped up. At the same time, the Englishman, Churchill, and the American, Roosevelt, agreed to pool their efforts to develop what was being called an "atomic bomb."

Before the Americans joined the war, British intelligence had issued a bulletin: "Detachments of a German expeditionary force under an obscure general, Rommel, have landed in North Africa."

Erwin Rommel, like George Patton, was clever, ruthless, and absolutely fearless. A delicate child educated at home during his youth, he was awarded for his exploits during the First World War, the *Pour le Mérite*, a decoration reserved for senior officers. Rommel was twenty-seven when the Great War ended, and he would endure nine long years as a captain. The Treaty of Versailles limited the German army to a hundred thousand enlisted men and four thousand officers. And during those years, this most decorated soldier remained a member of the middle class, as he was refused entry into the upper class of Germany. He remained forever a man outside, and because of this benign neglect, Erwin Rommel took chances on the battlefield no one aspiring to be a member of the German general staff would ever take.

One of his favorite tactics was to smash through the

enemy's lines, assault their rear, and cause a surrender of those units behind his enemy's front lines. Rommel at war threw off the trappings of the typical burgher, and wreaked havoc and destruction before him. Later those tactics would become what was known as the German Blitzkrieg.

Rommel, like many members of the German middle class, was not unhappy with the election of Adolf Hitler as chancellor. He, like so many others, saw Hitler as the man to lead Germany out of its postwar misery and, at the same time, keep the communists at bay. By now Rommel was a full colonel in charge of the battalion serving as Hitler's personal bodyguard. It didn't hurt that Rommel was not only a military hero, but blond and blue-eyed, the perfect image for posters going up all over Germany.

Rommel was thrilled to be named commander of the Seventh Panzer Division, the division that thrust through the Ardennes and made the French sue for peace. This was the secret of the German Blitz: assaulting at one point against the enemy and thrusting into its rear. It suited Erwin Rommel just fine, though it made Hitler and his general staff a bit nervous. Rommel's lust for battle was insatiable. But he got results, racing toward his goals and crushing a disoriented enemy, and always, which really alarmed those in Berlin, Rommel led from the front.

And in Europe, he faced a foe he would face again in North Africa when Bernard Montgomery almost captured him. Rommel returned the favor by counterattacking and almost cutting off Bernard Montgomery from the rest of the British army. Now Hitler called upon Rommel to rescue Mussolini's army in North Africa. *Der Führer* wanted a man of action, not someone who would plan his way to victory.

Benito Mussolini had seized power in Italy with quite passionate but empty rhetoric. Now, almost twenty years later, he was responsible for over four hundred new bridges, over four thousand miles of new roads, and for more than six hundred new telephone exchanges. *Il Duce* had built schools, hospitals, and low-cost housing for his people. He introduced maternity benefits, social security, and the forty-hour workweek but took away the right to strike. All these accomplishments were touted in the Fascist-controlled newspapers, which never once did an in-depth story about the squalor many Italians lived in behind some of the most magnificent structures built since the days of the Roman Empire.

Italian ocean liners streamed across the Atlantic in record-breaking time, and *Il Duce* had finally settled Italy's differences with the Church of Rome, if not intimidating its Pope. Leaders from all over the world came to Rome to pay homage to a man who had come to power by employing gangs of unemployed veterans of the Great War to club the opposition into submission. Watching from Germany, Adolf Hitler learned a lot from Benito Mussolini, the most important being that people would give up their civil liberties for order in their everyday lives. Mussolini, for his part, raged against this German upstart who openly imitated the trappings of the modern fascist party created by *Il Duce*.

Remembering the glory that was once Rome, but had become a country overwhelmed by a population explosion, Mussolini took charge of the Italian army and launched an invasion of Ethiopia in violation of the League of Nations. In Ethiopia, Mussolini believed he would find a home for over a million surplus Italians and a rich source of raw materials. For this transgression, the League of Nations imposed economic sanctions upon Italy, and world leaders openly derided him as his military became bogged down in mud against a bunch of spear-carriers. When a professional soldier was sent in, the Ethiopian military finally collapsed.

Next, Italian "volunteers" appeared fighting alongside Nazis under the fascist Franco, who was attempting to overthrow the government of Spain. Following this, Mussolini flew to Berlin—where he was shown how to really organize an army to conquer the world—and he signed a pact in which the Japanese, Germans, and Italians agreed to eliminate the threat of world communism. This was followed by a "pact of steel" that promised each country would follow the other into war.

Still, Italy did not follow the Germans into war but waited until France had sued for peace and England was on the ropes. Only then did Italy declare war, and Mussolini announced he would ride a white horse in triumph after each Italian victory. Unfortunately there were none. After the British ran Mussolini's army out of Greece, he focused his attention on North Africa. Even worse luck. A small number of English drove across North Africa and seized Tobruk. Within days, the English had turned the port city into a resupply point for their own forces.

North Africa secured, Churchill pulled out most of these troops and sent them off on a fool's errand to the Balkans. There seemed little to worry about. Some obscure German general had taken charge of the Axis effort in North Africa.

Because of the reduced British forces, Rommel encountered little resistance as he drove toward Egypt. When his Panzers finally broke through British lines, the British generals, who only weeks before had been responsible for dazzling victories against the Italian army, were captured. Upon meeting his counterparts, Rommel took a pair of sand goggles from his opposite number and adjusted the goggles above the gold-braided rim of his hat, a symbol that would become as recognizable as FDR's cigarette holder or Churchill's cigar.

Then it was on to Egypt, with Rommel capturing increasing numbers of British troops. Tobruk fell in one day, along with tons of food and equipment. For this, Hitler awarded Rommel a field marshal's baton. Rommel is said to have commented that he "would rather have had another division."

Hitler would never send anything like what the Desert Fox needed. Berlin was concentrating on their invasion of Russia, and while Rommel became a world celebrity, Berlin treated his victories as nothing more than a necessary evil to keep the Italians in the war. So, for two years, across the north of Africa, the English and the Germans, because of the flat and open country, leapfrogged back and forth, assaulting each other and claiming great victories or suffering miserable defeats.

When news of the fall of Tobruk reached Washington, Churchill was meeting with Roosevelt. The prime minister, for once, was too stunned to speak. Roosevelt filled the embarrassing silence by ordering several light bombers, fighter bombers, and hundreds of tanks sent to Egypt. A pretty gutsy move on FDR's part, given that a Japanese submarine had just shelled Fort Stevens in Oregon, the first attack by a foreign power on an American military installation since the War of 1812.

On the Russian front, the Germans had begun their summer offensive. There were a few hitches, such as cities that preferred to fight to the death rather than surrender, but the Nazis brought in flame-throwers and burned out the defenders. In Paris, a thousand Jews were rounded up and shipped by train to Auschwitz. In Berlin, Hitler believed the Red Army was sapped of its reserves. That might be true. The Germans had crossed the River Don and were headed for Stalingrad. In North Africa, the British got their backs up and inflicted heavy losses on the Germans, pushing them back. That same day two thousand Dutch Jews were deported to Auschwitz.

Heinrich Himmler, overseer of concentration camps, flew into Auschwitz to watch the unloading of Jews, the selection of fifteen hundred to be tattooed and sent to the barracks, and the gassing of another five hundred: old people, children, and the infirm. Hitler's leader of the SS wanted to see if there were any snags when the corpses were dragged from the chambers, thrown into pits, and the chamber cleaned and readied for the next group. Satisfied with what he had seen, Himmler ordered the total cleansing of the entire Jewish population from Greater Germany. This he wanted done by Christmas.

What a pleasing thought, mused Himmler, winging away from Auschwitz. Not a Jew in Europe. How long had right-minded people dreamed of a Europe without Jews, but only the Nazis had the nerve and the will to accomplish it.

In the Warsaw ghetto, thousands of Jews were rounded up and sent by train to Treblinka. There, all but those needed to service the camp were gassed. In the first seven weeks more than a quarter of a million were killed. Toward the end of July the remaining men and women inside the ghetto were determined to resist, so they set up a Jewish fighting organization. Deborah Geller was one of the first to join.

The Germans were less than a hundred miles from Stalingrad, pushing toward the Caucasus, a mountainous area rich with oil. Instead of capturing Moscow and cutting the Soviet Union in half, Hitler had opted for slicing out the most important pieces of the Russian economic pie. In this, Hitler was violating the cardinal rule of Otto Von Bismarck, the creator of the modern German state: Never attack Russia.

In Cairo, Churchill's staff told the British prime minister that if the Germans took the Caucasus, they wouldn't be far from the Persian Gulf oil fields. The British chiefs of staff recommended North Africa be abandoned and British forces there be sent to the Persian Gulf. If the Germans seized those oil fields, it would reduce British military fighting strength by twenty percent. Churchill didn't have long to make up his mind. The German army had crossed the Kuban River, pressing toward the Caucasus.

The most vulnerable leader of the Allies was also the most experienced. Winston Churchill, whose mother was an American, had reached his first cabinet rank at only thirty-four years of age. This had happened because of Churchill's skill at self-promotion and because Churchill had actually escaped from the Boers in South Africa while reporting from the Dark Continent.

Winston Churchill was one of those rare individuals who understood that you took chances when you were young, found out if you were lucky, and went on to conquer your chosen world. Churchill's world was politics, and even when out of favor, and out of the government, he continued to stay abreast of the buildup of the German war machine during the 1930s. At that time, no one was listening.

Once he was in power, Churchill demanded everyone listen to his ideas, and only those who had the nerve to stand up to him earned his respect. Realizing that Great Britain could not defeat the Nazis on its own, even with the assistance of the Russians, he repeatedly prostrated himself before Washington for aid from America. When the Japanese attacked Pearl

Harbor, Churchill was heard to remark: "So we won after all!"

However, this was before Tobruk fell and the German war machine was on the march to link up in the Mideast at the Persian Gulf oil fields. A member of his staff reminded the prime minister that England had a rather slim hold on food and armaments from the United States. German U-boats were sinking one or two ships in every convoy from America, sometimes entire convoys at a time. Using slave labor, the Germans had built concrete submarine pens on the coast of France. From there they struck at will at American shipping.

※   ※   ※

Wolfgang Topp stood on his U-boat, taking the last few drags off his cigarette. The protective red undercoat of the metal boat showed in streaks through its gray surface paint. Rust was everywhere, even laying siege to the 8.8-cm gun on the foredeck, though the gun was always heavily greased. Algae had formed on the wooden deck and made footing treacherous. Wolfgang and his fellow crew members had spent the past few months training in the Baltic. Now they were on their way to more serious business off the west coast of England.

If Wolfgang had thought the members of his crew were tough, meaning the ones who had stood beside him the day their boat had been christened, today those men were an even more solid unit. The captain, a veteran of the Spanish Civil War, had whipped the new men into shape. Submariners who had hit their heads on every pipe and duct as they moved through the sub, or grabbed handwheels and instruments to keep their balance, had become part of a smooth-running unit. They could actually move through the ship during heavy seas with only a touch here or there to steady themselves.

Their captain was a stocky man in his thirties, blond hair under the peak of a navy cap. The captain's green-blue eyes matched his cap's brass ornament, which could never stay properly shined and was always greenish-blue. He wore a long leather jacket, leather boots, and a seaman's braid on his left epaulet. The captain had been topside as the U-boat had been maneuvered into navigable waters by electric motors; then the diesels had taken over.

Breakers hit the port side, throwing up a fine spray, as Wolfgang took one last drag on his cigarette and flicked the butt over the side. After making way for the shift coming topside, he slipped down a ladder in the forward hatch and then headed for his bunk, where he found his excited bunkmates. Two sleep periods from now they would be in the hunting grounds of the North Atlantic.

While the Germans marched on the Caucasus, and more Jews were gassed in Poland, and Rommel ran loose in North Africa, a debate broke out within the military leadership of the United States. General "Hap" Arnold, a member of the Joint Chiefs of Staff, wanted to break the air corps away from the army and form a separate air force, maybe absorb the navy's pilots into an American air force. And Arnold wanted to transfer those navy pilots to the European Theater.

Naval aviators were incensed. After all, the carrier-based aircraft had inflicted most of the damage at Midway. Naval aviators would like to see army pilots take off from a runway rising and falling before them, and upon return, drive full-throttle into an arresting wire. Even in an era of radar, sometimes it was dumb luck if you found your way home over the endless miles of ocean stretching before you.

If all that wasn't enough, MacArthur—whom the admirals feared more than any Japanese—demanded his own task force. MacArthur believed the Jap navy was finished after the Battle of Midway, and he wanted to seize the stronghold at Rabaul. So the army hatched a plan whereby the navy and army would work together . . . well, that's as far as the plan got. The army and the navy would never work together.

MacArthur and the naval aviators weren't the only broken record. Everyone was sick and tired of hearing Ernest King say "Japan must be checked," but Ernest King wasn't prepared to shed the blood of American boys, or lose what ships he had left, to prop up a collapsing British Empire. Eisenhower, now a force in the War Department, stood up to King and said that they could not allow England to fall because there would be no place to stage an invasion of the continent. Not to mention that Russia had to be kept in the war or the Germans would continue their march on the oil fields of the Caucasus, perhaps even as far as the Persian Gulf oil fields. Every member of the Joint Chiefs of Staff remembered how Russia had collapsed during the Great War and opened the door for the Bolsheviks to seize control of the government.

Then, code breakers in Hawaii learned the Japanese were moving into Guadalcanal. Already a fighter airstrip had been built in Bougainville, the largest island in the Solomons. From that strip, and the one the Japanese were building on Guadalcanal, the enemy could control the sea-lanes to Australia. A seaborne invasion could be launched against Australia as early as mid-August. Something must be done. Admiral King went before the Joint Chiefs again and said "Japan must be checked."

That created a rather ticklish situation. Most of the Solomon Islands were in Douglas MacArthur's sphere of influence, but Ernest King—one of the most even-tempered men in the navy, Admiral King was always in a rage—demanded Guadalcanal become a naval operation. So the Joint Chiefs moved the dividing line between Nimitz's and MacArthur's commands so that Tulagi and Guadalcanal fell under Nimitz's command, and then ordered Admiral Ghormley to Australia to give MacArthur the bad news. MacArthur was stunned. *Time* magazine called him "A Hero on Ice."

Ghormley remained in the rear, leaving Frank Jack Fletcher and Admiral Richmond Kelly Turner, the amphibious landing commander, to sort things out regarding the disposition of ships, men, and equipment for Guadalcanal. Kelly Turner had been shipped to the

Pacific when it was determined that he could not work with his opposite number in the War Department. Kelly Turner had a foul mouth and a nasty temper. He wasn't called "Terrible" Turner for no reason.

Other instructions came down from the Joint Chiefs: Major General Alexander Archer Vandegrift and his First Marine Division were to seize Guadalcanal in five weeks. Vandegrift would have to complete this mission with his force "scattered over hell's half acre," many still at sea. Most of his troops hadn't been thoroughly trained. The practice landings on the beaches of Fiji had proved that. A complete bust.

And where the hell was Guadalcanal? For this, Vandegrift's intelligence section employed the Australian coast watchers' service, made up of former plantation owners, missionaries, and ships' captains who had sailed into about every port in the South Pacific. Still, the invasion must come no later than August 7, 1942, reiterated the Joint Chiefs. The Japanese were that close to completing their airfield.

Frank Jack Fletcher had lost the *Lexington* in the Battle of the Coral Sea and the *Yorktown* at Midway. When General Vandegrift met him, Fletcher was in command of the *Saratoga*, along with the carriers *Wasp*, *Enterprise*, and *Hornet*. These were the last American carriers in the Pacific, and Fletcher refused to go down in American naval history as the admiral who had lost five aircraft carriers in one war. Vandegrift's Marines would be allowed just three days to disembark at Guadalcanal. The soft-spoken and well-mannered

Vandegrift said he would need at least five. Admiral Fletcher shook his head and said he was leaving the third day.

Upon hearing they were headed for a palm-fringed, sandy-beached, tropical paradise, such as Fiji, many a Marine didn't think that was such a bad deal. Those Marines should've been privy to intelligence garnered from planters and missionaries who had lived on Guadalcanal. That information caused Vandegrift to begin referring to "Operation Watchtower" as "Operation Pestilence." His officers called it: "Operation Shoestring."

A hundred miles long by fifty miles wide, and slightly south of the equator, Guadalcanal is a jungle that just happens to be on an island. Hidden by dense vegetation, the environment is fed by rain from clouds trapped against the spine of an eight-thousand-foot mountain. There were open slopes where men could make their way through tall grass, even on the jungle floor where nothing grew. But under the jungle roof, the Marines found colorful birds that spent their days screeching their heads off and insects and reptiles the likes of which they'd never seen before. Those creatures fed on each other and the rotting vegetation of the jungle floor. The whole environment created quite a stink.

Because of this, the Japanese were building their airstrip on one of the few flat pieces of ground in a grassy field by the Lunga River, and it was also why the Japanese left their Korean slave labor on Guadalcanal to do the dirty work while they lived in the former British colonial headquarters across Sealark

Channel. Guadalcanal was about to go down in history as one of the most bitterly contested battles since the Union army had driven the Confederates out of Northern Virginia during the Civil War. That irony would not be lost on Alexander Archer Vandegrift. He was the grandson of Confederate soldiers.

Unable to pass the physical for West Point, he entered the University of Virginia, then reapplied for West Point. Sorry, all appointments had been taken; however, there were vacancies for the Marine Corps. So Alexander Archer Vandegrift became one of those Marines who, between the world wars, refused to accept the proposition laid down—because of the British defeat at Gallipoli in World War I—that hostile shores cannot be seized from the sea.

Invasions should be made over open terrain—for example, beaches—and should avoid ports and other facilities. And as Vandegrift and other Marines began to learn their new craft, the army and navy derided them as "beach jumpers." The Marines persevered, not because they wanted to prove any new theories, but because if they did not become expert at "beach jumping" they'd be nothing more than the navy's police force. So, while posted to Central and South America, the Marines learned the art of jungle warfare. Service with sailors taught them to appreciate the importance of ship-based air power, and duty in China taught them never to underestimate the Japanese.

It was from this "school" that Alexander Archer Vandegrift earned his second star, then command of the First Marine Division. And just as the submariner

Wolfgang Topp had been molded by more experienced hands, after the attack on Pearl Harbor old salts from around the world poured into New River, North Carolina, to whip the volunteers into shape and indoctrinate them into the proud history of the Marine Corps.

Cleveland Woodruff was among the new arrivals, and everyone on his train ended up in the same outfit. C Company had been a paper outfit until Woodruff's train had pulled into Parris Island for the Marines' notorious boot camp; then it would be on to the Marines recently acquired base at New River. With over a hundred thousand acres, many facing the beach, New River was an excellent facility for launching massive amphibious training exercises. During the trip, Cleve became friends with Harvey Meadors from New York.

New York City? asked Woodruff.

No, said Meadors, Upstate—whatever that meant, thought Woodruff, hearing the phrase for the first time.

During the physical back in Richmond, the doctor had found nothing wrong with Woodruff. Usually the doctor would send a young man to a train that would transport him to boot camp. But there was no way the Marines would be able to train and outfit the number of young men volunteering to fight the Japs.

"Woodruff, you have any last-minute business you need taken care of?"

"No, sir, I do not." Woodruff stood tall in front of a doctor who had been pressed into service because of the thousands of men who needed to be processed after the attack on December 7th.

The doctor regarded this gangly young man from the rural South. Cleveland Woodruff had been the brother chosen to go off to war. The elder brother had been refused enlistment. Someone had to stay home and take care of the family farm, over two thousand acres in the Shenandoah Valley. During the Civil War, that valley had been the breadbasket of the Confederacy. Now, Great Britain and Prime Minister Winston Churchill depended on those fields.

"Woodruff, you have no business interests . . . a girl you want to marry?"

"Doc, isn't it the Japs who should be worried about their interests?"

The older man clapped a hand on the young man's shoulder and pointed at the door. "Son, all I'm telling you is that when you pass through that door, there's no turning back."

Woodruff stood even straighter. "I'm ready to go."

"Son, don't believe for a minute what you hear about this war being over in a few months. You aren't coming home after boot camp. Maybe there's a week's leave for you in the future, but sooner or later you're going to be shipped to wherever the Marines need you."

"I understand the risk."

"What I'm trying to tell you is that there'll be plenty of Japs to kill wherever the Marines send you, but I can only promise you one week with your girlfriend."

Woodruff considered this. "Now that you mention it, Doc, I would like to get married."

Elizabeth Randolph was sitting at a window in her

bedroom when her father said she had a guest in the parlor. When told it was Cleve Woodruff, Elizabeth frowned.

"Tell him to go away. He didn't even tell me he was going to sign up." Elizabeth Randolph was blond, blue-eyed, and cute as the devil, but with the sensitivity of most attractive nineteen-year-olds.

"Elizabeth," said her father, "you are not going to be rude to a man about to go off to serve his country."

"I hate this war, Daddy. I don't think there'll be a Christmas party worth attending. All the boys have gone off to those awful boot camps. Just how long does it take for them to learn how to make their own boots anyway?"

"You will not dishonor the sacrifice young Woodruff is about to make for his country. Now come downstairs."

Four days later, Elizabeth Randolph became Mrs. Cleveland Woodruff, and once her husband shipped out, she moved in with Woodruff's family. That lasted through the first of the year. After the holidays, Elizabeth begged off, saying she would wait out the war at home. Her father was living alone and probably in his cups. Her decision did not please her new mother-in-law. There was a thing or two the senior Mrs. Woodruff wanted to teach her new daughter-in-law.

At home, Elizabeth became so restless and bored that her mother-in-law suggested the two of them join the Charity League, whose members knitted scarves and hats for our boys going overseas. Surrounded by women, the older the better, was just where Mrs. Woodruff wanted to keep her restless daughter-in-law.

Unfortunately, one of the members of the Charity League knew how to fly. The members were aghast that one of their own would pull on coveralls and ferry planes cross-country. Elizabeth Randolph didn't have any skills to speak of, but she had had enough of knitting scarves and hats. She applied for a job as a plane spotter along the Virginia coast. If the Japs could bomb Pearl Harbor, what was next? Norfolk Naval Yard?

Elizabeth was about to enter a rather tedious and boring profession where she would no longer be a volunteer but a member of a new government creation, the Women's Army Auxiliary Corps, or WAACs. The upside to Elizabeth's new job was that her mother-in-law could no longer meddle in her life.

※　　※　　※

The skies were overcast as the American invasion fleet sailed toward Guadalcanal. It was similar to the cover afforded the Japanese when they had attacked Pearl Harbor, almost to the day eight months before. On deck, sailors and Marines sweated as they went through their final preparations. In the tropics, you never stopped sweating. Sailors' shirts became as dark as their denim trousers. Large blotches filled the back of the pale green twill dungarees of the Marines.

Many Marines stood at the railing, dousing their smokes and watching their guardian destroyers disappear in the growing darkness. Tomorrow night they would not see those destroyers disappear. Tomorrow night, they would be ashore.

"You know, MacArthur's navy is out there some-where," said one of the Marines, turning away from the railing.

His companion stared at him. "MacArthur has a navy?"

"That's what I've heard. Some destroyers and a few cruisers."

The Marine nodded. "That sounds swell to me."

On grimy decks, riflemen sat, squatted, or leaned against bulkheads, pulling maintenance on their rifles under the watchful eye of China Marines—those who had served with the Fourth Marine Division in Shang-hai. Machine gunners double and triple-checked long belts of ammunition in cloth loops, then replaced them in oblong boxes. Packs were slung on backs, jostled around, then taken off and adjusted, only to be slung on again. The process was repeated over and over.

Marines played poker or threw craps, showed off the most recent jitterbug steps to the sound of short-wave broadcasts—and the laughter of buddies—or hunched over comics featuring their favorite heroes. Some were lost in thought, wondering if they would do as they had been trained or if they'd let their buddies down.

Cleve Woodruff was fashioning a camouflage net for his helmet and, once again, thinking of his bride. He had not expected Elizabeth to be so active in bed the two nights they had spent together. Her demands had made him blush. His thoughts of Elizabeth were inter-rupted when he and his platoon were summoned to another "Know Your Enemy" class. In this, lieutenants who had never seen combat would read to their charges from mimeographed and hastily stapled manuals about tactics that made the Japanese the most feared fighting men in the Pacific.

Then came the announcement: "All troops below decks."

As they descended into the bowels of the ship, few Marines had anything to say; even fewer cracked wise. Many headed for Protestant services or to priests who would hear their confessions. Woodruff had more important things on his mind. Another letter home. He banged down the middle bunk in the five-tiered sleeping arrangement welded to the side of the bulkhead of the transport, then climbed in and began writing to his Elizabeth.

Some Marines showered, and for the first time they didn't complain about being sticky from the saltwater tap. They simply pulled on their uniforms and lay in their bunks, but only after checking and rechecking that they had everything: clean socks and underwear, shaving or mess gear, bibles, paperback books, photos of a pin-up girl, or letters from home. It was so quiet down here Cleve could hear the throbbing of the ship's engines.

"I won a pile of money," said Meadors, returning to his bunk. Meadors was Cleve's buddy, as the Marine Corps insisted on everyone pairing up.

"What good will it do you?"

"I'll mail it home to my mom. If she's smart, she won't tell my old man. He'll only drink it up."

Woodruff returned to his letter.

My dear Elizabeth,

I hope this letter finds you well and that your folks and mine are also well. I wish I could tell you where I am and what I'm up to, but there is so much security—all I can say is that it's a mighty important job they've chosen us to do and I hope I have the courage to do my best for my God, my country, and especially for you.

Sometimes I think about our future and the number of children we'll have and what kind of house we'll live in and what kind of car we'll drive. Sometimes I can see you pregnant with our first child, laughing and giving me hell—sorry for the language—and telling me what chores need to be done.

I've been promised a job when I return, and I intend to make Old Man Davis keep his promise. Working in a hardware store might not seem like much, but who knows, maybe I could buy him out. Davis's sons don't want the place, and I have to tell you I don't like farming. I always liked that folks would come in and ask help finding the right tool, nut, bolt, or whatever. It gave me a good feeling to be of service, and not being responsible for everything that goes on around a farm. And worried about the weather and how it will affect our crops. I saw those worries wear down my father.

*I don't want you living with such a bitter
old man. Anyway, owning a store in town
seemed to be a keen way to provide for
our family. That's what I think about when
I think about you. Our future family. I know
I didn't talk much about these things when
I was home, but when you're—*

"Woodruff, would you do something about that light?"
asked Meadors.

"I'm almost finished."

"You know, Elizabeth's got a Dear John on the way."

"Harvey, I'm going to ignore that crack. I'm going to
give the Japs a chance to kill you, and if they don't,
then you and I can square off."

Meadors laughed, turned away from the light, and
was instantly asleep. Cleve wasn't so fortunate. Finishing his letter, he lay in the darkness. In that, he
suffered a similar malaise as his commanding officer.
Archer Vandegrift spent most of the night staring
through a porthole and praying for the clouds to remain overhead, at least until his invasion force had
closed with Guadalcanal.

SEVEN

Antonio Petrocelli, James Stuart, his new bride, and his adopted daughter had little trouble reaching Archangel. The Russians were running trains between Moscow and the port city twenty-four hours a day. Occasionally a train was sidetracked for an oncoming express, but still they made excellent time. Their papers made it possible for them to sail for England the day of their arrival.

If that was a good thing. U-boat wolf packs operated in these waters and sometimes it could be tough for a convoy to slip through. Nevertheless, they did have a better chance of reaching England than a ship sailing from the United States. Admiral Ernest King continued to rob ships from the North Atlantic for service in the Pacific, and American ships were being sunk regularly.

Petrocelli noticed Stuart and his wife didn't act like usual newlyweds. A remoteness had set in between

McKenzie Stuart, née Rivers, and her new husband. This was odd. Petrocelli could remember when Rivers and Stuart had schemed to be alone together. The lack of enthusiasm by his new bride, however, did not seem to bother Stuart. He busied himself with his report on the conditions in Russia, even having Petrocelli read it and make suggestions. Stuart had learned during the Louisiana Maneuvers that Petrocelli had an eye for what the average soldier might need. In addition, McKenzie kept busy composing articles for United Press.

Occasionally, Petrocelli would take Annie for a turn around the ship, hoping the two Stuarts would fall into each other's arms. At least talk. Upon returning, it didn't appear anything was different. No mussed hair, no black rages, no . . . well, nothing. Soon Petrocelli went looking for someone he could talk to and Annie was left to her own devices.

Her new father warned Anastasia that if there were any complaints from fellow passengers or members of the crew, she would spend the rest of the trip in their cabin. And where Annie might try to pull the wool over the eyes of Petrocelli or McKenzie, she dutifully said, "Yes, Papa," and did as Stuart instructed.

In their cabin were two sets of bunk beds. Petrocelli and Annie slept in one set while Stuart and Rivers used the other—until the first U-boat attack. That got McKenzie into bed with Stuart and one thing led to another.

The following morning everyone acted as if nothing had happened. Annie could sleep through anything, but with the second U-boat attack, Petrocelli went topside, ostensibly to watch the fireworks. What the Stuarts had been doing in that lower bunk sounded more like two people at war than two people loving each other.

All in all, Petrocelli was happy to reach England and looked forward to checking out the local pubs, along with any available gals. Instead, they were met at the docks and ordered to report to the supreme commander. McKenzie gave her new husband a peck on the cheek. Annie hugged each man and told them she would miss them. Then, it was off to Eisenhower's headquarters, Stuart never looking back. Petrocelli did and saw Annie waving good-bye and McKenzie instructing the driver how to stow their bags. When they would see those two again, the sergeant had no idea.

✳   ✳   ✳

Rising out of the mist as the Americans rounded Guadalcanal's northwest tip was cone-shaped Savo Island, the creation of volcanic action. This was the entrance to Sealark Channel, where the fleet would split up. Ships carrying the main body would take up stations off Guadalcanal's beaches. The lesser force sailed north, then east to a point off the islands on the other side of the channel. The lesser force's target was the seaplane base at Tulagi. MacArthur's B-17s had pounded all targets for more than a week, but that wasn't something the navy mentioned in its after-action reports.

At 4:30 A.M. Marines were piped to breakfast—the

officers had been up earlier—a meal some Marines found difficult to eat because of a severe case of the jitters. Others ate plenty. Who knew when they would eat again like this?

At dawn, a cruiser catapulted a scout plane into the air. Shortly after that, American cruisers and destroyers opened fire and Admiral Fletcher's planes lifted off and began dropping their ordnance. The Japanese on both sides of the channel woke up to find the channel filled with enemy ships. Seaplanes in Tulagi harbor were instantly turned into floating pyres. Shore batteries sprang into life only to be pounded to pieces. The Japanese on Tulagi radioed the Imperial Command that they were under attack and fell back to the caves in the hills, where they vowed they would fight to the death. Still, there was no answering fire from Guadalcanal.

Standing at the rail, Cleve could not help but be taken with the beauty of the island. A ridge ran down Guadalcanal's spine. Someone said Mount Austen was eight thousand feet tall. He hoped he wasn't going to have to climb Mount Austen. The practice run on the beaches of Fiji had been exhausting with all the equipment he had to carry. To Cleve, the island of Guadalcanal appeared lush and wet; a sea of grass on the ridges, blue waves washing over gray beaches, and coconut trees beckoning them ashore—until shells began crashing into them. The bombardment went on for more than two hours, and then the Marines were ordered over the side.

Cleve watched the stubby Higgins boats lowered

away, then the cargo nets unrolled. Cleve went over the side, and with all that equipment on his back, others quickly caught up with him, stepping on his fingers. Cleve finally let go and thumped to the bobbing deck of the landing craft. Loaded to capacity, the Higgins boat maneuvered away from the transport, rising and falling in the swells as it motored into position with others to head for what the Marines had designated as "Beach Red." They were to land at nine o'clock. In one of the boats was a coastwatcher, or an Australian who knew his way around the island.

Marines stared over gunwales in the direction of the emerald isle being chewed up by bombs, cannon fire, and red tracers from carrier planes. Many swallowed hard and muttered prayers. Behind them, and across Sealark Channel, it sounded like Lt. Col. "Red Mike" Edson's 1st Marine Raider Battalion was catching hell trying to secure the seaplane base at Tulagi. Still, there was no return fire from Guadalcanal, even the minesweepers were going about their work unmolested.

It must be a trick, thought Cleve as his boat roared toward a shoreline where palm trees collapsed onto the beach or were blown sky-high. The Japs were waiting for them to get closer, as in those movies where the Redcoats line up and fire all at once. Then a shout from his sergeant and over the side of the boat he went, pack and all. Cleve rushed into the surf, screaming his head off, and quickly found himself off the narrow beach, even more quickly experiencing the tropical rain forest.

Cleve went to one knee in the soft terrain and looked around. His buddies were equally puzzled. There was nothing here but the darkness and the vines, ferns, or other flora Cleve didn't recognize. Marines soon learned you did not want to bump into a vine descending from one of the huge trees supporting the canopy. When you did, from that jungle roof could fall scorpions or red ants. Still, there wasn't a single Jap in sight. From across the channel came explosions of dug-in Japs being dug out by "Red Mike" Edson's 1st Raider Battalion. Where the hell were the goddamn Japs?

Cleve sweated under the weight of his weapon, ammo, and other equipment. His denims quickly became soaked and he began to develop a rash between his legs. Alongside him, Harvey Meadors stumbled as the soft ground gave way beneath him. Before he could lift his foot, Meadors' boot passed through a log that shattered at his touch. The boot appeared on the other side, covered with ants. Meadors stomped them off.

Men were talking among themselves, their leaders unable to hush them as they moved under the canopy and toward the airstrip. Certainly they would run into Japs there. Someone said there were supposed to be twenty-five hundred of the bastards on the island. But not here. Only the quiet of the jungle floor, occasionally broken by the screech of an unidentifiable bird and the sound of cicadas, if Guadalcanal had cicadas.

On the beach, where supplies continued to pile up, General Vandegrift came ashore and listened to his division commanders' frustration about not being able to make contact with the enemy. It appeared the Japanese had taken to the hills.

Vandegrift said, "I'm beginning to doubt whether

there's a Jap on the whole damned island."

A few hours later Cleve's unit ran into its first green wall. It was as if God had plopped down a wall of tangled tropical growth in the middle of the jungle and lit it with sunlight for all to see. Older hands, experienced fighters from Nicaragua, told them that where the sunlight reaches the jungle floor, usually near rivers and creeks, the Marines would find undergrowth lining both sides. This had to be a branch of the Ilu. Still, they would have to find a way. The Marines were doing just that, with machetes, when the Japanese launched their first attack.

Cleve could hear the thud of bombs exploding behind them. Had the other Marines gotten off their transports safely? He was glad to be here, sweating like a pig, especially when the dive bombers hit. Several explosions could be heard coming from the general direction of the channel, different from the thud of bombs hitting the surface of the water, and then the fighting ended, the enemy driven off, Cleve figured, by the navy's carrier aircraft. Overhead, planes sped by and there was no sound from the jungle roof. Even the crickets, or whatever was making that sound, were quiet. Cleve's unit returned to the problem of crossing this branch of the river.

Their obstacle was filled with small trees, ferns, and vines, but worse were the centipedes that bit, along with snakes, crabs, and rats, all larger than anything Cleve had seen, and he had been raised in the country. The frigging wasps were as long as your finger, and in the trees, birds looking like vultures stared down at them, apparently waiting their turn.

Crossing the Ilu was as far as the Marines made it on D-day. When the sun went down they were well short of the airfield, so pickets were set out, foxholes dug, and guard shifts assigned. From their "Know Your Enemy" classes, Marines remembered how a Jap could slip into camp under cover of darkness, slit your throat, and disappear before your buddy knew you were dead. The Japs were real devils, and effective ones, too.

A hand shook Cleve awake. Or had it been the gunfire?

"Japs," explained Meadors.

Cleve and Harvey threw themselves against that side of their foxhole, secured their helmets on their heads, and returned fire.

The firing went on for more than half an hour, bullets zinging overhead, along with red tracers, and then someone who had access to a radio ordered, "Cease fire!"

Silence was followed by a loud snort of disgust everyone recognized as coming from a gunnery sergeant who had served with the Marines in China. Cleve and Harvey glanced at each other.

"What is it?" demanded more than one Marine.

"We were firing at our own men," was finally passed through the ranks, and then it was whispered up and down the line for those who had been hit to call for the corpsman to come forward. Ten minutes later, there was still no need for corpsmen.

Meadors shook his head. "I hope to hell we don't run into any damn Japs."

The following day, the Marines left the darkness of the jungle canopy for the bright sunlight of the airstrip. Despite warnings from their sergeants, they bunched up to hustle through a hole blown in the jungle by an errant bomb. Nobody wanted to hack or squeeze his way through another green wall.

On the other side of this wall, Marines spread out and went to one knee, brought up their rifles, and surveyed the strip. It contained several hangars, a dirt runway almost four thousand feet long, a control tower with an arching roof, and bulldozers and other construction gear, all intact. Ordered to stay off the runway, Cleve's unit entered a building with no sides and plenty of benches and tables, and found bowls of rice.

They secured the area and reported that the Japanese construction workers must not've been armed because they'd all hightailed it out of there. Upon further inspection, the Marines discovered the landing field had a power plant supplying electricity to an ice plant and a radio station. Inside one building, huge bins were filled with wormy rice.

Once the field was secured, General Vandegrift and his staff came forward in jeeps and trucks, and tons of equipment started arriving from the jammed beaches where "Terrible" Turner was nagging the Marines to move their gear off the beach. Japanese planes had already struck, so their navy couldn't be far behind.

Climbing down from his jeep, Vandegrift stared in

the direction of the mountains and jungle forest. "It looks like Nicaragua all over again."

A battalion was left behind to secure Henderson Field, named for a Marine bomber commander who had crashed his plane into a Japanese ship at Midway. For Cleve and his unit, it was up and moving again, heading in the direction of Mount Austen.

Sweat ran in rivers and several men passed out. God, but it was hot, and that grassy ridge seemed a long, long way off. Cleve's unit did not make the ridge but dug in for the night. After settling into their foxhole and removing their helmets, Cleve looked at Harvey with a broad grin; two blond and scrawny boys from different parts of the country who had been paired up and sent off to war. Damn, but it'd been easy to take Guadalcanal.

Kelly Turner, chief of amphibious landings, stayed on station, believing the Japanese cruisers too far away. Frank Jack Fletcher, however, radioed Admiral Ghormley that he had lost too many planes, actually one-fifth, during the recent Japanese aerial attack. Fletcher was pulling out without telling Turner or Vandegrift. The Marines had received not five, not three, but only two days' air cover. Also unknown to Turner was the fact that Rear Admiral John S. McCain, commander of land-based aviation in the South Pacific, had few aircraft in the air that might spot any approaching Japanese task force.

Rabaul is a port in New Britain, and the island of New Britain lies northeast of New Guinea; New Guinea is northeast of Australia. The port of Rabaul had been seized by the Japanese in January and had become a main staging area for Japanese operations, especially to the south. An old adage in the Japanese navy said, "An island is an unsinkable aircraft carrier."

Rabaul was fast becoming one of those unsinkable aircraft carriers as the Japanese added additional landing strips in preparation for seizing New Guinea and Port Moresby. That meant there were plenty of men and material in Rabaul to be thrown at the Americans when Yamamoto's orders came down to drive the Marines off Guadalcanal.

Gunichi Mikawa was the Japanese admiral who had sent the torpedo bombers Cleve Woodruff had heard being shot out of the sky by American flyers the day they landed on Guadalcanal. Mikawa's torpedo bombers had sunk an American transport and damaged a destroyer, but, unknown to Mikawa, his torpedo bombers had caused even more damage to the Marine cause: Frank Jack Fletcher had withdrawn his carrier fleet. Mikawa sent five troop transports to reinforce Guadalcanal. Unfortunately, an American sub discovered the convoy and sent one of the transports to the bottom. The remaining ships were recalled to Rabaul.

While all this was happening, Admiral Mikawa was pulling together a makeshift task force. So quickly was the task force formed that tactical information was blinked to each of the seven cruisers as they sailed down a sea corridor in the Solomon Islands. Mikawa's plan was a hit-and-run attack. He would enter Sealark Channel and smash whatever American ships were there, and then continue out of the channel and be gone before Fletcher's carrier aircraft could strike at dawn.

Because Mikawa's task force had to sail during daylight hours, an American search plane radioed the task force's location to Guadalcanal. The information came in during the midnight watch change and was not passed along to Admiral Turner, who was holding a flag conference with General Vandegrift and the leader of the British ships attached to the Guadalcanal landing. In addition, squalls had broken out at the entrance of Sealark Channel, giving the attacking Japanese more cover. It might not have made any difference. Most sailors had been at general quarters for over two days and were dead on their feet.

Dug in for another night, Cleve Woodruff and Harvey Meadors watched lightning flash in the distance. Now if that rain would come a bit closer. The two Marines got their wish. The rain finally did come, soaking them and filling their foxhole with water.

At 2 A.M. both men woke to the sound of airplanes overhead. The planes had their lights on and were dropping parachutist flares that turned the night sky green. Marines blinked in surprise and looked upward.

What the hell was going on? If the planes were theirs, and they had to be because they were flying with their lights on, why were they lighting up the channel?

Suddenly Sealark Channel rocked with the sound

of great guns. Flashes lit up the night in the direction of Savo Island. That was followed by more cannon fire, then searchlights scanned the night for targets. From the Marines' position, it appeared that someone was having a Fourth of July fireworks show to end all shows. And it was your usual fireworks show, brilliant flashes lasting a matter of minutes. Occasionally a shell exploded below the Marines' position or soared overhead, to be lost on the other side of the ridge.

Word was the Japs were landing on Red Beach. They might not make the grassy ridge, but one could never tell, so word was passed along for the Marines to stay alert. For more than a half hour, the big guns continued to roar, and then those same guns became muffled as the combatants sailed through Sealark Channel.

Jeez! thought Cleve, the navy must be kicking butt.

Before dawn, the channel went silent and the remaining fires were doused before first light. By that time, Cleve's unit was up and moving to secure the ridge before the Japanese did. During one of their periodic halts so that men in the unit wouldn't pass out in the tropical heat, their lieutenant spoke to squad-sized gatherings while the rest of the platoon pulled security. Around them, the air reeked of cordite drifting in from Sealark Channel.

"Men," said their leader, "I've been informed that there are no ships in the channel. They've all been sunk or sailed away."

"The Japs?" asked someone. "Are they there?"

"That's what I'm trying to tell you, Marine. There's nobody there, not a single ship left in the channel."

Now the platoon leader had their complete attention. "Listen up. We don't know when the good guys will return, so it's up to us to make do until they arrive. We've got half rations for five weeks and ammo for a four-day fight, but no radar, aircraft, or heavy guns."

By now, the members of the squad were openly staring at him.

"What I'm telling you is the Japs could drop bombs, land troops, or sit offshore and shell us all to hell."

The Marines looked at each other; some stared at the ground. Those with cigarettes didn't notice their smokes fall from their hands. Finally, one of the Marines screwed up the courage to ask, "This isn't going to be another Bataan, is it?"

EIGHT

A variety of Filipino watercraft instead of PT boats, which had taken MacArthur's family and staff off Corregidor, ferried Nicky Lamm through choppy seas to the southernmost island of the Filipino archipelago where twenty-five thousand Filipinos held out against the Japanese. Another boat was provided, a larger craft, for the longer trip to Australia.

When Nicky Lamm arrived in Australia, he refused all attempts to be hospitalized and insisted on being taken to see MacArthur. Not only was Lamm sick from his trip from Davao, but he hadn't been able to rid himself of a fever he'd contracted crossing from the northern Philippines to the south.

At headquarters Nicky made it clear that he would talk with MacArthur and only MacArthur, then stomped out of the office. Actually, Lamm staggered away and was caught by MPs before he collapsed. He was being ordered not to leave until he had been debriefed when the officer doing the ordering realized the young man had passed out.

Nicky was rushed to the hospital, where he was treated for the aforementioned fever, extreme sunburn, and dehydration, and placed under guard. When he regained consciousness, a young, blond Australian nurse told him what he had heard before. Nicky was safe, the horrors he had seen were all behind him, and she wouldn't try to steal him from his true love.

"What are you . . . talking about?"

"You have suffered a great deal, Lieutenant, and it's only right you be cheered up by your girlfriend. I can get a wheelchair and take you to a phone."

"Thank . . . thank you."

"But," said his angel of mercy, not smiling now, "before you can speak to Nurse O'Kelly, you must be debriefed by General Sutherland's staff."

"Tell Sutherland to go screw himself." Nicky paused. "Sorry for the language."

"Oh, Lieutenant Lamm," said the angel with a smile, "we are becoming used to the ways of you Americans—your language, too."

It wasn't long before the Great Man arrived to interview Lamm. MacArthur sat on the bed next to Nicky's and listened to what the flyer had to say about the Death March; then he nodded, got to his feet, and left with his entourage. Everyone noticed that the Great Man's shoulders were slumped, his gait not so spry, and his countenance grim.

What they never learned was that when MacArthur

reported Lamm's tale to Washington, he was forbidden to speak of the Death March. Washington feared the American public would demand a greater reaction against Japan, and Washington wanted to whip the Nazis first. For that reason, Charles "Doc" Ryder's 34th Division had been sent to Northern Ireland the first of the year.

❇   ❇   ❇

Once James Stuart left Eisenhower's headquarters, Ike turned to the other man in the room, a thin, sickly man who would barely live to see the end of the war. Harry Hopkins was literally working himself to death. FDR's friend and devoted slave, Hopkins tolerated the doctor assigned to him by the president.

"Just who is this Major Stuart?" asked Eisenhower, "if you don't mind my asking."

"Stuart's father went to prep school with the president. Stuart's great-uncle was the Confederate cavalry officer Jeb Stuart."

Eisenhower nodded. Everyone knew "Jeb" Stuart. Stuart had literally run rings around the Union Army—twice—until Phil Sheridan had begged Grant for the opportunity to track down and kill the rebel general.

"Who does he report to?" asked Ike.

Hopkins smiled. "Why, he reports to you, Ike."

Eisenhower grunted. Politicians and their games. When Ike had reached Washington only days after the attack on Pearl, he heard a story about an officer who had tried to warn those in the War Department about the impending attack. Ike never did get a name, and he quickly learned it wasn't anything a rising general wanted to inquire about.

The reason the story wouldn't die was because the officer in question had been shipped off to the Russian Front. That part of the tale had been true, and now Harry Hopkins, which meant ultimately FDR, knew more about the Russian situation than did Stalin, who was kept up to date by lackeys and bootlickers.

"At least Stuart comes from good genes," Ike said.

"Just barely," said Hopkins. "Stuart's father was killed doing intelligence work during the Great War. Stuart's brother and mother were killed by the Spanish flu. If that young man wants his line to continue, he'd better start a family soon."

"Well," Ike said, "if his escapades in Russia didn't put that message across, where he's going next should do the job."

"Isn't that what you do with a decent scout, General?" asked Hopkins with a grim smile. "Send him off until one day he doesn't return?"

A few days later, on the continent, the patients of a mental asylum for Jews were put on trains to Treblinka, where they would be gassed and buried in mass graves along with homosexuals and the disabled. When the news reached the Warsaw ghetto, Deborah Geller wept once again. Where were the Americans?

Well, a little over fifty of them, including her former lover, James Stuart, and Antonio Petrocelli, were with Canadians from the South Saskatchewan Regiment. Everyone was hunkered down in an assault craft approaching the coastal village of Pourville, two and a half miles west of the French port of Dieppe. The invasion of the continent was under way, the first major amphibious landing in Europe, an action taken to assure people such as Deborah Geller that they had not been forgotten. It would also show the Germans that their Atlantic defenses could be breached, and if the Nazis had any sense, they would fortify the beaches of France and halt their march on the Caucasus.

Or perhaps this whole operation had been set in motion because five thousand Canadians had itchy trigger fingers. Still, this all-volunteer force had had enough of the English countryside, enough of its women and its beer. For almost a year they had been waiting for action. Besides, an in-and-out operation would provide valuable experience in modern landing techniques and set the stage for the upcoming invasion of France set for the following year. Except that the British and Canadian military leaders had dismissed the need for bombers to soften up the Dieppe defenses before their troops hit the beach.

Dwight Eisenhower was a proponent of an across-the-channel attack, and so he sent along a platoon of rangers to observe. Five different points would be hit along a beach twenty kilometers long, or about twelve miles. Five thousand Canadian soldiers would be offloaded onto assault landing craft and cross ten miles of water under early-morning darkness.

The length of a mile Antonio Petrocelli could understand, but kilometers? You had to learn a different language to fight this war. Even more curiously, there was a buzz of anticipation when a scrawny guy wearing a blue RAF pack climbed out of a staff car before they left Southampton. Who was this guy? The South Saskatchewans he and Stuart were detailed to came from some place in Canada across the border from North Dakota. Jeez. This really was shaping up to be a world war.

"Brave man to go on such a mission," murmured James Stuart.

Petrocelli glanced at the assembled Canadians. "I figure they're all brave. We're the fools."

Actually, Antonio Petrocelli hadn't thought much of Canadians, didn't think much of them at all, except during Prohibition when Canadians made sure his father had plenty of scotch to drink.

"He's Jewish," stated his immediate superior.

Petrocelli stared at the Englishman as a Catholic blessed him with his rosary. A representative of the Anglican Church also gave him his blessing.

"Make sure that man returns. If not, make sure he's not left for dead either."

"Because we don't want Nazis capturing a Jew?"

"Because he knows more about the British radar system than anyone on this planet. His name is top secret. The Canadians have nicknamed him 'Spook' because he is so pale from working indoors."

Two units of British commandos were assigned to destroy the coastal batteries to the east and the west. Unluckily, the eastern unit had run into a German convoy and the radio crackled with disaster. Others in their party could see flashing guns.

This wasn't supposed to be happening, thought Petrocelli as he stared over the gunwale to the east. Dieppe had been chosen because a German radar unit was perched on the cliff at nearby Pourville, but also because the port was rumored to be not as heavily defended as the larger ports.

"I don't like the way this is shaping up, boss."

Stuart nodded. For years, the armies of the world had taken whatever the Nazis had thrown at them and never stood fast. This morning, as dawn broke over the French horizon, the Allies would stand fast. Still, there was an onshore crossfire the British fighter planes couldn't seem to extinguish . . . .

The weather was clear, the seas calm, and the spray in your face invigorating. The boat was filled to capacity with Canadians and their Lee Enfield rifles, web belts and packs, and camouflaged steel helmets. The gunwale was about eye level and you could see what was ahead of you. It appeared to be just as they had been briefed: With the tide in, there would be a narrow pebble beach, then a seawall. Heavily defended by Jerry.

From the rear of the boat boomed a voice. "General quarters, blokes."

Ahead of the Canadians, minesweepers swept the coastal waters within ten miles of the coast. Several mines could be there: those which detonated on contact, those which "heard" a ship passing and exploded, those which reacted to a change in water pressure, and those set off by the metal hulls of ships.

Overhead, the RAF hit the coastal defense and the air-field nearby. Spitfires would also interdict troops trying to reinforce the garrison along the cliffs. Offshore were the destroyers, giving cover so the minesweepers could do their work, dropping lighted buoys to mark cleared paths. Then came the LCA—that is, landing craft, assault. Each a little more than forty feet long, these armored boats could reach a maximum speed of ten knots. The LCA Stuart and Petrocelli were in held a platoon of Canadians but no tank. The tanks were with the main attack force that would hit Dieppe fifteen minutes after the infantry did.

How Stuart longed to be operating a Churchill tank coming ashore at Dieppe. Throughout the Louisiana Maneuvers, Stuart had been used by George Patton as a motorcycle scout. Stuart actually had more time in Panzers from his stint at the German War College than he had in any American tank. In this regard, he wasn't the only frustrated officer. Dwight David Eisenhower had never experienced combat.

Reports of heavy fighting to the east made the South Saskatchewans wonder what the hell they'd run into, but there was hope. The British commandos operating to the west had spiked the guns at Varengeville and were preparing to withdraw. LCAs had been dispatched to pick them up. Then the armored front ramp lowered and Stuart and Petrocelli followed the Canadians ashore, rushing toward the seawall and Pourville.

Where they found no opposition.

Why was this? The Allies knew there were several German radar stations mounted on the cliffs overlooking the English Channel.

Petrocelli watched the RAF radar expert and his Canadian security detail, with apparently no thought for life or limb, race up the pebble beach, alongside the seven- or eight-foot seawall dotted with pillboxes. Stuart and Petrocelli went after them, both Americans holding their Thompson machine guns across their chests, their heavy packs slapping into their backs.

The South Saskatchewans headed inland to cross the River Scie—where they were stopped cold. The Germans held the high ground, in this case, the higher floors of former resort hotels. Mortar and artillery support were called for, and as the South Saskatchewans waited for support, any sign of support, the Germans poured on mortar and machine gun fire of their own. The decision was made to push forward, but as the dead piled up at the bridge over the River Scie, the attack bogged down.

There was even worse news to their east. Landings at both Berneval and Puys had failed. Even though there were Allied destroyers and planes hitting targets up and down the coast, reports were coming in that the Royal Regiment of Canada and a company of the Black Watch (Royal Highland Regiment) of Canada were pinned down on the beach outside the town. Theirs was a mortar section that would be sorely needed. There the seawall was thick with barbed wire and few had been able to cross it. The Canadians' tanks remained on the beach at Dieppe, blasting away at enemy positions but unable to cross the seawall.

The South Saskatchewans knew they must cross

the bridge, enter Dieppe, and put pressure on the Germans from the rear, giving their companions to the east some relief. Still, no one wanted to endure the mortar and machine gun fire from the Germans. Dead Canadians floated in the Scie or lay on the bridge. Many of the wounded called for stretcher bearers.

Lieutenant Colonel Charles Cecil "Cec" Ingersoll Merritt, commanding officer of the South Saskatchewan Regiment, came forward to see what was holding up the advance. What Merritt found were men lying dead on the bridge or trying to swim across the river. He knew that his pinned-down men were likely to be slaughtered if they remained in their current positions.

Merritt took off his steel helmet, ran to the center of the bridge, and yelled, "Come on boys! They can't hit a barn door. Let's go!"

Constricted throats swallowed, and then—screaming their lungs out—the South Saskatchewans fired on the run as they charged across the bridge.

While the first wave secured the buildings on the other side of the river Scie, or the high ground, Merritt returned for another group, and finally a third. That time Merritt was wounded as he raced through the withering machine gun and rifle fire from Germans who had not been dug out of positions along the river. Once bandaged, Merritt took another group across the bridge. Later, as his unit pressed toward the center of town, and under the cover of smoke, Merritt took out a German machine gun nest.

As Merritt's unit was moving toward the center of

town, the radar specialist and his bodyguards fought their way, under heavy fire, in the direction of the radar station east of Pourville. Several of the bodyguards were wounded or killed in the process. The approach to the station was open grassland from the village on up, and without proper fire support, it was suicidal to cross. Still, the radar expert, his bodyguards, and the two Americans tried, until driven back, finding cover in a house with "A" Company of the South Saskatchewans.

Someone said they should call for fire support from one of the ships at sea. Ridiculous, said the radar expert. He wanted to enter that building and learn what Jerry was up to. It was a moot point. None of the SSRs had radio contact with any ship.

They tried flanking movements, but the Germans were ready for them, pushing the Saskatchewans back. The ships at sea had no idea where the friendlies were and chose not to fire. Still, Petrocelli saw the radar expert smile after another failed attempt to flank the station.

"I cut their telephone lines."

"So they can't call for reinforcements?" asked Petrocelli, scooting over beside the man.

The radar expert shook his head. "It means they have to use their radio, and anything they say and do can be picked up by ships at sea or back in England."

"Uh-huh," said Petrocelli, not really sure he understood what the hell this guy was talking about.

"Er—Tony." James Stuart beckoned him over to the other side of the room of the building where everyone was staying close to the floor.

Petrocelli scrambled over. "What is it, boss?"

"I wouldn't get too close to that guy."

"I don't understand," said the sergeant, glancing at the scrawny man who lay on his back. "Don't we want to make sure he gets back alive?"

"Tony," said Stuart, gesturing at the remaining bodyguards that accompanied the radar expert, "those guys aren't just there for security."

Petrocelli stared at the Jew, who had changed his mind about the radar site and was trying to convince the company commander to find a tank and level the building.

"What are you saying? That they'll kill him if he can't return?"

"Why do you think I'm here? If the security detail should falter . . . ."

"Jesus," Petrocelli said, staring at Stuart. "And just when I was beginning to think you were human."

"I'm going to ignore that remark, Sergeant."

"I really don't care if you do or not. Sir."

Petrocelli returned to the side of the radar expert, where he learned there was to be no tank. Unless it came from the Germans. Panzers were on their way, and that meant that the radar specialist and his remaining bodyguards must return to the beach. Spook wasn't pleased, but he went along. When the word was given to move out, the surviving bodyguards surrounded him and off they went, with Petrocelli and Stuart pulling up the rear.

❋   ❋   ❋

"Nicky?"

Lamm opened his eyes. Evidently he was dreaming, and it was always the same dream. Lamm closed his eyes. It was dark outside. He should be dreaming.

"Nicky, can you hear me?"

So what if it was a dream. After what he'd been through, wasn't he allowed a delusion or two? Lamm lay there, dreaming that Katie O'Kelly stood beside his bed. The white dress with the troublesome belt . . . her gorgeous, long black hair . . . and the dark skin from being one-eighth Cherokee. A tanned hand took one of his own as the woman he thought was Katie O'Kelly knelt beside the bed and lay her head on his chest. She was crying.

Nicky put a hand around the woman's head and held it tight. He didn't know which one of the nurses was participating in his dream, but he was pleased with the woman's choice of medication.

The woman raised her head and looked at him. "Nicky, don't you recognize me?"

"Yes," said Lamm with a dreamy smile. "You're the gal everyone tells me I'm in love with."

"I love you, too." Tears appeared at the corners of the woman's eyes and ran down her cheeks.

"You do, Katie?"

She raised her head to shake it. "I didn't realize it until I thought you were dead."

"Well, you'd better be in love with me because I've been through . . . ." Nicky sat up and looked around the ward. "I'm not dreaming this?"

"I certainly hope not," said O'Kelly, wiping the tears

away. "That seaplane MacArthur sent for me, well, the pilot was another crazy flyer just like you."

✻   ✻   ✻

Vivian Riley sat at one of the long tables in the mess hall with her hands folded in front of her. There were just over fifty American nurses and they had no idea what the future held. They were members of the military; of that there was no doubt. They, however, were about to be the first American women to fall into the hands of the enemy. As she sat there with the other nurses, the too-tall, and very scrawny woman wondered if Nicky Lamm had reached Australia or if she'd end up nursing him once again in a prisoner of war camp somewhere on Luzon.

Their commanding officer had given them very simple orders: Always wear your uniform with your Red Cross armband on your sleeve and stay together. Never go anywhere alone; if possible never leave your tunnel. In addition, keep your gas mask handy.

Rumors filtered in. The women were members of the Red Cross and would be sent home. They were prisoners of war and would be treated as such. The Rape of Nanking was often mentioned. No one knew what would happen. Outside, a bed sheet replaced the Stars and Stripes on the flagpole while "Taps" was played. Inside the tunnel, it was thought the nurses should leave something behind, so they scrawled their names on a bed sheet. The Rape of Nanking was making a major play for the hearts and minds of these soldiers.

The American flag had been lowered at noon, and at 2 P.M. the Japanese entered the nurses' tunnel, accompanied by American officers who ordered the women to form up. Hastily they did, many forcing back tears, others gulping down air they didn't know if they would ever breathe again. When they could see clearly, these women, who had seen the worst and the best of men, saw eyes filled with curiosity, not desire.

Vivian Riley returned the stares of her captors, realizing the Japanese had no idea why the American nurses were there. Plain and simple, they were a curiosity, but not to all Japanese. Several of the women, including Vivian, were hustled out of the tunnel and into the light of day.

A Japanese officer bowed and gestured at a photographer. "This soldier is to photograph you so that General MacArthur will know that you are being well taken care of." He gestured at men at the end of their column: Japanese soldiers with rifles and bayonets. "And these men are here to make sure that you smile."

*　　*　　*

Everyone in the unit was pulling back. The South Saskatchewans had run out of rounds, and the mortars were being returned to the beach. Still, it was an orderly retreat, the last man with a Bren light machine gun covering those falling back. The Brens were a favorite of the English, and the Americans had one of their own called the Browning Automatic Rifle (BAR).

The landing craft arrived, and the personnel who

were to assist the Canadians aboard were immediately pinned down along the seawall. The tide was out, and the LCAs hovered in the water on the far side of a no-man's-land of pebble beach under heavy mortar and machine gun fire. German soldiers had reestablished their positions on the cliffs, overlooking what was now the evacuation beach. From higher ground, they fired relentlessly on those trapped on the beach below.

Colonel Merritt motioned James Stuart over. "I'm going up there. I want you and that security detail on the next boat out of here."

Stuart glanced at the heights. The wounded and others had to be evacuated because more Germans were on their way.

"Sir," said Stuart, "I've been leaving people behind an awfully long time."

"I know all about Dunkirk, Major, and your foray into Russia, otherwise you wouldn't have been brought along. Now, take what you've seen back to Eisenhower and see if you can talk some sense into that man. Without proper air and artillery support, any mission such as this is destined to fail."

Merritt clapped Stuart on the shoulder before turning away to organize his men. "And don't wait too long establishing that second front." To his fellow SSRs, he said, "Okay, who's with me? These people need some time to move the wounded aboard the LCAs."

To a man, the Canadians struggled to their feet. Though they were dirty, tired, and hungry, they followed Merritt in the direction of the heights. In the surf, LCAs moved away from the beach under heavy mortar and machine gun fire. When the LCAs were either sunk or out of range, the Germans returned their attention to those on the beach. It was those German positions Merritt intended to subdue.

Several long minutes later, and over the cries of the wounded on the beach, came the sound of a firefight, screams of hand-to-hand combat, and finally silence. Now there was no more firing. The LCAs saw this and headed toward shore again. Stuart slung his Thompson machine gun over his shoulder, picked up one end of a litter, and started toward the landing craft.

"It's time to go."

Merritt's rear guard held the cliffs as their fellow South Saskatchewans carried their wounded aboard the LCAs. With the tide out, it was a good seventy-five to one hundred yards of open pebble beach. Stuart and Petrocelli had hold of a stretcher with—ironically— a stretcher bearer on it. The Canadian smiled as he looked up. Both legs were covered in blood and much of his pants had been blown away, exposing deep cuts.

"Looks like I'm only along for the ride this time."

After such a wearing day, during the trek to the LCAs, Petrocelli or Stuart occasionally stumbled. Petrocelli did now, going down. He had been hit, and the rear of the stretcher collapsed to the ground. Despite Petrocelli's pleas not to leave him behind, Stuart dragged the stretcher into the water, where another Canadian climbed out of an LCA and pulled the injured stretcher bearer into the boat. When Stuart returned to his companion, Petrocelli had raised himself to his knees and was staring in disbelief at his side. A bright red streak had formed there.

"Come on, Tony," said Stuart, pulling his friend to his feet. "It's only a scratch."

"Yeah, but it hurts like a bitch."

Stuart put the sergeant's good arm around his neck and hauled him across the pebble beach and aboard the boat. Dropping his Thompson machine gun and pack on the deck of the LCA, Stuart left Petrocelli and returned with another stretcher bearer to the beach. There were snipers up the coast, perhaps a hundred yards from the Canadians' position, and now they peppered the beach with shot. Panzer tanks, unable to get a good site picture, left it to mortar units to bombard the beach.

Stuart and the Canadian didn't have to go far to find a man holding his guts in. They each took arms and legs and hoisted him on the stretcher. Before they could lift the stretcher, the Canadian, who had taken the rear of the stretcher, pitched forward on the wounded man. Stuart put a couple of fingers to the wounded man's neck and, feeling a pulse, pulled away the hands of the man holding in his guts with his own hands. The wounded man didn't give up without a protest.

"Wrap your hands around this man," ordered Stuart. "He'll hold in your intestines by lying on top of you."

A mortar round hit so close that Stuart was knocked to the beach. Dazed and on his hands and knees, he looked around, trying to figure out where he was and what he was doing there. A bullet whistled by. Another nipped the blouse of his uniform. He saw the men on the stretcher, one lying on top of the other. Farther out, a landing craft being boarded by men sloshing through the surf.

"Well, Yank," said the wounded man lying face up on the stretcher, new shrapnel wounds on the side of his body and that of the man who lay on top of him, "are you going to get us off the beach or what?"

Stuart struggled to his feet, put his back to the stretcher, bent down and took the two handles. Dragging the wounded men into the surf, he sloshed toward the LCA where the last of the SSRs were beckoning for him to come aboard. A glance up and down the shore told Stuart the other boats were gone.

Clambering along behind him in the surf came four more stretcher bearers with two stretchers filled with wounded men piled on top of each other, stacked like cordwood. Half stumbling, half swimming, Spook and his last remaining SSR bodyguard were pulled from the water into the LCA.

"We need to get out of here, blokes," came the call from the captain of this very small craft.

Hands reached out for Stuart, but he stepped aside and let them pull the two injured men aboard, and then the others carried by the other bearers. Stuart saw a man floating in the surf, face up. He struggled over, found the man was dead, and ripped off his dog tags.

From where he sat on the deck of the LCA, Petrocelli stared at his friend, companion, and immediate superior. The stupid bastard was intentionally trying to get himself killed.

There were more shouts that the "damn Yank" should board the LCA, that they had to get out of there. A round from a German mortar encouraged Stuart to finally climb aboard. Once all were aboard, the ramp came up and the LCA backed away from the beach. With a bit of distance from machine gun fire, mortars, and artillery rounds, the tone of the men on board changed.

"We should all stay and fight."

"We're cowards," shouted another.

Noticing he was the senior man, Stuart said, "You had your orders, as did I. We were told to return to England."

"And leave our comrades behind?"

"Orders are orders."

"Who are you to talk?" asked a Canadian from his place on the floor. "I grew up with those people we're leaving behind."

"I knew damn few of the men I left behind at Dunkirk," said Stuart, turning to stare over the gunwale, "but I still left the beach when ordered."

Men stared at him. Some nudged their buddies, asking if what they had just heard was what they thought they had heard.

"You were at Dunkirk?" asked one of them.

Stuart continued to stare over the gunwale at a beach little different from one a couple of hundred miles to the north. The only difference was that on this beach he hadn't been peppered by a German grenade and been carried aboard a fishing boat that ferried him to the evacuation crafts.

Goddammit! Next time he wouldn't cut and run. Next time he'd stand and fight. And die if necessary.

Petrocelli was on his feet and holding his side where

a first field dressing had been applied. Anyone cold-blooded enough to kill a fellow soldier like the Spook should be able to answer a question that had always been on Petrocelli's mind.

"Sir, there's something I've always wanted to ask you about Dunkirk."

"Don't, Tony," said Stuart, shaking his head. "Please don't."

*   *   *

Weeks passed, and the rules in the tunnels never changed. Make sure you were on your feet and bowed when you were around any Japanese. Keep that Red Cross armband on. Some of the nurses almost broke down, but they were brought back to the reality of the situation when Japanese soldiers herded the wounded Americans from their bunks and out of the tunnel. Soon there were fewer than five hundred Americans in the hospital.

One night, foraging for food, Vivian Riley found a hole in the wall; it led to a crawl space and ended in another tunnel filled with canned goods stored there before the Rock fell. Several of the nurses fainted from their good fortune; then a schedule was set up in which someone would go through the tunnel and return with the food. GI can openers would be passed around and the gorging would begin.

One day, they received orders that they could take their wards topside. The old Fort Mills Hospital was to be their new home. Vivian Riley felt as though she had been reborn. She could see the sun and sky and feel the wind on her face. Vivian stood outside the shell of the hospital and let the air, heat, and light wash over her. It was too much. She trembled with anxiety. What if the Japs returned them to the stinking tunnels of Corregidor? She would fight that. She would die to . . . die under the open expanse of the sky, the clouds, the blue, the breeze . . . . It was then that Vivian Riley finally understood Nicky Lamm's desire to fly.

Not long after that, when the nurses were loaded on ships for the trip to Manila, the trucks that met them at the harbor took the nurses in a different direction from those carrying the wounded and injured. A nurse tapped the driver on the shoulder and told him the truck was headed in the wrong direction. When a bayonet was stuck in her face, the nurse sat down, and no one met each other's eyes as the truck continued down the dusty road in the opposite direction from their patients.

NINE

When Stuart left his new wife and daughter at the pier, McKenzie realized she and the girl were totally alone. Not that there wasn't a plan; she was to report to the office of United Press for her next assignment. Cables had provided that much. Cables she had sequestered in the same piece of furniture where all that food had been hidden. What had she been thinking? Had she been thinking at all?

"What do we do now, Mama?"

Opening her purse and taking out a cigarette, McKenzie said to her new daughter, "We take that taxi Tony called for us."

Leaving behind the great ships and the antiaircraft guns lining the harbor, they were driven to the Claridge Hotel through a London pockmarked with bomb craters, gutted buildings, and sandbagged positions. There a room waited for them, a room on the top floor. Most hotel guests didn't care to stay on the top floors. It made for a long walk down to the air-raid shelters, and fire marshals made damn sure everyone left their rooms. For that reason rooms on the upper floors were always available.

At the desk, McKenzie snuffed out her cigarette in an ashtray and took a handful of telegrams from an elderly man. Another elderly man had struggled with their bags, bringing them into the hotel.

McKenzie glanced through the stack and then stooped down to the little girl. "Annie, I need you to be a grownup while I do some work."

"Not at all," said a man wearing the attire of a British flyer: blue uniform with a cap cocked at a jaunty angle. Around his neck was a white scarf.

The aviator stooped down and scooped up Annie, causing the child to drop her bag to the lobby floor. Anastasia's mouth fell open as she flew into the air.

"Allow me to introduce myself," said the aviator with a slight bow. "I am Wing Commander Mark Elbert of His Majesty's Royal Air Force and I haven't seen many children in the last few years. Most were moved to the country during the Blitz."

He was tall and blue-eyed—the one eye that remained. The other was covered with a black patch strapped around the back of his head. Elbert appeared to be in his late thirties. His slicked-back black hair showed a bit of gray at his temples. His face was quite narrow, there were hollows in his cheeks, and his color was poor.

"McKenzie Rivers, er—Stuart," said McKenzie, remembering her married name.

"Quite a bit of Scot in you, is there?" said Elbert with a sly smile. "Will the king be able to trust you in our fair country?"

"My husband is a Stuart from Virginia. I'm sure they came from the Highlands, as did my father's ancestors. He's in the newspaper business in New York." McKenzie flushed. "I'm sure you're not interested in all this."

"On the contrary," Elbert said, lowering Annie to the floor. "Will your husband be joining you in London?"

"I have no idea. What he does is hush-hush. I'm not even privy to that information. I work for United Press."

"Well, Mrs. Stuart," said the flyer, almost bowing again, "there is no reason why Annie cannot be in my care while you finish your business." Elbert inclined his head toward the telegrams, then toward the rear of the lobby. "With your permission I'll take her into the dining room where they might even have some ice cream."

"Ice cream!" Annie's eyes lit up as she was lowered to the ground.

"Yes," Elbert said, "many delicacies are available now that your General Eisenhower has arrived. He dines here regularly."

"Mama, may I go?"

"You wouldn't happen to know why your President Roosevelt sent such an unproven general to save our country, would you, Mrs. Stuart?"

McKenzie evaluated this lean, tough-looking soldier, and then glanced at the wad of yellow paper in her hand. "It appears I am at your mercy, Commander.

Just make sure you return Annie to the wireless office if she becomes a bother."

"I'm sure she won't," said Elbert with another smile.

"I won't, Mama," said Annie, gripping the aviator's hand.

"And to answer your question, Commander, you only have to ask what is the task at hand. For Ike, that is."

"Ike?"

"Eisenhower. Why is he here?"

"We assume he was sent to coordinate the counter-attack against the Axis powers."

"Then the president has sent the right man."

"I certainly hope you are correct."

After another slight bow, Mark Elbert crossed the lobby with Anastasia and disappeared into a dining room filled with bare tables and worn seat coverings. McKenzie watched them go, then she had her and the child's bags sent up to their room. She asked for a place where she might work and was shown into the manager's office.

"I can't take your office," she protested as an older man pulled himself and his pot gut to his feet. The office was much like McKenzie's father's, with its heavy wooden desk, a narrow table behind it hosting a phone, and plush chairs, except that all the furniture looked worn, as did the carpet.

"I assure you it is no problem, Miss Rivers."

"You—you know my name?"

"Well," the manager said with a chuckle, "we have been receiving your telegrams for the last month." He brought his bulk around the desk. "And I think you will find that the American press can have about anything it wants in my country. All you have to do is ask."

Numbly, McKenzie sat down and sorted through the telegrams, arranging them in order. On the top she placed the one from her father.

MCKENZIE

WOODWARD DEAD IN BLITZ STOP WILL YOU FILL IN STOP NO RESTRIC- TIONS STOP HOW LONG BEFORE WE WILL HAVE YOUR RUSSIAN MATERIAL STOP

FATHER

McKenzie blinked back the tears and swallowed hard. That was about as close to a compliment as she'd receive from her father. As for the "fill in" business . . . .

She leaned back in her chair, brushed down the hem of her dress, and absentmindedly took another cigarette from her purse.

Let's consider the situation realistically. United Press's man in London is Ed Beattie. Beattie's more experienced than you, kiddo, and he's on a first-name basis with Steve Early, Roosevelt's press secretary, not to mention he knows Harry Hopkins, the president's aide. Either you play second fiddle to Beattie or strike out on your own, if that's what it could be called, returning to work for your father.

McKenzie sat up and lit the cigarette. The "Russian

material" could be leverage. If she could remember anything. After throwing up at Stalin's dinner, everything was pretty much a blank. McKenzie shivered at an image of Leningrad flashing through her mind.

After a long drag off her smoke, she placed the cigarette on the lip of an ashtray and picked up a blank yellow form.

> *FATHER*
>
> *RUSSIAN MATERIAL SENT UPON CON-*
> *FIRMATION WHO RUNS UK BUREAU*
> *STOP CHANGE SURNAME ON PAY CHECK*
> *TO STUART STOP*
>
> *MCKENZIE*

A smile played at the corner of her lips. Two could play this game. Still, her father wouldn't be far wrong to say she'd fallen for another exciting young man. Had she? She'd been pretty liquored up when she'd married James Stuart. Maybe it'd all been a big mistake.

❉   ❉   ❉

Though the American public could not pronounce Guadalcanal or locate it on a map, they were pleased, eight months after the attack on Pearl Harbor, that their country was finally going on the offensive. The American public didn't realize that the Marines on Guadalcanal had no heavy weapons, very little barbed wire, and were using Japanese rice bags for sandbags.

In Japan, Rear Admiral Mikawa, leader of the devastating attack on the American ships in Sealark Channel, was treated as a hero, and headlines announced that Australia had become an orphan in the Pacific. His superiors were not as easily impressed. They knew Mikawa had come within a single blow of eliminating the American threat in the Pacific. Mikawa was told that Guadalcanal must be retaken by no less than Prime Minister Tojo, who told Mikawa that one breach in their defensive perimeter would put their whole southeastern area at risk.

Because of this, Yamamoto ordered Admiral Kondo's Second Fleet and Admiral Nagumo's strike force to Truk, a Japanese base the equivalent of Pearl Harbor. The two admirals were ordered to give the army whatever assistance it needed to retake Guadalcanal.

On the army side, General Hyakutake sighed, shook his head, and took time from his offensive against New Guinea to dispatch to Guadalcanal twenty-five hundred men from Colonel Kiyano Ichiki's unit who were veterans of the Borneo campaign, thirty-five hundred men from General Kiyotake Kawaguchi, and a unit of Imperial Navy Marines. Since one group would lag behind the other arriving at Guadalcanal, General Hyakutake signed off on a two-stage landing involving mixed units—with no rehearsal time. After that, Hyakutake returned his attention to driving MacArthur's Australians from New Guinea.

Hyakutake had no idea why the Americans were on Guadalcanal. The few who had landed weren't enough to hold the island, and the airstrip was well on the

Japanese Empire's flank. Or perhaps General Hyakutake was simply another soldier who didn't understand the value of airpower. It would take Dwight David Eisenhower quite a while to learn this same lesson.

❋　　❋　　❋

"Can the Marines hold?"

It was the question on everyone's mind. Even Secretary of the Navy Knox expressed reservations. Knox knew of the disastrous results of the battle in Sealark Channel, results kept from the American public. He also knew the waters on three sides of the island of Guadalcanal were controlled by the Japanese, and that the Marines were being bombarded from ranges none of their weapons could reach. Those bombardments, at one o'clock each afternoon, became known as Tojo Time.

Some of the material dropped on Guadalcanal was meant for Japanese soldiers: wicker baskets with cushions to soften the landing. They contained food packages, candies, ammunition, and leaflets. Written in Japanese, the leaflets could not be deciphered.

"If it's in Japanese," explained Harvey Meadors, "it can only mean that help is on the way."

"For us?" asked Cleve.

"No, dummy. For the Japanese."

With the Japanese poised to strike from Rabaul, a little more than six hundred miles away, General Vandegrift had a laundry list of things he wanted accomplished, and very quickly. One group of Marines was to dig in and form a defensive perimeter along Henderson Field, and at the same time establish 75-mm and 105-mm cannon so they could fire on any section of the line, especially the beach. Machine guns were part of these fortifications, along with 75-mm half-tracks, machines whose front ran on wheels, their rear on tracks.

Another group of Marines began moving all those supplies from the beaches to dumps inside the new perimeter, while another group commandeered a Japanese bulldozer and other road-building equipment to complete the airstrip. Between tropical rainstorms and the daily arrival of Japanese bombers at Tojo Time, it was slow going.

As for barbed wire, which had not been landed in any great quantity, the Lever Brothers' plantation on Guadalcanal had its fences liberated, and that fencing was deployed along the beach. And because there were not enough Marines to man the southern side of the perimeter protecting the airfield, members of the Tractor Battalion, the Pioneers, and Engineers took up guard duty when not otherwise employed.

It took about a week, but finally the beaches were cleared of supplies and the airstrip's runway completed. None of this could have been accomplished if not for the accommodating Japanese. The enemy had left behind all the necessary equipment, not only to finish the airstrip, but also to extend its length to almost four thousand feet.

One of the Marines tinkered with the enemy's radio

and contact was established with the outside world. General Vandegrift reported to Kelly Turner, amphibious commander in the Pacific, that only five days of rations remained. The navy quickly shot back that they had landed more than fifty days of rations on the beaches of Guadalcanal. The navy had—at low tide, and when the tide came in, the supplies went out. Marines were soon reduced to eating fish and rice, fish and rice, and more fish and rice. Extra requirements of protein came from tins of meat and smoked oysters left behind by the Japanese or an insect found in the wormy rice. Two meals like this each day soon had the Marines down by twenty or thirty pounds per man.

As for the enemy remaining on the island, most were enslaved Koreans sent to Guadalcanal to build the airstrip. All were willing to surrender. The remaining Japanese dug in, one group establishing machine gun positions west of the airstrip, and the bastards were tough to dig out. The good news was that in only a few days, American fighters were landing on Henderson Field via the *Long Island*. As a result, planes flying out of the Japanese stronghold in Rabaul met heavy resistance from the "Cactus Air Force," a name derived from the island's code name—when the Cactus Air Force could get aloft.

Torrential rainstorms could ground the Americans while the Japanese flew in from Rabaul and bombed the island with impunity. And because the landing strip had been built on ground in the middle of a coconut plantation, navigational aids were nothing more than beer bottles placed at intervals on each side of a dirt airstrip and lit with flares.

The loss of planes, however, was not always from a Japanese attack. A plane trying to take off after a rainstorm might strike a hole in the runway that hadn't been there before the storm and end up in shambles— which then had to be cleared. In addition, there were the Japanese submarines that surfaced during the day and lobbed shells into the Marines' perimeter. Nighttime brought destroyers ripping into the Marines' planes and their support units, especially those not benefiting from hard cover. Then there was the occasional shell that missed Henderson Field and fell into the jungle where the Marines had established fuel dumps. Not to mention that after a month on Guadalcanal, pilots, underfed and dogged by malarial mosquitoes, lost the quickness of hand and eye that it took to bring down enemy planes.

One day, a patrol, including intelligence officers who should have known better, launched a mission late in the day. Though the Goettge patrol would reach their target area well after dark, they insisted on pressing on—into an area where the Korean slave labor said there were more of their kind, along with a heavy concentration of Japanese.

A white flag had been seen. Perhaps more Koreans wanted to surrender; a captured Japanese prisoner agreed with this evaluation. However, without any breeze, the Japanese flag with its red circle on a field of white could *appear* to be a flag of surrender. Goettge and his troops evidently didn't consider the fact that the enemy across Sealark Channel had fought to the death, and that the only Japanese taken prisoner were those dazed or unconscious.

The ambush was sudden and severe. Only three members of the Goettge patrol survived, and those who escaped did so by swimming through pockets of water or crawling across the coral reef. The survivors returned to speak of "sabers flashing in the sun," meaning the Japanese had given the wounded Marines a rather savage *coup de grace.* From that day on, Marines seldom took prisoners. Or spoke of the unmitigated disaster that became known as the Goettge patrol.

Just before Henderson Field became operational, five hundred Japanese came ashore ten miles east of the airstrip. This was one side of a pincer attack. The next night, the other pincer landed to the west. Colonel Kiyano Ichiki commanded this second thousand-man unit. Ichiki's regiment had been scheduled to occupy Midway. When that mission was scuttled, his unit had cooled its heels on Guam until ordered to retake Guadalcanal from the two thousand or so Americans thought to be on the island.

Not waiting for reinforcements or artillery support, Ichiki radioed Rabaul that he was setting out with nine hundred of his very best soldiers to close his side of the pincer. And just as in the case of the Goettge patrol, instead of remembering how stubbornly American Marines had held out on Corregidor, Ichiki chose to remember how Americans stationed in China seemed to think the nighttime was made for dancing. He would soon surprise them with another form of dancing—at the end of a Japanese bayonet.

Vandegrift was informed by one of his scouts that the Japanese were on their way, but with the Marines' perimeter extending for miles, the general needed to know the Japanese point of attack. Vandegrift learned the answer to that question when a patrol sent out to destroy a Japanese observation post ran into a unit of Japanese strolling through the palm trees along the beach. When the engagement ended, it was a moment before the Marines realized the dead men lying at their feet wore new uniforms. This could only mean they had routed an advance party of the Japanese attack force.

From their direction of travel, Vandegrift deduced that the Japanese would have to cross a thirty-foot-wide, shallow creek that ran into a sandbar at the edge of the ocean. Vandegrift ordered the last rolls of barbed wire strung across the creek and more machine gun emplacements added.

Where was the kill zone? asked Marines setting up their guns. Their gunnery sergeant pointed to the sandbar crossing the smelly, stagnant creek.

It was hot, humid, and just after midnight when—from his position above the sandbar—Cleve Woodruff thought he heard something. It sounded like metal on metal, and when he listened closely, Cleve thought he could make out the sound of someone slogging through the surf on the far side of the sandbar. He touched Harvey on the shoulder.

Meadors nodded, but only after wiping the sweat

away. "Japs. They don't like fighting their way through that green wall any more than we do." Word was passed down the line that the enemy was moving into the kill zone. Marines held their fire and their breath.

The Japanese knew there were Americans ahead of them, but they declined to charge until enough of their force was in position to attack. That came around 3 A.M., when Japanese could be heard chattering in front of the Marines' position. Cleve wiped his forehead and pointed his rifle in the direction of the noise. Down the line, a corporal who had served in Nicaragua and China put a hand on the shoulder of a nervous Marine.

"Steady, Marine."

The young man swallowed his fear and peered into the night. The overcast made it impossible to see what was happening on the sandbar, in the surf, or along the creek. But they could hear it. The Japanese were at the wire and muttering, first in whispers, then aloud.

"What the hell?" Meadors looked over a fallen palm tree, which had been chopped down to reinforce his and Cleve's position.

"Harvey, for God's sake, get down."

Meadors did, but not from what Woodruff said. From down the line came the order: "Open fire!"

Meadors ducked, and then joined the explosion of rifles and machine guns firing in the direction of the sandbar.

Despite seeing their comrades mowed down, the remainder of the Japanese column rushed forward, throwing huge firecrackers and shouting "Banzai!" They, too, became caught in the barbed wire that had stopped their companions. Very quickly grenades were jerked off harnesses, pins pulled, and thrown in the direction of the red tracers flying in their direction. Still, the barbed wire held and the Ichikis withdrew. It would be another hour before they made a second attack.

Once again it was under heavy fire. This time, however, the Japanese had Bangalore torpedoes—long pipes packed with explosives—brought forward and shoved beneath the barbed wire. American howitzers answered this challenge. Shells flashed, lighting up the creek and its jungle backdrop and ripping apart the Japanese bunched up at the wire. Many of the enemy tried to skirt the American lines and slug their way through the surf to attack the Americans' flank. They, too, were repulsed.

Cleve and Harvey expended the rounds in their clips, reloaded, and went back to work firing at the shadowy figures at the wire. Then the Bangalore torpedoes did their work, and Japanese came rushing through the gap, led by sword-waving officers shouting "Banzai!" The Marines shot them down easily.

While jamming another clip into his Springfield, Cleve saw that the number of Japanese splashing across the creek had increased to platoon size. These numbers were not so easily repulsed. Upriver, machine guns protecting the Marines' flank were swung around and brought to bear on the creek. However, this took time.

As the Japanese charged the hill, Harvey Meadors was first to his feet, slashing at the bayonets coming his way. Cleve followed, leaping from his foxhole to seize the high ground. Cleve planted his bayonet into the chest of a Japanese soldier, but before he could pull it out, another of the enemy blundered into him, knocking him to the ground. Meadors cleared the man off Cleve with the butt of his Springfield.

No one was firing now. Empty rifles all, it became a contest of wills. Would the Marines hold or be driven back? From upriver came machine gun fire as the Marines opened up on the creek. Behind the Ichikis, American mortar rounds landed. Now the Ichikis' advance party was trapped on this side of the creek and there was no choice but to move forward. Or die.

Possibly both.

Cleve had gotten to his feet again, his rifle pointed in the wrong direction. He snapped the butt into the face of an oncoming Japanese, keeping the man's bayonet at bay. More Japanese closed with him so quickly that Cleve began swinging his rifle around to keep the enemy away. He and Harvey were being pushed back, but unlike some of their comrades they were still on their feet. The Ichikis followed, tripping over the Marines' emplacements in the dark, and then stumbling to their feet to meet Meadors, and Woodruff's bayonets. Still, the Ichikis kept coming.

With arms aching from swinging his rifle, Cleve finally lowered his weapon, tripping up the next Japanese who charged him. The two men went down in a tangle of arms and legs. Both men lost their weapons, or realized there was little advantage to having them.

Cleve struck out with his fists and connected with bone. The man screamed, and before Cleve could overcome the shock of actually being in hand-to-hand combat, the Ichiki threw himself on the young Marine. The Japanese got his hands around Cleve's throat. Cleve returned the favor by gouging the Japanese in the eyes with his thumbs. Before either man could seriously injure the other, the Ichiki was bayoneted through the shoulder and jerked away by a group of Marines held in reserve to fill any hole in the perimeter.

Cleve gulped for air, looked around, and saw Meadors resting back on his arms, dead Japs on both sides of him. Sweat ran down the men's faces as the reserves pushed the Ichikis down into the creek—where, once again, the Japanese were hit with murderous machine gun fire.

As the Ichikis ran for the safety of the jungle, they were shot down by the machine guns or blown apart by mortar fire. The smart ones used piles of their dead companions as protection to low crawl in the direction of the embankment along the ocean.

At dawn, the Cactus Air Force was brought to bear on the Ichikis' position. Then the Marines flanked the Ichikis with tanks and literally rolled over the few hundred of the enemy that tried to escape into the jungle. Before those tanks reached Kiyano Ichiki, the colonel committed hara-kiri.

The Marines didn't know it but the commander whom they had forced to commit suicide had been the commander of the unit on the Marco Polo bridge in China where Japanese and Chinese soldiers, reacting to the discharging of a weapon, created the incident that precipitated the Second World War in the Far East. At that time, the Americans had been in junior high school.

More than eight hundred Japanese bodies lay in the foul-smelling creek, but only thirty-five Marines died in what was America's first victory over the premier jungle fighters in the Far East. It also set the tone for further engagements between the two opponents. As Admiral Yamamoto commented: "The real battle is now a competition between Japanese discipline and American scientific technology."

✳   ✳   ✳

At Maikop and Krasnodar in the eastern Soviet Union, the Germans found that the Russians had blown the fields. Hitler wouldn't find the oil he needed there, so the Germans pressed on. In North Africa, Rommel was having troubles of his own, and those also dealt with oil. The British had successfully resupplied the island of Malta in the Mediterranean. This meant that the British could continue their submarine raids and aircraft attacks against Rommel's supply lines. Churchill went to Moscow to explain that there would be no second front in Europe but a landing in North Africa. Stalin snorted and asked if the British were afraid of the Germans.

"Not at all," said the British prime minister. "But the Americans are untested in warfare, and to throw the ten percent of American units who have arrived in Great Britain against German veterans would do little to draw many Germans from the Russian Front. However, with only a quarter of what we need to cross the English Channel, we can seize North Africa, wipe out Rommel's

Afrika Korps, and cross into Italy, which *will* draw Germans away from the Russian Front. The Italians do not want this war. Fighting in North Africa has proved this."

Churchill paused to let this sink in. "Besides, with the number of planes and ordnance the Americans are beginning to produce, we should be able to destroy every building in Germany before our troops ever reach Berlin."

Stalin grunted in agreement. He had good reason to want to pound hell out of Germany. The Nazis were less than two hundred miles from Stalingrad, and only one hundred fifty miles from the oil-rich Caucasus. There was even talk that Moscow might be abandoned and the Soviet government withdrawn into the Ural Mountains.

Hitler, too, was concerned about a second front and expected the Allies to land on the beaches of France. He ordered an Atlantic wall to be built: over fifteen thousand concrete bunkers in all. "The German blood these fortifications will spare is well worth the money spent."

TEN

Dwight David Eisenhower reached England after the fall of Tobruk in northern Africa, when British morale was at its lowest point. The staff he inherited was the outgrowth of a special observer's mission assigned to London while America was still neutral. James Stuart had been part of the special observer's group as he had made his way, with phony documents, around Greater Germany before America joined the war.

It was not Ike's first visit to England. During an inspection regarding the impact of American troops arriving in England, Eisenhower had his first meeting with Bernard Montgomery, commander of British forces in southeast England. As Monty raised his pointer to a map on the wall of the farmhouse, he sniffed the air.

The lieutenant general, who had informed his American visitors that he had taken time from his busy schedule to brief them, asked, "Who is smoking?"

Eisenhower admitted it was him.

"Put it out!" came the command from the man with the pointer.

Ike did so, and when his new staff began arriving from the States he understood their complaint: the British were arrogant toward Americans; the Germans they feared. Furthermore, what the English were doing didn't make sense. The British planned for the Germans and the Russians to bleed each other white. Only then could the Allies land in France and succeed in defeating Germany.

Once Eisenhower arrived in London, he instituted the seven-day workweek. Not everyone was pleased, and as George Marshall, chief of staff of the army, had overhauled the War Department, Eisenhower had to clean house. Ike even had the audacity to move his command into the country. The general was sick and tired of returning to a hotel room every night after the unrelenting demands put on him from two different governments while he had to make life-and-death decisions. Eisenhower ended up in a townhouse with a garden adjoining a golf course, and his staff ended up in the countryside. Soon, the requests for transfers to the States began, and Eisenhower was glad to see those men go.

At a conference with the press, McKenzie took a seat beside Helen Kirkpatrick of the *Chicago Daily News.*

The older woman smiled. "McKenzie, I heard you got married. James Stuart's quite a catch, if you can get a word out of him."

"You . . . you know him?"

"Of course."

Stunned by this casual revelation, McKenzie didn't see the cigarette-smoking Ed Murrow slip through the rows of chairs in her direction. The chief of the Columbia Broadcasting System's European news service removed the cigarette from his mouth and said, "So this is the girl who caught James Stuart?" The thin man smiled.

McKenzie hastily got to her feet. "Er—Mr. Murrow. So nice to meet you." McKenzie had grown up on this man's voice. Murrow had defied the Germans by broadcasting from British rooftops during the Blitz. He had the ability to make you see over the radio what he could see from those rooftops.

Murrow gave her the once-over. "And James Stuart did well, too." McKenzie wore a blue skirt and jacket that matched, wide-shouldered and fitted. Her skirt had three pleats both in front and back. Her blouse was white, her black hair cut in a modified bob.

"You know my husband?" she asked her hero.

"Only by reputation, my dear." Murrow inclined his head in the direction of Helen Kirkpatrick. "Like Helen, most reporters would like to buy your husband a drink or two and ask him even more questions. You watch out. When Helen asks you to go shopping, it'll be more than shopping that she's interested in."

"Aw, Ed," said Kirkpatrick with a grin, "you know I'm not that kind of gal."

"You women have an advantage . . . ." His voice trailed off as Eisenhower entered the room with his aide. Ike saw Murrow speaking to the women and waited for him to take his seat.

After a few niceties were exchanged between Ike and the press, Ray Daniell of the *New York Times*, president of the Association of American Correspondents, presented a list of complaints about army censorship and the army's public relations office.

"General, they look down on our work here, and it takes forever to get anything through the censors."

It was McKenzie's first look at Eisenhower since the maneuvers. In Louisiana, Eisenhower's headquarters had very quickly become a hangout for savvy reporters. Ike was a treasure trove of information, and he didn't appear to view the press as an adversary. The general was thinner than she remembered and he had his third star. McKenzie's husband said if the powers-that-be had any sense, Eisenhower would be made Supreme Commander.

"One commander?" she had asked James Stuart.

"Someone has to be responsible for the implementation of the war."

"But the British, the French, the Free Forces fighting the Nazis—one commander for all?"

"Someone has to be in charge."

Curiously, her new husband had not tried to take charge of her life. McKenzie wondered if that was because she already had a job he thought important to the war effort. Or if he was so busy reading and talking with people that he forgot about her. McKenzie was expected to care for the child; it seemed James never gave Annie a thought until she broke through his concentration. If there was a "father figure" for Annie, it was Tony Petrocelli.

But how did these reporters know her husband? In the States, James Stuart had been a mere lieutenant of armor; in Russia he wore the rank of major. When she inquired why the sudden promotion, Stuart had replied that "investigative officers" were generally majors or light colonels, so that is the rank he had become.

McKenzie had smiled. "You make it sound as if you can pick and choose your rank as you please."

"Not as I please, but as the mission dictates."

"And what is your real rank, James?"

With a rare smile, he asked, "McKenzie, are you saying only field grade officers can turn your head?"

Helen Kirkpatrick touched McKenzie's knee. "You must have a remarkable memory not to be taking notes."

Hastily, McKenzie drew a steno pad from her purse and focused her attention on Eisenhower. Although she'd had plenty of food hidden in a wardrobe, along the way she had lost her camera equipment. No problem. Her father had acquiesced to her terms, even providing her with her own Jimmy Olsen, who at that very moment was on one knee snapping shots of Eisenhower.

Concentrating on what Ike was saying, McKenzie learned Ike had suggested the US Army accept the invitation of thousands of British women who wanted to take American GIs into their homes and acquaint them with British family life. Ike concluded his remarks by encouraging the American press to aggressively tell good stories about the American troops in Great Britain.

"May we see the colored troops?" asked someone across the room. McKenzie couldn't tell who. The man had not stood and there had to be over thirty reporters in the room.

"Of course, and you should know that my policy for handling colored troops would be absolute equality of treatment."

"Does this mean no segregation?" blurted out McKenzie before she realized she had asked the question.

Eisenhower located where the question had come from. "The colored troops will have as good as our white soldiers, but there will be segregation where facilities afford themselves." Then Ike flashed that incredible smile of his. "And best wishes on your recent marriage, Mrs. Stuart."

McKenzie flushed as everyone in the room turned and stared. There was a smattering of applause, and when the applause died down, a reporter asked if he could report about the friction between the black and white soldiers.

"Yes," said Ike with a nod.

This reply caused someone to be bold enough to ask if the press would be allowed to report about black servicemen dating English women.

"I don't see why not," Ike said.

With that, the conference with the press was concluded. Moments later, the dumbfounded reporters remembered who McKenzie Rivers had recently married and that they should congratulate her. Or they might miss forever the chance to buddy up with James Stuart.

✻   ✻   ✻

In the South Pacific, the Japanese landed fresh troops on Guadalcanal and let loose with a barrage from their support ships before slipping away under cover of darkness. The route the Japanese used among the Solomon Islands was called the "slot" by the Americans, and the regular run of Japanese soldiers deposited by Tanaka was called the "Guadalcanal Express" or "Cactus Express." Admiral Tanaka dubbed this eight-week maneuver "Operation Rat."

Eventually these two navies would run into each other, which they did off the eastern Solomons. Once again, the enemies used their air arms against the other's carriers. Involved in this battle was Nagumo for the Japanese, who had blown the opportunity at Pearl Harbor and Midway to destroy the Americans' naval fleet. His opponent was Admiral Frank Jack Fletcher, who upon being told by naval intelligence that there were no Japanese near these waters, sent the *Wasp* off to refuel. It was a perfect match—of timid admirals, that is.

Therefore, Fletcher was left with the *Enterprise* and the *Saratoga* to meet Nagumo's *Zuikaku, Shokaku,* and the small carrier *Ryujo*. The *Ryujo* didn't last long. Naval aviators found and sank her while she was refueling her planes. While the American planes were away, Japanese planes found the *Enterprise* and the *Saratoga*.

Three bombs hit the *Enterprise* and soon she was smoking. The Japanese reported they had sunk one, maybe two, carriers. By the time the Japanese returned to their carriers, the *Enterprise* was steaming back to Pearl for repairs, but not without some nervous moments. For almost an hour, she remained in those waters, and Admiral Nagumo sailed within fifty miles of the crippled ship while she remained dead in the water.

Admiral Tanaka had his own bad luck. When he sailed to Guadalcanal to land troops, the Cactus Air Force was waiting for him. After intercepting the planes from the *Ryujo*—before the Japanese light carrier had been sunk—the Cactus dive bombers sank a troop transport and hurt the *Jintsu* enough that Tanaka had to transfer his flag to a destroyer. As sailors on Japanese destroyers pulled sailors from the sea, American Flying Fortresses arrived and sank another ship. Tanaka was told to retire from the field and leave those in the water to fend for themselves.

On the other hand, Kelly Turner's convoys *had* reached Guadalcanal, as had Mason Monroe who had been shot down. After being washed ashore, and after a few Japanese beers, Monroe was told that the reason the Cactus Air Force was so effective was because of the loss of so many American carriers in their waters. The Cactus Air Force already had a good number of navy pilots in its ranks.

At Truk, General Hyakutake wondered why the Americans were putting so much effort into Guadalcanal. The keys to Australia were New Guinea and Port Moresby.

The Imperial navy went so far as to tell the army to let Guadalcanal go; but the navy was ordered by the Imperial Command to supply the army with whatever it required to retake the island. Guadalcanal would take precedent over pushing MacArthur's Australians out of New Guinea.

This wasn't what the navy wanted to hear. A new American battleship was roaming the waters around Guadalcanal. Not only did the *Washington* have more firepower, but she could do thirty knots and keep up with any fast carrier.

This time, Ichiki's rear echelon—fifteen hundred men—plus another thousand from the Yokosuka Fifth Naval Landing Force would be used in the new offensive. Hyakutake believed twenty-five hundred soldiers were enough to defeat the ten thousand Americans on Guadalcanal. It appeared Japanese estimates of the number of Americans on Guadalcanal had increased, but this had not changed their contempt for the American fighting man.

Sailing in support of this effort was the Combined Fleet under the command of Admiral Yamamoto. Navy aircraft would soften up the Marines with daily bombings while destroyers and cruisers bombarded them at night. There should be little resistance when the next Japanese force went ashore.

This change of strategy by the Imperial Command required that General Hyakutake abandon troops who had fought their way through the jungle of New Guinea and come within a few miles of Port Moresby. Without reinforcements, these soldiers were forced to turn back.

Most died in the jungle. Shortly after this, Australian "diggers" destroyed a Japanese amphibious force before it could land on New Guinea.

✳   ✳   ✳

When the German Sixth Army arrived at the Volga River north of Stalingrad, the Nazis had conquered almost as much of Russia as Genghis Khan's hordes had in the thirteenth century. The swastika flew from the Pyrenees to the Caucasus. North Africa was in Hitler's hands and the Mediterranean was now a Nazi lake. It was possible that the Nazi war machine might roll through central Asia and finally into the Persian Gulf oil fields. Only one thing stood in their way: Hitler himself. Instead of ordering his men to bypass Stalingrad, he ordered his armies to seize the city.

Because Stalin had saved Tsaritsyn from the White Army, Joseph Stalin commemorated his victory by giving the city his name and began to convert it into a model city with modern plants, municipal buildings and parks, and tall apartment buildings overlooking the River Volga. Proud of how the Soviet system had turned their city into one that could compete with any city in the West, or so said the propagandists, the citizenry was totally unprepared for the fate to befall them.

Stalingrad had no natural defenses. The city curved for twenty miles along the bank of the Volga, meaning, though there was an open body of water behind its defenders, all supplies and reinforcements would have

199

to cross that body of water. Stalingrad could have been neutralized by being bombed or starved into submission, but Hitler ordered the German Sixth Army to enter Stalingrad and slaughter the male population; the females were to be shipped off for use elsewhere.

Stalin replied in kind with his "Not One Step Backwards" order. Simply put, the order decreed that any Russian soldier who surrendered to the Germans would be shot, as would their families back home. That decree would be sorely tested as the *Luftwaffe* hit the city for the first time while citizens lounged in gardens along the Volga or strolled along the broad streets.

It was a carpet-bombing at its most effective, the Germans dropping high-explosive and incendiary bombs that soon sprouted monuments to the death of homes, only their brick chimneys remaining. The apartment buildings overlooking the Volga quickly turned into shells of their former selves with floors collapsing and burying families alive. Gasoline dumps became columns of black smoke that could be seen over two hundred miles away. Essential public works, such as the waterworks, the telephone exchange, and the hospitals had their windows blown out, their equipment destroyed, and its personnel abandoning their stations, which included patients who lay helpless in their beds— if they hadn't been blown out of them.

Outside the city, women manned the antiaircraft guns, leveling those weapons at the approaching Panzers, who returned fire. One by one, these batteries were silenced.

German soldiers stopped their tanks, stuck their

heads from their turrets, and stared at the Volga, the beginning of Asia. It was true. No one could stand before the army of the Third Reich. Many soldiers took time for photographs, then another antiaircraft battery opened up and the Panzers leveled that position. The Germans, after silencing these guns, were shocked to learn their cannons had wiped out battery after battery of female defenders.

The Germans were to face an even more tenacious foe: women who would leap into just finished tanks in the former tractor factory and charge into the mouth of the German war machine. There was no shortage of volunteers, despite the number of political commissars slipping across the Volga to safety.

When women and children were given the chance to flee, the *Luftwaffe* had no idea these were refugees and blew their boats out of the water. Cries from the women and children in the Volga could be heard on shore, but German soldiers were denied permission to send rubber boats to rescue them. Morning came, and tentative Russians slipped boats in the water under the watchful eyes of their opponents. In Moscow, the US embassy reported Stalingrad had surrendered. The Soviet Union had been cut into two parts, north and south.

Not only his army, but also Hitler had been affected by "victory disease," as much as any Japanese had. As the Sixth Army moved on Stalingrad, Berlin ordered all Jews in unoccupied France to be deported, including one hundred fifty children.

The local *gendarmes* collaborated, but the French

were sickened by the action taken by their government. Priests took Jewish families into their homes, and soon an order was issued to arrest all Catholic priests sheltering Jews. Upon learning of the deportations, the Swiss announced they would no longer turn back Jews crossing from France into Switzerland.

In North Africa, the depleted British and the undersupplied Germans went at each other repeatedly until Prime Minister Winston Churchill, surviving a vote of censure in Parliament, realized something had to be done and done fast. Command of the British Eighth Army was turned over to another obscure general, this one wearing not goggles but a beret. Berets didn't fall off a general's head and make him look foolish as he climbed in and out of tanks. In addition, that beret made for good copy. Bernard Law Montgomery thought that a leader was a man who spent many an hour among his troops, inspiring them. The general staff could work out the details.

After Montgomery took command, a rumor swept throughout the British Eighth Army that "Monty" had told officers devising plans of retreat to tear them up. He also ordered men working on an emplacement to stop digging. The Germans would not reach this far. It was to become a policy of "no withdrawal," and very quickly word spread that someone quite different from the Old Guard was in charge.

"If we are attacked, there will be no retreat," Monty was to have said. "If we cannot stay here alive, we will stay here dead. Two new divisions have arrived. In a week the situation will be stabilized, in two weeks, we will be sitting pretty. In three weeks the issue will be certain."

You had to admire a man who could settle the matter of North Africa in a few sentences. Two weeks and five days after Montgomery arrived in the desert, he lured Rommel into an ambush at Alam al Halfa ridge to destroy him. If he could stop Rommel there, the German general was lost. Through broken encrypted communiqués, Monty knew Rommel's tanks were down to their last few gallons of petrol.

There was more. Montgomery's tanks outnumbered Rommel's two to one, and three hundred of Monty's tanks were the new American Shermans. Not only that, Montgomery had air superiority, and British units were equipped with a new antitank gun. In this battle, Rommel would be outgunned while also having to contend with a swollen liver and infected nose. Still, Rommel came on at the head of three veteran German divisions and an Italian division guarding one flank.

British minefields slowed his advance, and the soft sand burned up his remaining fuel. The Royal Air Force tried to destroy him, but luck always favored the Desert Fox. Rommel swung north under cover of a sandstorm, and when that movement faltered, Rommel fell back south into the Ragil Depression. Now, with the sandstorm gone, British aircraft and artillery pounded his position through the night.

When dawn broke, Rommel struck again, but everywhere his units found New Zealanders, British, or landmines waiting. Pounded by the British for a second night, the Desert Fox received more bad news. One of his divisions had run out of fuel. The following morning, Rommel called off the attack, and weary Germans crept away to the west under heavy air and artillery bombardment, the rear guard glancing over their shoulders. Any minute British tanks would close with them and destroy the remains of the *Afrika Korps*. That did not happen. Bernard Montgomery, not to mention Winston Churchill, needed a victory untarnished by British units being destroyed by one of Rommel's antitank screens as his predecessors had been.

✳   ✳   ✳

On the first of September, German troops entered Stalingrad and sent the Russian defenders reeling. Marshal Georgi Zhukov, who had been selected by Stalin to defend the city, pulled his troops together and counterattacked. Marshal Zhukov was a new kind of Russian general: full of energy, angry at the humiliation suffered by his country, and not a bit afraid of political commissars or the secret police.

Still, the Germans pushed Zhukov's units back and prepared to thrust deeper into the city. Before they could, Soviet reinforcements arrived from across the Volga and the German advance was halted. German planes dropped thousands of bombs in an attempt to make Stalingrad submit. That was the Germans' second mistake, leveling the city; their first being not bypassing Stalingrad and continuing toward the oil fields of the Caucasus.

✳   ✳   ✳

During the voyage to Guadalcanal, a quarrel broke out between Admiral Tanaka and General Kawaguchi, the man chosen to rid Guadalcanal of the American Marines. The quarrel was over how to get Japanese forces ashore. Kawaguchi wanted his men landed in barges. Tanaka said he had been ordered to put the general's forces ashore by destroyer. They split the difference, and over the coming weeks the forces brought in by Tanaka's destroyers, which included General Kawaguchi, reached Guadalcanal safely. The Cactus Air Force killed many going ashore by barge. More than four hundred men died at sea.

Ashore, Kawaguchi split his men into three attacking battalions, and because of the jungle, those units lost contact, were slowed down, and failed to coordinate their attack. The main body was supposed to smash into the rear of the Marines' defense perimeter while a secondary force drove against the airfield from the west. The contingent of Imperial Navy marines was to attack the other side of the airfield. This lack of coordination gave the US Marines the chance to cling to their tenuous hold on Guadalcanal.

Rumor had it the Seventh Marines were on their way, that the Marines on Guadalcanal had to hold on for a few more days. Kawaguchi also heard the rumor, and if the rumor was true, it was imperative that he seize the airfield before the Seventh Marines arrived. Something that wasn't a rumor was the order by Chester

Nimitz, commander of the Pacific Fleet, that all the Marines in the Hawaiian Islands that weren't "doing a man's work" were to be immediately shipped out to fill out new raider battalions. It would appear that the "navy's police" had taken a giant step toward respectability.

The new name for Sealark Channel was Ironbottom Sound, and the name fit, as the *Vincennes, Quincy, Astoria,* and *Canberra* all rested on its bottom. Crossing Ironbottom Sound was "Red Mike" Edson's raider battalion to shore up the defenses of Guadalcanal. With the exception of isolated snipers, Japanese positions had been destroyed on the islands across the channel. American reporters mobbed the red-headed Edson when he landed, asking what it had been like to secure the islands across the former Sealark Channel.

"The Japs were in caves. The only way you could pry them out was to toss in sticks of dynamite, then go in and dig out the survivors with machine guns." He paused, either out of exhaustion or for emphasis. "There are two thousand dead Japs on Tugali. We only took twenty-three of them alive."

On Guadalcanal, Edson's raiders were sent by boats to hit the Japanese buildup. The raiders got lucky. Before they landed, a line of American cargo ships, escorted by destroyers and cruisers, passed the raiders' target. The Japanese thought this was a major American landing and took to the jungle.

Edson's men swept up the coast, meeting little resistance, until the enemy opened up with 75-mm cannon, protected on its flanks by machine gun fire. Edson called in air strikes from Henderson Field, and then his raiders flanked the Japanese position and went in to mop up.

In a village, the Marines destroyed much of the Japanese stores, confiscated the medical supplies, and took with them an ample stash of British-made cigarettes, along with tins of food and a radio transmitter. When the raiders returned, Vandegrift hurried them to positions along a ridge overlooking the jungle. Local scouts had reported up to five thousand enemy troops to the east. The ridge and the raiders' backside was to the airstrip, just above Vandegrift's command post.

The raiders weren't the only new arrivals inside the Marines' perimeter. As usual, "Terrible" Turner was on Guadalcanal and giving General Vandegrift advice about the disposition of his troops, such as that Marines should be scattered in outposts across the island to repulse the invaders, not stretched around Henderson Field's perimeter. Turner was in the middle of one of his harangues when the first unit of General Kawaguchi's troops reached the airfield and launched its attack.

Preceding this had been a bombardment from Japanese bombers. The Cactus Air Force went up and nailed ten of the lumbering bombers and three Zeros. That night, "Washing Machine Charlie"—the name for Japanese planes because of the sound of their engines— dropped a flare to light up Henderson Field for naval bombardment.

The bombardment went on for a half hour, and those on the far end of the perimeter held their breath and listened to the southern end being hit. As the bombardment ceased, the firing became stronger; rifles, machine guns, mortars, and grenades were heard. Then the Japanese ships turned on their searchlights and combed the coast for targets. At midnight there was another flare and the naval bombardment began all over again. At the command post, Admiral Turner's voice could be heard over the firefight. "What are they doing to my boats? That's what worries me."

The following day, Japanese planes and ships stayed on station later than usual. The Marines figured another attack was imminent, when in fact Admiral Tanaka thought the airstrip had been taken and he was there only to offer support. Japanese pilots, who had hoped to land on Henderson Field, turned back, disappointed and harassed by the Cactus Air Force.

"Red Mike" Edson told his officers that what had happened the night before was only a test. "They'll be back. Get our men dug in, make sure the wire is tight, and give the men a good meal. They're going to need it."

ELEVEN

Very quickly McKenzie Stuart learned that Wing Commander Mark Elbert of His Majesty's Royal Air Force was a story himself. Elbert had been in France fighting the Germans before Dunkirk, and then had flown his plane back to England and taken up the defense of his homeland.

On Eagle Day, August 13, 1940, Hitler's air chief, Hermann Göring, began an intense campaign against the Royal Air Force's facilities. Göring planned to destroy as many English planes as possible on the ground and turn his *Messerschmitts* against any British fighters that made it into the air.

That particular day, Mark Elbert was flying over the English Channel. He was there for convoy support, as the Germans would pounce on anything in the water. Suddenly, Elbert's headset crackled with a message that Fighter Control's radar had detected Germans approaching from the south. Elbert waited for orders to abandon the convoy, which was nearly in port, and head south. The order never came. This did not surprise him. He was used to Air Vice Marshal Hugh Dowding's tactics.

Dowding had seen the devastation wreaked on the air forces of the Dutch, French, and Poles, and Dowding had planned accordingly. What the Germans were doing on Eagle Day was what they had done against their previous enemies: launching a sneak attack to catch the English napping. For that reason, Dowding spread his forces across the country, and he made it a rule never to stake his inferior force on one roll of the dice. Hermann Göring could send wave after wave of planes in an attempt to lure the English into a showdown, but Hugh Dowding knew that all his country had to do was remain in the game.

Eagle Day never came close to defeating the Royal Air Force "in four weeks" as Hitler's air chief had predicted. Göring never caught the English on the ground or in the sky. When faced with superior numbers, the Brits simply avoided combat and the Germans had to go looking for other targets. Many times there were none and precious fuel was wasted. Sometimes the RAF would hit the *Luftwaffe* hard at the point of no return— when German fighters had just enough fuel to return to occupied France. The British had another thing going for them. Their bases were only a short distance away, not some airstrip across the English Channel. Many a German pilot was shot down with his eye on his gas gauge instead of looking through his gun sight.

On Eagle Day, Mark Elbert ran into a pack of

Messerschmitts, downed two, and then was shot down himself. Actually, the Germans shot up his cockpit, sending shards from the windscreen into the aviator. Blinded in one eye, his career as a pilot over, Elbert began a fit of drinking while recuperating that no one could talk him out of. He considered himself a penguin, someone in uniform who struts around Piccadilly Circus but cannot fly.

A chap on Air Vice Marshal Dowding's staff had attended Sandhurst with Elbert and ran into the drunken pilot in one of the many bars near the Circus. This man had just the cure for Elbert's despondency: an invitation to view Fighter Command.

Fighter Command was the British operation that detected and plotted the direction of enemy aircraft. And just as a dedicated core of sailors and soldiers had banded together to preserve their proud history and look forward to better days, a group of RAF officers and scientists had nurtured Fighter Command during the lean years of the 1930s.

Elbert happened to be at Fighter Command when the first warnings came in from the eastern and southern coasts of England. Mark Elbert watched with his good eye, mesmerized, as the approaching German planes were first detected by radar. He had heard of this "radar" and knew his planes wore an IFF device to let "radar" know he was a friend, not a foe. Now, as he stood on the balcony overlooking the huge grid map on the massive board below, radar became very real to Mark Elbert.

He watched as WAAFs, wearing uniforms blotted with

sweat and revealing the intensity of the women's work, used sticks to solemnly push colorful blocks of wood across the huge table. Mounted on the wall was a strange-colored clock segmented into five-minute triangles. As Elbert watched, differently sized wooden triangular blocks with flags were pushed across the grids. A plastic arrow designated the direction of attack and the arrow matched one of the colors on the odd-colored clock on the wall. Then word was flashed to the sectors expected to come under attack, and this would dictate the response by the air squadron commander responsible for that particular sector.

Elbert's friend leaned over and whispered that the size of the attack determined the size of the wooden block pushed across the table map of England; the flag was the number of the attack, and the arrows changed color as each five-minute segment elapsed on the multicolored clock.

In the balcony sat two more WAAFs with the air controller who gave vectors to the intercepting British squadron. Sometimes the controller spoke directly to the pilots in the air. Over a loudspeaker on the wall everyone could hear both sides of the conversation. Other than that, the room was silent. When the women working the board were spoken to, they replied matter-of-factly. As Elbert stood on this balcony in Stanmore, just north of London, he hung on every word coming through the speaker. That could be him up there. Hell, that had been him up there. He'd spoken to Fighter Command before.

Now the Germans were close enough for the Observer Corps to weigh in, and over secured lines, English men and women along the coast strained their eyes skyward, filling out "radar's" initial support. Then the sector leader took over, guiding the RAF fighters to their targets and safely returning the surviving planes to their home base. This was the edge Hugh Dowding had against Hermann Göring when the Third Reich's huge bombers attempted to bomb England into submission.

So, as American reporters stood on the beach and watched the *Luftwaffe* have its way with their targets, these same reporters would return to their desks and churn out more pessimistic reports for their stateside papers. McKenzie Stuart's reports were much more upbeat. McKenzie had visited Stanmore, and while she could not report what she had seen, her copy infuriated her father in the States.

"Communist propaganda" is what he termed reports that the Soviets could hold out until the Allies launched their Second Front. Gilbert Burns went on to lambaste his daughter's vain hopes for the survival of England. "You sound like a cheerleader more than a reporter."

"They didn't have cheerleaders at the prep school I attended," shot back his daughter on the crackling overseas connection.

"McKenzie, do you remember that argument we had several months ago when you said my paper would be marginalized if I didn't get behind Roosevelt's war effort—before we were ever involved in this war?"

"Of course." That had been a real knock-down-drag-out fight about whether she would cover garden parties or the coming world war. The argument had ended with McKenzie's resignation from *The Record* and her subsequently joining United Press.

"That's what's happening to you," said her father now. "There isn't a person at this newspaper who believes the Soviets can hold out against Jerry. It's even rumored that Ike doesn't think they'll last. What makes you think you know better in this matter than General Eisenhower?"

"Ike hasn't been to the Russian Front. I have."

"My God, McKenzie, your arrogance—"

"And where do you think I came by that arrogance, Father?" She cleared her throat. "I can back up everything I say," said McKenzie, pressing the limits of censorship.

Unknown to McKenzie, the censors knew of her exploits in Russia, the American military officer whom she had married, and most importantly, how difficult it was to make McKenzie's father and other editors back in the United States believe in the Soviets.

"Actually, Father, I remember our conversation quite well. You didn't think I could do this job. I have. Now why don't you let me continue, and if you and Doyle want to blue line most of what I write, you'll miss one of the biggest stories of this war: the steadfastness of the Russian soldier."

For a moment her father didn't reply, and McKenzie thought she had lost the connection. Then he asked, "You are assuring me that this isn't some youthful exuberance on your part?"

"Father, I'm twenty-six years of age, I'm responsible

for a child and a husband, and I have been where other reporters have not gone. I expect to be treated like an experienced and reliable journalist. If you can find anything inaccurate in my stories, please bring it to my attention. Otherwise, let me report this war as I see it." And for the first time McKenzie hung up without saying "good-bye" or telling her father that she loved him. McKenzie was still trembling when she left the booth.

Mark Elbert put an arm around her, pulling her in tight. "Drink?" he asked.

McKenzie nodded. "More than one."

Flashing a small smile, Elbert asked, "Perhaps this weekend is the proper one to visit the countryside?"

McKenzie nodded. "Yes. Perhaps it is."

✳   ✳   ✳

Wolfgang Topp was shaken awake by the cry "Dive." The alarm bell sounded throughout the ship and that got Topp moving. He stumbled to his position as the men topside slid down the aluminum ladder and thumped to the deck. Machinists grabbed handles of leverage valves and hung on, using their weight to blow the ballast into the sea. All around Wolfgang, people turned hand-wheels desperately, and there was a noticeable "swoosh" as the air rushed out of the ballast tanks and the sea roared in. Before he could reach his position, Wolfgang was thrown to the floor of the control room and sat there, stunned. Someone shouted a warning.

"An outboard air induction valve didn't close!"

Topp tried to get to his feet, but a shipmate stepped on his hand. The boat tilted and appeared to drop sharply, headed for the bottom. From what Topp remembered, they were along the coast of England.

Another voice shouted through an opening in the stern of the boat. "The head valve is jammed. It will not close properly."

Properly, thought Wolfgang as he sat on the metal deck. A peculiar choice of words. Either the valve closed or it did not. If not, they would sink like a stone.

"Blow all tanks!" came the order from the captain. Then, "Surface."

From where he sat on the deck, Wolfgang could see the needle on the depth gauge drop from seventy to one hundred meters. The boat was sinking stern first and anything not lashed down flew in the direction of Wolfgang. And there was plenty to fly. Every millimeter was used in a U-boat, with every seat a locker. Foodstuffs hung everywhere, so because of the suddenness of the movement, more than other submariners came tumbling in Wolfgang's direction.

Topp threw up his hands as canned goods, boxes, and fellow shipmates fell on top of him. A roar came from the rear of the boat, and then a jarring thud as the U-boat hit the bottom of the North Atlantic.

The lights went out.

The ship went silent.

"Inboard air induction valve secured."

Under his feet the deck swayed in one direction, then the other.

"The stern is stuck in the mud," whispered the man lying on top of Wolfgang.

Topp said nothing. He could barely draw a breath.

"All crew to the bow," ordered the captain.

Once his fellow submariner climbed off him and he could brush away the fallen items, Topp scrambled to his feet. Using the auxiliary lighting, figures ahead of him moved forward. A last glance at the depth gauge read one hundred twenty-two meters. What would they do if the English found them stuck down here?

On his hands and knees, Wolfgang climbed almost straight up. He used valves, pipes, or pumps to steady his feet and pull himself up by his hands. He glanced behind him, actually below him and down the shaft, past the radio room, the commander's quarters, the lavatories, and returned to his quarters shared with extra torpedoes mounted over bunks or hammocks. Behind him, it was like looking out the window of a tall building, seeing his fellow crewmembers crawling up the gangway into the bow.

Beyond the wet and bearded submariners, their faces smeared with oil and grease, came the sound of the captain and the hopeful voice of the chief as they waited for the ballast provided by the submariners to level the submarine and free it from the mud.

It was a short wait, and Wolfgang did not know if that was a good or bad thing. Then his ship wagged its stern, freeing itself from the bottom of the North Atlantic—to surface in the face of what? What was waiting topside? Why had the order been given to dive?

Once the ship righted itself, level once again, the

crew nodded, smiled, and returned to their posts. The Papenberg depth gauge read 80 meters, then 60, then 40, and finally 20 before orders from the captain stopped the ascent. Now what?

※　　※　　※

James Stuart was on the phone, trying to get through to his wife when he was summoned by the British high command. In a spartan room with a single officer seated behind a mahogany desk, a British colonel said, "You come highly recommended, Major."

Stuart said nothing. He was thinking of those he had left behind at both Dunkirk and Dieppe. What was there to be said but that he was a coward?

From behind the desk, the colonel continued, "In the Channel Islands there is a lighthouse occupied by the Germans. We thought you might like to go along and see what British commandos can do in a pinch."

Stuart stared at the general. Why was this happening to him? True, he had survived Dieppe with minor scrapes and bruises, but to send him out this soon—why?

Stuart cleared his voice. "Whatever the Crown thinks is necessary, sir."

An eyebrow was raised before the British officer dismissed him.

James Stuart figured his number was up. Even Antonio Petrocelli's face darkened at the news.

"Are they trying to kill you, sir?"

The sergeant had not been ordered to go along because he was recuperating from a German bullet that had sliced open his side and cracked two ribs. For that reason, Petrocelli spent a good bit of time standing, and he was standing beside the desk assigned to James Stuart—when he was in England.

"If I don't come back would you see what you can do for Anastasia?" said Stuart, staring out a window in Eisenhower's command center. The English countryside was quite beautiful. It was very much like the plantation he had grown up on in Virginia. A place he really believed he would never see again.

"Yes, sir," came the resounding response. "I'll see what I can do for McKenzie, too, sir."

Stuart looked at the man with whom he had shared so many adventures, someone who probably knew him better than anyone. "What do you hear of McKenzie? And the girl?"

"Both are well," said Petrocelli with a poker face.

Stuart pressed his subordinate for more information.

"Well, sir, I don't see much of McKenzie. Most of the time I'm with Annie, and she's been sent to the countryside." Petrocelli smiled. "McKenzie's keeping hours like Eisenhower."

Ike was famous for being at his desk at eight each morning, even when Churchill kept him up talking until past three the previous night. Ike also came in and worked a few hours on Sunday.

"Tell me what you know," encouraged Stuart, his voice softening.

"She runs her father's bureau in London."

"Yes, yes," said Stuart impatiently, "but is she part of the social scene?"

"Only to see what information she can pick up," observed Petrocelli dryly, "then she's in the office the next morning."

"And who escorts her to these functions?"

"She has her own Jimmy Olsen."

Stuart eyed his subordinate. "Tony, is there something you'd rather not tell me?"

A long pause, then, "Sir, permission to speak freely?"

"Of course." Stuart felt a tug at his heart and it wasn't one of love.

"How many times have you seen McKenzie since we arrived in England?"

"Tony, you know the demands of my job."

"Sir, just answer the question."

Stuart stared at the empty desk in front of him. "None."

"Or phoned her?"

Stuart's head came up. "Several times."

"Ever get through?"

"You know how the phone system is in this country."

"Sir, everyone needs someone. I once thought there was someone who didn't need anyone, but now I'm having second thoughts."

There was a silence between the two men.

Finally, Stuart asked, "What do you suggest?"

"McKenzie is like any other woman," Petrocelli said with a shrug. "She only wants to know that she's on your mind all the time."

"All the time?"

"That's all women want. The rest they can do without. Why don't you write her? Every day. Well, at least the days when the brass hats aren't trying to get you killed."

❋   ❋   ❋

Wolfgang Topp returned to his position in the control center of the boat—about twenty by twenty feet—at the same time his commander demanded to know what the hell all that had been about. The control room was crammed with levers, buttons, and spinwheels. The commander's eye was at the Zeiss attack scope, hat turned backward, checking the surface for danger, demanding to know why they had submerged.

"Sir," said the 1st officer, "the lookouts reported a ship. An English destroyer."

"Did you confirm it?" the captain demanded of the officer who had just transferred in.

"Yes, sir," said the younger man, almost coming to attention near the scope.

The commander pulled his eye from the scope, turned his cap around, and swung the scope around to his second-in-command. "Tell me what you see."

The exec reversed his cap, took a very long look, and then pulled his eye from the attack scope. "Er—nothing, sir. Perhaps some clouds in the distance."

"Nothing that looks like a ship."

"No, sir. Nothing that appears to be a ship."

"That is correct." Looking around the bridge at the

assembled submariners. "Who was standing duty with you?"

The offending parties were pointed out, three men with heads bowed, wet binoculars and towels around their necks, heavy oil clothing dripping water from their shift topside.

Ignoring the men and his 1st officer, the captain turned to one of the ten petty officers responsible for the topside watches. "Someone should be on report."

"It will be done, sir."

"Sir, I really—" started the exec.

About to return to his quarters, the captain faced the younger man. "It is not you the chief will write up. That is my responsibility." Disappearing in the direction of his quarters, the commander added, "Find out why that valve would not close. Do not wake me until you have done so."

"Yes, sir."

"Who's going to be written up?" whispered Wolfgang.

"The petty officer has to write himself up," said one of the older hands. "Two of the three on lookout are never to be topside together. They have too much imagination for observation duty."

Wolfgang stared at the three submariners. The petty officer was really dressing them down, and as he did so, it dawned on Wolfgang that simply being at sea could get you killed. You didn't have to make contact with the enemy.

Later, they would learn that someone had left a wrench in the outboard air induction valve, causing it to become jammed. No one came forward to say how the wrench had gotten there, and the crew manning that section of the boat, along with the chief engineer, had their duties doubled.

* * *

The connection was poor between the office of the *New York Record* and Honolulu. Over the line, Jacob Nye heard Doyle ask him, "What have you got, Nye?"

"Admiral Kimmel and General Short might be stateside, but the committee's going to hang them, possibly quite literally. That's it. Plain and simple."

"Then why are you still in the Hawaiian Territories?"

"I thought Mr. Burns wanted me here."

"We need you in New York. There's another job waiting for you."

"And that is?"

"Are you questioning your instructions, Mr. Nye?"

"With my eyesight, Mr. Boyle, I will never fight in this war, but there are plenty of newspapers who need reporters for combat coverage."

Jacob Nye had been sent to Pearl Harbor to follow the inquisition being held by the United States government into the surprise attack on Pearl. He had done that job and was eager to get out of Honolulu and into the field. The place still stank of the Japanese attack and there was an air-raid drill about every day. Not to mention the navy wasn't all that forthcoming to reporters stuck in Honolulu. But if a reporter sailed with the troops that would be a completely different matter.

Nye cleared his throat as he sat in the public telephone booth. A line of reporters and civilians was waiting to use the phone and the editor in chief of his newspaper was toying with him. Very much like the navy. "I'm not interested in returning to New York, Mr. Doyle. I want to follow the army to Guadalcanal."

"Our paper has more important issues to settle than the outcome of some battle. Take the next flight back to the States."

"That's your opinion. What does Gilbert Burns say?"

"Burns' opinion isn't the one that counts."

Jacob Nye didn't know what to say. Gilbert Burns owned the *New York Record,* lock, stock, and barrel.

"Nye," said Doyle over the crackling line, "every newspaper needs an SOB to run it. Since our only other options are a girl and a fag, you're the obvious choice." Doyle was speaking of Gilbert Burns's daughter and son.

"The board of directors concurs in this?" asked Nye, plainly astonished.

"I can put it in writing if you prefer."

"Then do it—Western Union knows my address—or tomorrow I'll ship out to Australia."

That afternoon, Jacob Nye received a telegram from Gilbert Burns ordering him home.

✳ ✳ ✳

When Nicky Lamm was summoned to MacArthur's headquarters, he still walked with a limp from a tumble he had taken down a Filipino hillside. He was also weak from a bout of malaria contracted *after* he had escaped from the Philippines. This made Nicky wonder how Vivian Riley was faring. Had she been sent to a camp? Or worse—to some Japanese comfort station, as Japanese whorehouses were called? And what had happened to Terray del Mundo, the woman who had nursed him back to health, or the Filipino scouts who had assisted him while he made the trek south to Davao? And "Big Bertha" and the malingerer Pendergrass?

Nicky had plenty of time to consider this. He was kept waiting more than an hour. Nicky quickly learned MacArthur's sycophants were running this war like they'd never been given the boot from the Philippines.

Finally, he was ushered into a captain's office. A mere captain? Evidently, he wasn't as important as the fawning nurses and awestruck sailors and soldiers he ran into daily.

"Lamm, you're being reassigned." The captain was middle-aged, going to fat.

"Yes, sir." Nicky had not been given permission to stand at ease.

"There's a ship heading for the States. Be on it Tuesday morning."

"Sir, I didn't escape from Bataan and Corregidor to be shipped back to the States. I want to—"

"The United States Army doesn't care what you want."

"But I'm not well . . ." was all Nicky could think of to say.

"Then a long sea voyage is just the ticket." The captain paused. "And that's just what our ships have to take to avoid the Japs."

"Sir, this is not how I expected to be treated—"

"I'd say you've been quite lucky not to be brought up on charges."

"For what? Sir."

"For whatever General Sutherland's staff can dream up. You pissed off the wrong man, Lamm. Best thing that could happen were those orders from Washington."

"Washington?"

"It appears the War Department doesn't want to lose one of its genuine heroes by the off chance that you might fall into enemy hands while flying around the Pacific. Besides, there's only room for one hero in the South Pacific, and you and I both know who that's going to be."

"But I want to fight the Japs, sir."

"That makes two of us, but we do what the army tells us. Your next duty will be selling war bonds."

✳   ✳   ✳

Katie O'Kelly had been reinstated into naval service, though it had been noted on her permanent record that this was a probationary period.

"Yeah," laughed one of her shipmates, a nurse who had married an enlisted man and immediately been shipped to the Pacific for fraternizing with enlisted men. "Just don't get your rear end shot off before you expunge your record."

All the girls in the quarters laughed. Everyone knew the bum rap on Katie. Assigned to duty with a Japanese-American doctor to perform abortions on American officers' wives—there was always a lonely officer's wife who would take comfort, usually with an enlisted man so whatever the sailor said could be so much scuttlebutt—Katie had the bad luck to draw the wrong duty. The woman had to be rushed to the base hospital and someone had to take the blame. That turned out to be Katie O'Kelly.

What these new friends of hers didn't know was that she'd tried to take her life by walking into the sea, until Nicky Lamm had intervened. She had seen Nicky again, and her life was complete. A bubble of joy rose in her heart each time she thought about him, and that was what she had needed: a good dose of hope. In Canberra, she had done the same for him.

Katie smiled at the thought of Nicky trying to make love to her. Nicky couldn't perform. What did he expect? The man was just out of the hospital. The army had given them the use of an open car to tour the city, but Katie and Nicky wanted to spend time alone. They did, lying alongside each other in a hotel bed, talking about their future. Not the immediate future. No one knew what that held. The future they envisioned had children, a home, a white picket fence, the whole nine yards.

Several months before, upon reporting aboard ship, Katie had been assigned a bunk and told to clean the operating room. Their ship was steaming south to a harbor off the island of Tongatabu, where they expected a great number of American ships to arrive. Rumor had it these ships were headed to the Coral Sea where they would meet the Japs head-on. Nobody knew for sure, but, as an injured sailor told her, the Coral Sea was the lifeline to Australia. Evidently the sailor, who was missing a leg, was correct in his assumption. The next day he was sent to the brig, and over his bunk was posted a sign: Loose lips sink ships.

Instead of the Battle of Coral Sea, one of the nurses was reminiscing about King Neptune's Court. The nurse, who had long blond hair, was holding out her hair and laughing. As their ship had approached the equator, signs had begun to appear saying "Polliwogs, beware!" "Polliwogs" were those who had never crossed the equator. "Shellbacks" were those who had. It made the women, even those who had treated the carnage at Pearl Harbor, a bit nervous.

One day, the shipboard communication system ordered: "All polliwogs fall in at your quarters. Davy Jones is coming aboard."

Nurses glanced nervously at each other. What was there to do but return to their quarters and stand at attention as a sailor they recognized passed in review. He wore a pirate's wide-brim black hat, a mustache smeared on with paint, and a non-issue cutaway coat that fell below his wide non-issue belt. In his hand was a sword, over one eye a patch. But Katie wasn't about to laugh at this man or the one who followed him. "Peg Leg" Pete, who thankfully had both legs, wore a similar black-paint mustache, but he looked more like one of those English policemen you saw in *Life* magazine during the Blitz.

All the nurses were sent to various parts of the ship, and some were put in stocks, to the general laughter of the captain and his staff, who watched from the bridge. Every nurse had to take a turn in the barber chair where Davy Jones or "Peg Leg" Pete went about the task of lifting their locks and snipping here and snipping there.

The shellbacks laughed as they saw the look of horror on the nurses' faces when Davy Jones or "Peg Leg" Pete shoved what appeared to be locks of their hair in the nurses' faces. It was all a joke—no hair of the women's had been cut. The men's hair was another story. Theirs was butchered and it took weeks to return to normal.

Then it was on to the Royal Tub where everyone took a turn being dunked, like at a county fair. The only difference was that each time the luckless nurse came to the surface gasping for air, one of the shellbacks exclaimed, "What? Still breathing?" and down the nurse would go until it was time for another candidate.

Thinking the worst behind them, the nurses stumbled down the stairs through a line of shellbacks—where they were stuck in the rear with an electric pitchfork. Yelping, nurses and their male colleagues attempted to escape, only to be trapped by a net. That was when fire hoses were turned on them.

There was no escape, and polliwogs, both male and female, ended up in a jumble of arms and legs against the netting before the hoses stopped their wet work. When the nurses went to their quarters, they were in total agreement: They could not wait until they had a chance to torment the next group of polliwogs to cross the equator.

✳   ✳   ✳

The boat took them to the lighthouse under the cover of dark. After disembarking, the leader of the British commandos said, "Now if you will please follow me, Major Stuart. And no cowboy antics."

Stuart nodded. For some reason he was feeling particularly vulnerable without Tony watching his back. However, Petrocelli was on medical leave in London, and probably visiting Anastasia.

Anastasia Stuart. His daughter. And his wife? What was McKenzie up to? Stuart had made the suggested phone call from his office before leaving for this latest raid and had met with devastating results.

He had finally gotten through to the *Record*'s bureau in London and, frustrated by the long wait, had failed to properly identify himself.

"She's with the wing commander in the country."

"And which wing commander would that be?" asked Stuart, straightening up in the chair where he sat.

"Mark Elbert of His Majesty's Royal Air Force."

"They're visiting one of the RAF bases?" Stuart was aware of Vice Air Marshal Dowding's scheme of scattering the RAF around the country.

"Perhaps," said the voice on the other end of the line, now more guarded. "Whom shall I say called?"

"It doesn't matter. I won't be here when she returns."

Stuart hung up and stared at the phone. Around him

people hurried here and there. Operation Torch was underway; troops from the States had sailed days ago.

Aware that Petrocelli was watching him, Stuart said, "Tony, have you ever seen me drunk?"

"No, sir. I have not."

"Then come along," said Stuart, getting to his feet. "I'll show you how it's done."

Petrocelli said, "I think we have time for a note before we leave."

Stuart glanced at the phone. "I don't think a note's going to do the job."

Petrocelli took a sheet of paper and a pen from the desk where Stuart had sat and handed these to his boss. "Either write McKenzie, sir," said Petrocelli, "or my mother about the terrific job I'm doing over here for my country."

Stuart smiled and quickly scribbled a note to his wife, then stuck it in an envelope provided by Petrocelli. The sergeant sealed the envelope and called for a courier.

To the soldier, he said, "Get this to the bureau of the *New York Record* right away."

"Sir, the censors—"

"Soldier, the major and I will be in North Africa while you're in the rear. I've written a letter to my mother, and now the major wants this taken to his wife who works at the London bureau of the *New York Record*. As a secretary," added Petrocelli, glancing at James Stuart. "Think you can handle that?"

"Yes, Sergeant!" The young man almost clicked his heels, then turned and left the two men.

"Why are you doing this, Tony?" asked Stuart, getting to his feet.

"Sir, we have finally been assigned to a tank unit, and I would prefer that you have your mind on your job and not be worried about what your wife's up to."

Wearing dark gear and with pistols at the ready, the British commandos left their dinghies behind and moved toward the lighthouse. The Germans manning the lighthouse were housed in the lower level. The commandos seized this area with ease, and then entered the radio room, where an astonished German soldier scrambled to his feet.

One of the commandos stepped forward and clubbed the man upside the head. The soldier fell to the floor, and as he fell, another commando was scooping up the codebooks. Another was kneeling alongside the radio and was applying enough explosives to blow the top off the lighthouse, never mind blowing up the radio.

Sailing away with seven prisoners, the leader of the commandos said, "That's how it's done, Major."

"Why?" was all Stuart could ask.

"So you could see that the debacle at Dieppe wasn't what you should expect when our two nations assault the Nazis' Atlantic wall."

TWELVE

On Guadalcanal, General Vandegrift ordered one of the battalions covering the Lunga River flank to reinforce "Red Mike" Edson. Sick and exhausted Marines who had not slept for two days stumbled into positions to shore up the raiders and await developments. The Japanese leader, Kawaguchi, threw everything at the Marines defending the ridge because whoever held the ridge held the airfield.

Another bombardment by Japanese ships at sea, another flare dropped by Washing Machine Charlie, and then Kawaguchi's men charged out of the jungle: two battalions striking between the Lunga River and the ridge. Of the three groups attacking the Marines, the largest had the mission of driving across the ridge and reaching the airstrip. Those in the command post could hear the enemy slashing through the underbrush, trying to scale the ravine to reach the command post.

With superior numbers, the Japanese broke through

the Marines' lines, cursing, tossing firecrackers, and yelling "Banzai." One platoon was cut off, red tracers flew in both directions, marking targets for death, and the Marines were pushed back.

Kawaguchi called in mortar fire, and rounds rained down on the Marines' position. The Marines returned the favor with 105-mm howitzers south of the airstrip. The howitzers were under orders from "Red Mike" to "walk their rounds back and forth."

Yes, the Japanese controlled the ridge at that moment. The area between the jungle and the ridge became one vast killing ground, with the sound of the Marines' '03s cracking in response to the Japanese's .25s and chants of "US Marines dead by tomorrow!"

Mortars and howitzers poured rounds on a ridge that was grassy no more; the night was shattered with the flash of gunfire, those huge firecrackers of the Japanese, and the eerie green of flares dropped by Washing Machine Charlie.

Cleve Woodruff's unit fought its way into position, filling the break in the line with men and machine gun fire. Cleve gaped as one wave of Japanese was mowed down, then another. The suicidal charges forced Edson's lines to be bent into a semicircle around the knob at the top of the ridge, a mere thousand yards from Henderson Field.

Again the fighting became hand-to-hand, and once again the Japanese had to climb, sometimes trip, over their dead comrades to reach Harvey and Cleve. It was probably good that the fighting was hand-to-hand because the Americans were almost out of ammo.

More rounds were hustled forward, including belts for machine guns. By 3 A.M. Cleve and Harvey's unit had closed the Marines' broken lines and were no longer simply holding the knoll but had pushed the Japanese back. That was when another group of Japs rushed out of the jungle.

What assault was this? wondered Cleve as he hastily reloaded. The seventh? The ninth? Overhead, Washing Machine Charlie continued to drop flares, and from the jungle came the cry of "gas." While Harvey and Cleve were fumbling for their masks—that cursed piece of equipment soldiers always wonder why they carry until it's needed—Meadors took a bullet through the heart.

Cleve neither saw nor heard his friend fall. He was fumbling with the mask, then, upon learning the "gas" was only smoke, Cleve snatched the suffocating thing off and faced Japanese flanking the Marines' position.

As sniper rounds opened holes in the canvas of Vandegrift's command post, "Red Mike" called the general and told Vandegrift that his raiders could hold. When Woodruff later heard of this, he thought it was the craziest remark he'd heard since landing on Guadalcanal. In the coming weeks he would hear crazier things, and more buddies would die.

Hugging the ground of his command post, Vandegrift said to his staff, "It's just a few hours till dawn, then we'll see where we stand."

Cleve's unit moved again, this time to the left flank where the Japanese were threatening to break through again. Cleve noticed he had become separated from Meadors, and called to him until someone told him to hold it down. Cleve slugged forward, hoping for the best, expecting the worst.

A mile to the east, another of General Kawaguchi's prongs ran into the wire on a grassy field bordering the Tenaru River and some nicely dug-in Marines, who pushed the Japanese back. To rub salt in the wounds of the Japanese, the Marines went after them with tanks—and lost half their armor. The Nips appeared to still have some bite. This was borne out when Kawaguchi's third prong attacked a hill held by the Fifth Marines. They were driven back into the jungle but remained where they could snipe at the Marines' position.

Dawn was approaching, and that meant mechanics and maintenance personnel would be running across Henderson Field and checking for holes in the landing strip. Once these were filled in, the Cactus Air Force was airborne.

Because Kawaguchi's men had retreated, corpsmen were sent to fetch those Marines who lay in the open and were subjected to continuing sniper fire from the jungle. Grass fires smoldered, and farther down the slope they saw a sight too horrible to comprehend: hundreds of Japanese blown apart by artillery fire. Burned fuels, cordite from weapons, and the smell of bodies filled the air.

Marines on the retaken ridge, dirty and exhausted, hunkered down to avoid the snipers taking potshots at them. Finally, the Marines had had enough. Under cover from the Cactus Air Force, they raided the jungle in a mopping-up operation. As they did, Japanese planes flew in over the mountain to bomb the "Pagoda," a rectangular-shaped building with a curved roof that was used as the operations center for the Cactus Air Force. They were driven off.

More planes from Henderson Field went on sorties against Japanese positions, including those at sea. Marines searching the jungle found few snipers, but they did find plenty of equipment. Captured Japanese begged for knives, gesturing at their stomachs as if to indicate they wanted to disembowel themselves. When not given the requested knives, the prisoners appeared greatly relieved.

The Seventh Marine Regiment was ordered to reinforce Guadalcanal. Unfortunately, a Japanese boat, the sub that had turned the *Wasp* into a blazing inferno, spotted the transports carrying the Seventh. This time that same sub damaged the new battleship *North Carolina*, and even got lucky with a hit on the *O'Brien*.

"Terrible" Turner was adamant, and made his point, expletives not deleted, that the Marines on Guadalcanal must be resupplied. Turner had become a true believer, and luck was with him. When bad weather kept Japanese planes on the ground in Rabaul, and the Japanese navy failed to sail to intercept the Seventh Marine Regiment, more than one hundred and fifty vehicles were landed, tons of rations, and hundred of drums of aviation fuel for the First Marine Air Wing, which now joined the Cactus Air Force.

With a jaunty wave, Mason Monroe saluted his former comrades in arms, happily leaving this hellhole to return to carrier duty, where there was always clean water, chow, and a decent bunk. Mason Monroe had good reason to want to leave Guadalcanal, and it had more to do with a good bath and time for his mosquito bites to heal. Backed by reinforcements, General Vandegrift couldn't let well enough alone and planned to extend his perimeter.

No go. The Japanese were heavily dug in down the beach. Then came news the Marines on Guadalcanal didn't want to hear: The Japanese were massing units at Rabaul, Truk, and Bougainville. Moreover, these were heavy units, meaning they weren't a bunch of riflemen supported by mortars. All in all, it made what "Terrible" Turner had landed on Guadalcanal look pretty puny.

❇   ❇   ❇

The lieutenant in charge of the plane spotters along the Virginia coast wanted Elizabeth Randolph Woodruff to move to Washington. He said he had an important job in the Pentagon, that monstrosity being built along the Potomac. He would be in charge of security, perhaps even after the war when the building would be turned into a veterans' hospital.

Elizabeth was intrigued by the thought of living in Washington and bored to death with coast watching. What did it matter if she or others watched the coast? The Germans had sunk enough tonnage—a new word for her—to close beaches all along the East Coast.

Who would want to live along the coast if you couldn't

bathe in the ocean? Elizabeth had seen pictures in *Life* of naval nurses sunbathing topside on their hospital ships. Now that didn't look like such bad duty. One thing for sure: She was ready for a change.

The young blonde turned her binoculars toward the sky over the Virginia coast as the lieutenant approached her position. The hem of her A-line dress flapped in the breeze off the ocean. A cotton jacket had been thrown over her shoulders to shield her from that breeze and her blond hair was worn in a ponytail.

"Elizabeth?"

She continued to search the sky for enemy aircraft, then the ocean for U-boats.

Again he called her name.

Elizabeth lowered her glasses and faced him. "Rodney, what is it you want this time?"

The officer glanced at the sand making up the dune. He was a pimple-faced young man who wore shiny new gold bars of a second lieutenant on the shoulders of his woolen khakis. On his head was the narrow garrison cap. "I've been transferred. I won't see you again."

Elizabeth felt a hole open in her heart. It was not anything like love; it was more like a loss of a family member. No. Not like *her* family. Her father was drunk out of his mind whenever she visited him, her mother-in-law a true bitch, and her father-in-law always giving advice to anyone who would listen about how to increase crop yields during wartime. Elizabeth could abide none of them. That was why she was here, staring over this fucking ocean!

What language! She'd never spoken like that before.

Maybe a "damn" or a "hell," but that was okay. Scarlett O'Hara had used such words. She, however, had moved much further than Scarlett. Elizabeth Randolph Woodruff had gone well beyond that when she had invited this young lieutenant to her bed. Now he had returned. Could he actually be the white knight she waited for?

"I want you to move to Washington with me."

"Do you realize how preposterous that sounds? I'm a married woman."

"I have found a room for you."

"You have?" Despite herself, hope rose in her throat. If there was anything she wanted, it was out of Virginia. The whole society, the Old South. Everything that had once filled her life with joy and a sense of stability now suffocated her. "It's probably in some brothel. That's how much you think of me."

"No, no," said the young man, waving his hands to protest, "it's a boarding house. One of my bosses at the War Department helped me secure lodgings for you. He thinks you're my fiancée."

"Well," said Elizabeth, facing the ocean again, "I cannot go. I'm a married woman."

"Yes, yes, and you are forbidden by law to divorce any man serving overseas. But there is still hope."

"That he will die," said Elizabeth with obvious sarcasm.

"Oh, Elizabeth!" The lieutenant seized her arms and pulled her against him. "I didn't mean anything of the sort." The smell of this woman in the salt air made the young man fumble for words. "It's just . . . I want us to be together . . . however it must be."

The fish had taken the hook. "I will consider your proposal." She gestured at the ocean with her glasses, and his hands slid off her. "There is my work to consider . . . ."

"The paperwork is finished. You can leave anytime you wish."

Below her the surf crashed into a dark and nasty beach, oil marring its natural beauty. "There's my family. . . ."

"Yes, yes," said the young man, turning her around and taking her into his arms. "Whatever you must do."

Then he kissed her gently. That was how you knew if you had really hooked a man. He would be gentle. The real bastards you could never control.

Two days later she was summoned, not to Washington, but home. Her father was dying, and his attorney informed her there were matters demanding her attention as the only heir of the Randolph's plantation home.

Elizabeth wondered if she still had an ancestral home? The most common people had been building nearer and nearer the Big House. Her father said you should always keep the common element, meaning the colored and the rednecks, at bay. Now these people lived only a few hundred yards from her home. Perhaps it would be necessary for her to defend her home as Scarlett had Tara. If so she would do it!

At the train station in Richmond, a Packard sedan was waiting for her, manned by a very young black servant. Its only passenger: her mother-in-law.

While Elizabeth's luggage was placed in the trunk, Mrs. Woodruff said, "Mr. Woodruff had business at the bank. I will send him along for this conference. It's not ladylike for you to be forced to attend to such matters without a man present."

Elizabeth looked the old bat squarely in the eye. "I'll need no help handling this attorney. He's a man, is he not?"

Her father's lawyer was a fat man with a belly barely restrained by his belt, pants, and seersucker jacket. His name was Walter Stuart Fulmer.

"I am here to settle my father's accounts," announced Elizabeth once she was seated in front of the attorney's desk and had forgone the offer of an iced tea.

Once the door had closed behind the clerk, the attorney said, "Elizabeth, I don't wish to dwell on the sad state of affairs you find yourself in."

"Pardon?" The young woman leaned forward.

"Your father insisted on living in the world of the Old South and his accounts are far behind." The fat man had not moved beyond half rising when Elizabeth had been ushered into his chambers. Now he leaned back in his chair.

"What are you telling me?" asked Elizabeth, not so sure of herself now.

"Yankees want to buy what is left of your estate."

"Then sell it! I have another life." Her back straightened and her chin rose. "One where I can be free of all these insufferable relationships."

"Very well, I will prepare the papers. It is a decent

offer and will clear up the indebtedness your father has incurred over the years." He went on to add, "You are a very fortunate young woman to have a family to take you in."

"I'm not about to be lorded over by that old bitch."

"Elizabeth, please, such language."

"Mr. Fulmer, if you persist in failing to grasp what has happened to our world, perhaps I should take my business elsewhere."

Now the attorney sat up. "I have a very good grasp of what has happened to *your* world, young lady. There won't be any money after your father dies. Creditors are just waiting for the right opportunity. Since you can move in with your in-laws, they will show you no pity."

"I have a job with the government. I am not without means."

Across the desk, Fulmer decided to lean back and listen to what this child had to say. He got an earful. Elizabeth Randolph Woodruff and her lover had had many a conversation as they held hands overlooking the ocean washing more spilt oil ashore.

"You may think this is just a war," explained Elizabeth, "but more than that is happening. Women are taking men's places in the workforce. I have done this myself, and now have a chance to move to Washington and further my career."

"Your career . . . ?"

"Mr. Fulmer, in the future women will have careers."

"You're wrong, my dear. I was in the Great War. When that was said and done, all I wanted to do was to return to Virginia and start a family. Fortunately, I found a wonderful woman I've been married to for over thirty years. You think women want careers, that they want to leave hearth and home? No, Elizabeth," said Fulmer, shaking his head, "you are doing this to serve your own devices. Not once while growing up did you ever hear the word 'no.' Not only that, you are your father's daughter and you will waste your life with no thought for the future. Just as your father has done."

The girl twisted around uncomfortably in her chair. She really could use a cigarette. "You are such a fuddy-duddy, Mister Fulmer."

"Don't interrupt me when I'm speaking, young lady. I'm not your father, and I'm certainly not that simple-minded young man you married." Fulmer gestured at the office with its dark wood, thickly covered seats, and rows of law books lining the shelves. "While building this practice, I watched your father waste every cent he came into when he married your mother. I can understand why your father doted on you. You were the youngest, and the only remaining child after the Spanish Fever took your mother and sister. Yes, he doted on you, but he also doted on himself, denying himself nothing. Now your father has left you with nothing. Less than nothing since you and your father will have to move in with the Woodruffs once the sale of the house is complete."

"We have . . . nothing?"

"Your home and the land it sits on is mortgaged to the hilt." Fulmer leaned forward on his desk with both arms. "You can't say you didn't see this coming, my dear. Piece by piece the plantation has been sold off for years. So forget about Washington and make peace with your mother-in-law. They have a farm to run and not enough help. Too many black servants have joined up."

"Black men in our army?"

"There were black men in the Confederate Army. They also served in the Great War."

"I never thought . . . ."

"You'd best learn to think because you are a married woman with responsibilities. No, Elizabeth, there will be no Washington for you."

✳   ✳   ✳

The gonging of the alarm, then the "General Quarters" bugle through ship-wide loudspeakers brought Nicky Lamm out of a deep sleep. He had been dreaming of Katie again, about their time together in Australia. It had been only a seventy-two-hour pass, but it had been a godsend.

Before going topside, Nicky took down his life preserver and a small pack that held everything he owned, including several photographs of Katie O'Kelly. Still walking with a limp, he made his way topside with others catching a ride on this destroyer on its way to Pearl. From there, he would sail on another ship for San Diego, then by train across the country to Washington. Nicky appreciated that his orders gave him a week's leave near St. Louis, where he could visit with his family. There was a very special gal he wanted to tell his folks about.

As Nicky struggled up the ladder, he realized the ship was dead in the water and there was no sound from its engines. They were still moored in the harbor where they had arrived late yesterday afternoon. Still, there was the call to general quarters.

Because of his limp, Nicky was one of the last to arrive topside. Topside, he looked down the line of men at the railing; all were wearing life preservers and many carried musette bags. Bags that would do nothing but drag them under if they went over the side, and bags that the navy would certainly not allow to be taken along if "away all boats" was called.

The night was dark and quiet but for the mumbling of the men at the railing and those at the cannon chambering a round. Then came the word "fire." Nicky flinched as the cannon exploded.

"What are they firing on?"

"Putting a round across the bow of a ship trying to sneak into the harbor."

Lights immediately came on a thousand yards away, revealing a hospital ship running in the dark as it was required to do whenever inside a harbor.

Below deck on that ship, Katie O'Kelly realized they were going to need more gauze. She never heard the ship go to general quarters. Very early on, she learned to focus on the job at hand. She, the other nurses, the doctors, and the corpsmen had been working for three days with little sleep. Their patients, Marines, had been in one hell of a battle.

"Gauze?" demanded the surgeon, straightening up

at the operating table. "How the hell can we be short of gauze?"

The anesthesiologist sat at the head of the table; the patient lay on it. The sailor was missing both legs. A corpsman had just left with buckets filled with the remains of the sailor's limbs.

Katie ignored the remark as she blotted the surgeon's forehead before leaving. Usually there was plenty of gauze, but earlier in the day they had even run out of dressings because of the number of patients arriving with belly or chest wounds. Paper cushioning the ship's dishes and china had been pressed into service. Usually, though, there was plenty of gauze.

Katie stepped into the corridor and down the hall to the nearest ward, a huge open room lined with bed after bed of sick and injured Marines.

"Gauze?" she asked Ann Anderson, the head nurse.

Anderson, who had won the Silver Star by boarding damaged vessels at Pearl Harbor on December 7th to treat the wounded, looked up from where she leaned over the bed of an unconscious Marine with an IV in his arm. The ward was filled with wounded; nurses were needed everywhere at once. "Check the stores. And get back into uniform, O'Kelly."

Anderson was referring to the wide belt nurses wore around the middle of their cotton dresses. The dresses had long sleeves and were the nurses' duty uniforms. Most doctors, however, allowed the nurses to remove the belt in the operating room. A nurse's back was always damp with perspiration, and taking off the belt was the only way a woman could get some air under her dress.

Re-entering the operating room, Katie strapped on her belt. "I'll get the gauze from the stores, sir, if the mate hasn't gone topside with the others."

The doctor looked around the operating room, then at the anesthesiologist. His fellow doctor shook his masked face. Aseptic technique had gone out the window with the onslaught of the wounded, and now the navy expected them to go to general quarters in the middle of a procedure?

✳   ✳   ✳

McKenzie jerked her blouse shut. The caress of Mark's hands had been stimulating, her nipples becoming erect, but something was wrong. Her body had deceived her into thinking that being at this quaint inn, that leaning back on this overstuffed sofa and sipping wine—all of that was okay.

"I—I can't do this." She scooted back from the flyer as a perplexed look crossed Elbert's face.

Thankfully, Mark did not press her. He simply reached for his wine glass and finished his drink.

Entering this inn in the English countryside, McKenzie had wondered if this was where Mark brought his lovers. After all, the old lady at the front desk had not once met their eyes but had slid the key to their room across the desk and disappeared into the back room. On the radio Churchill was giving the Nazis hell, but what else was new? She and Mark were here to put all that behind them. At least for a weekend. Now she'd faltered when all it took was for her to surrender to this man who had done so much for her.

Perhaps that was what was wrong.

Only minutes after stepping into their room, McKenzie had taken the wineglass offered by Mark and accepted his first kiss. Nothing was rushed. Once they were seated on the sofa, there had been that bit about how he had his eye—the one good one he had, he said, laughing—on her the first day he had met her in the lobby of the Claridge Hotel. She was one of the most intriguing women he'd ever met.

McKenzie brushed this off with the simple statement that she doubted Mark Elbert had met many American women, or could form such a judgment on the spot.

This brought another smile and chuckle. Did James Stuart ever smile? Did he ever think about her? A long pull from the wineglass, and then Mark was kissing her throat, being gentle and kind.

McKenzie placed her glass on the coffee table. She didn't need more wine to enjoy this. Still, all she could think of while Mark unbuttoned her blouse was that her louse of a husband had left her to fend for herself in a city as large as New York—until Mark Elbert took time away from his work to make sure she was able to report the most fascinating stories. He even took her places she *couldn't* report about.

Her bastard of a husband knew people and knew his way around Europe. Probably knew his way around this new Europe better than Mark Elbert. Had James Stuart ever offered to share any of that information with her?

Mark had done all those things, even arguing with her about the choice of Eisenhower as supreme commander. "The man has dangerous ideas."

"During the maneuvers, Eisenhower was generally correct in his assessment of the situation."

"My dear, you know how much I trust your judgment, but if Eisenhower is wrong about this cross-channel landing he so strongly desires, thousands of young men will die."

Because he trusted her judgment. Because she could be trusted not to report everything he had shown her.

"What is making you so uncomfortable?" asked Elbert, pouring another glass of wine. "You wanted to get away from the city. We've been talking about this for weeks."

"Yes, yes, I know that," said McKenzie, looking around for a cigarette.

Mark offered her one and then lit it. Looking at the cigarette, he said, "First time I had an affair I was consumed with guilt."

McKenzie let out a smoke-filled breath, almost choking on it. She coughed, then said, "You were?"

Now he looked at her. "It's not natural to cheat on your husband, or in my case, my wife."

"Then you understand why . . . ."

"I understand that you and I may not live to see tomorrow, and it is only natural that people will cleave to each other." Elbert lit his own cigarette. "And not consider the consequences."

"Except for that first time."

"Yes," he said with a nod. "That first time is the most difficult."

"And your wife . . . ?"

". . . is so far from danger I will not see her or my children until after the war ends. Actually, I may never see them again."

"Where?"

"Kingston, Jamaica. I'm very serious about protecting my family."

McKenzie gestured at the room with its cozy fire in the fireplace. "Then what is this?"

Elbert shrugged. "Nothing more than we make of it. If you can live without the attention and the touch of the opposite sex, you are a much better man—I mean, person—than I."

Elbert snubbed out his cigarette and got to his feet. "I will take my turn in the bath, then sleep here," he said, gesturing at the couch. "If you become lonely during the night I shall be here for you. It won't be love. It won't be romance. It will simply be two creatures clutching each other and hoping they reach the morning light."

"And if your wife . . . ?" McKenzie couldn't finish the thought.

"I would never ask such a question. It would be assumed on both parts that we took our pleasures where we could find them."

"I—I don't understand that kind of relationship."

"It is the most modern of relationships," said Elbert with his winning smile, "or shall we say, the relationship of the present." With that he headed for the bedroom and the bath.

McKenzie snubbed out her cigarette in the ashtray.

Where was that damn James Stuart when she needed him? The stress of the bombing, caring for the child, and running the office of her father's paper was simply too much. So what if she cheated on her husband? Perhaps James was lying in the arms of another right now, just as Mark Elbert's wife might be doing on the beaches of the Caribbean.

Water began to run in a tub. McKenzie glanced at the closed door and gritted her teeth. There was a war going on, dammit! Things *were* different. Lots of people were finding solace in the arms of those they weren't married to, especially soldiers stationed overseas. The English whorehouses runneth over, and the British soldiers hated the Americans for their money, smokes, and candy bars. When was the last time an English girl had a new pair of nylons?

Yes, thought McKenzie with a nod to herself. The American servicemen had a distinct advantage over the local boys. Even Eisenhower played on that weakness when he arrived. What had Ike brought for his opposite numbers? Fruit. Something the English were short of and desperately desired.

McKenzie leaned back against the sofa. Mark Elbert had done the same for her. Providing what she needed. Stories she could file that would make her reputation. Did she actually owe him something? Something she could also enjoy?

As Mark Elbert splashed in his bath, McKenzie took in the bookcases filled with books, the area rugs, the curtains and sheers, and best of all, the fire. The furniture was worn, as were the rugs, but it was a cozy place, a place where Mark said they could escape the dreary monotony of the danger in London.

Not such a bad spot to be in. And she *would* be lonely in her bed again tonight. Mark Elbert knew of that loneliness, spoke openly of it, whereas her husband was like a rock. No, a stone wall would be more—

There was a knock at the door.

Startled, McKenzie gripped the arm of the sofa. Should she answer the door?

The splashing continued in the bath.

Another knock. This one more insistent.

"Coming." McKenzie brushed back her hair and went to the door, checking the alignment of the placket of her blouse as she did.

"Who is it?" she asked.

"Miss Rivers, I have a telegram for you."

Miss Rivers? McKenzie opened the heavy door.

The woman who owned the inn was old and thin, and was bowed. She had to look up at McKenzie as she handed the yellow envelope to her. "Please do me the courtesy of informing me if the information in this telegram will cause you and Commander Elbert to depart early."

"Er—yes. Yes, I will."

"Very good," said the crone, nodding. "There is considerable demand for rooms outside London, and even though the commander is a regular, I always like to know when a room will be free. There is a waiting list, you see." With that the woman with the arched back went down the corridor to the stairs.

McKenzie was left standing there, her mind racing. Mark Elbert a regular! And if they were finished with the room, would they be so kind as to inform the crone at the desk? She looked at the bedroom door. The son of a bitch!

But by the time McKenzie had closed the door, she realized she was as much of a hypocrite as Elbert. Mark had offered no illusions about why they were spending the weekend together.

What was it he had said? What they would do in this room wouldn't be love. It wouldn't be romance. It will simply be two creatures clutching each other and hoping they reached the morning light.

What a line! And she had almost fallen for it.

Did she hate her husband that much?

McKenzie realized the telegram was in her hand. She ripped open the envelope, then opened the folded paper.

> *MCKENZIE*
>
> *SORRY TO REPORT YOUR FATHER DEAD FROM HEART ATTACK STOP BOARD OF DIRECTORS APPOINTED JACOB NYE INTERIM EDITOR STOP*
>
> *DOYLE*

McKenzie crumpled up the telegram as she stumbled over to the sofa and sat down. Her father was dead. But that was impossible. Except there had been all those rages leading to red faces and gasps for breath. She had to fly home and make funeral arrangements.

What was she thinking? Her father, if he were still alive, would think she was shirking her responsibilities. She had a bureau to run, and memorial services could be held later. There were a hell of a lot of memorial services being held these days, usually for dead or missing sailors and soldiers.

That wasn't all the telegram had said. *Jacob Nye has been appointed interim director of the paper because the board believes in him and not in you. Face facts, McKenzie. The board wants a man to run the paper.*

But you've worked at *The Record* since you were a kid, hawked papers, written stories, edited—hell you deserve to run *The Record*. And you've been to the Russian Front, suffered London and Leningrad under siege, not to mention interviewing Churchill and Stalin.

McKenzie nodded. It's all a matter of credentials. With a journalist it always came down to credentials. Credentials could play a role here, especially if she could add another one. One that showed special nerve and resolve. It might be enough to prove to the board that she had the toughness needed to run a big-city newspaper.

When Mark Elbert came out of the bathroom, he was wearing his bathrobe. "McKenzie, I was thinking . . . ." He looked around. The fire flickered in the fireplace, but the room was empty. "McKenzie?"

Another knock at the door.

Elbert answered the knock. It was the old woman, and she had several questions for him.

"Will you be leaving in the morning, Commander?"

"I don't believe so."

"Then someone else will be joining you?"

"I really don't think that's any of your business."

"Well," said the crone with a sigh, "it appears we are both the losers in this case. The woman you arrived with has left in your motorcar."

THIRTEEN

Another VIP flew into Guadalcanal and became a true believer. Admiral John S. McCain, commander of land-based aviation in the South Pacific and a man whose son would later run for president, went away recommending that no effort be spared in upgrading the facilities of Henderson Field. McCain had the vision to see beyond the dusty airstrip that became a swampy bog on rainy days. Up to seventy-five percent of the damage done to American aircraft was occurring during landings and takeoffs.

The true heroes of Guadalcanal were becoming the Marines who would grab a shovel and fill in craters or potholes—while working around bombs that had failed to detonate or might be time-delayed. In addition, conditions were primitive: Ground crews had to fill tanks by pumping gas from fifty-five-gallon drums, and they had to arm planes with bombs and ammo using muscle power. Exhausted after shifts that seemed to last for-

ever, ground crews and pilots lived like infantrymen
dug in for the duration.

General Kawaguchi had been ordered to seize
Henderson Field before Marine reinforcements arrived.
In this he had failed because of his tactics, the jungle,
or by the sheer force of will of the American Marines.
Now, the Seventh Marines had arrived. More than three
thousand healthy and well-equipped men stood ready
to fill any breach, and, once again, if Admiral Turner
had his way, these reinforcements would seize several
points around the island and halt the landing of any
further Japanese. Instead, Vandegrift strengthened the
Henderson Field perimeter.

Turner said he was going to send a couple of com-
panies of the 2nd Raider Battalion to eliminate several
Japanese observation posts. Once again, Vandegrift re-
spectfully disagreed. The 1st Raider Battalion was ex-
hausted from seizing the islands across Ironbottom
Sound, not to mention two hellish nights on Bloody
Ridge. If anything, the 2nd should relieve the 1st Raider
Battalion.

Or not. Less than a week after taking thirty percent
casualties, the 1st Battalion was back on the job—at
Vandegrift's request. "Red Mike's" reward was command
of the Fifth Marines. In that, Edson would have his
work cut out for him. The Fifth hadn't performed up to
expectations—because "Red Mike" had skimmed the
cream from the Fifth Marines to make up the 1st Raider
Battalion.

The Japanese stronghold on Guadalcanal was a point where the Matanikau River entered the ocean. There, like the Lunga, another sandbar stopped its flow, except during the rainy season when, fed by its tributaries, the Matanikau raced downhill to the sea.

About four miles inland stood some huts, and the Japanese controlled that village. Through this grassy, marshy, and hilly area the Matanikau meandered or raced, depending on the time of year, and the Japanese defended the area around the Matanikau as fiercely as the Americans did Henderson Field. In this the Japanese had an edge. They could disappear into the jungle and wait to fight another day, whereas the Marines had to hold Henderson Field at all cost. Therefore, the Marines' *modus operandi* became sweeps through the area, then hasty returns to the perimeter at the slightest hint of any threat to Henderson Field.

Three Marine companies swept through the Matanikau and turned up a few Japs who wanted to fight. A week later, Vandegrift sent in a battalion with instructions to clean out the area. These met heavily dug-in Japanese who did not turn and run. By the middle of the afternoon, the Marines' battalion commander had been relieved, and by nightfall, the Marines, out of range of American artillery, dug in for the night. The next morning the Japanese were gone and the Marines returned to Henderson Field to bicker among themselves. Someone was overheard to say that when Marines begin to quibble among themselves, it is time for the army to move in and the Marines to find another beach to jump.

1st Battalion, Seventh Marines headed across Mount Austen to seize the opposite bank of the Matanikau, where, from this position, they would push across the river and into the village. "Chesty" Puller, a colorful character who would rather not hear from Division HQ but make decisions on his own, was in charge. Puller soon made contact with the enemy and casualties were high. Not only that, it took four men to carry one litter to the rear. The 2nd Battalion, Fifth Marines rushed to the rescue, but probe after probe were machine-gunned down as the Japanese refused to disappear into the jungle.

Well, when all else fails, send "Red Mike" in. Edson had similar results. Marines attempting to seize the mouth of the Matanikau were immediately pinned down. "Red Mike" told his men they had to go in there and dig those Japs off the riverbank or the Japanese would come for them with bayonets and knives during the night. The Japs did and the fighting turned nasty. Finally someone had the sense to bring in a half-track with a 75-mm cannon and blast the Japanese out of their position. Many of the enemy tried to flee across the Matanikau and were shot down in the same manner as the Ichikis who had fled across the Lagona.

Farther upstream, Chesty Puller's men discovered a battalion of Japanese bivouacking in a ravine. Chesty called in artillery on the far side, and when the Japanese tried to climb out of the ravine, the Marines mowed them down. More than four hundred Japanese died in that ravine.

The Marines had finally broken the Japanese hold on the area, but with little to show for it. Warnings from Admiral Kelly Turner about a buildup of enemy troops, ships, and planes in Rabaul caused the Marines to abandon their newly won positions. Rumor had it this attack was to be the biggest offensive ever mounted by the Japanese against Guadalcanal.

※　　※　　※

The Allies—Franklin Roosevelt, that is—had promised the Soviets (read the American people) that they would open a second front in 1942. But following the fall of Tobruk, FDR had to rush more machinery and weapons to the beleaguered English. The American president didn't want to have to ask Congress for more machinery and weapons for what looked like a lost cause, especially with midterm elections looming on the horizon.

The British officer corps wanted to land in North Africa and mop up what was left of the German and Italian armies. To Eisenhower this made little sense. Why in the world should you go all the way to Africa to fight Germans when you could cross the English Channel and find more than you cared to deal with? It just didn't make sense, so Ike touted Operation Sledgehammer, first proposed by George Marshall and Harry Hopkins as a stopgap measure if the Soviet Union should collapse.

The British officer corps pooh-poohed the idea of landing "green" Americans on the beaches of France and—once the beachhead was secured—feeding more "green" Americans into the breach. The breach would never occur, as Dieppe had proven. The Germans had more than enough men to throw any number of divisions back into the sea. Besides, the *Luftwaffe* had air superiority over France.

Both the American chief of staff of the army and the chief of naval operations, not to mention Harry Hopkins and the president's press secretary, were flown in to assist Eisenhower in presenting Operation Sledgehammer to Churchill and the British high command.

It simply wasn't going to happen. The British had had enough of failure, sixty thousand Englishmen had died in one day during the First World War, so Marshall turned to FDR to cast the deciding vote. This was an easy call. FDR wanted American boys fighting somewhere, anywhere, before midterm elections.

Eisenhower was told Operation Torch would be launched against North Africa; the good news was Eisenhower would command the whole shebang. Marshall believed Eisenhower could get along with anyone. Still, this did not sit well with Ike. Leaving the hotel, Eisenhower told his aide this was a political move, but he intended to make it work.

It was also a political move to make the supreme commander an American, as the French blamed their humiliating defeat on lack of aircraft support from England. Perhaps, if an American was in charge, the traditional Franco-American friendship would be rekindled and cause French soldiers in North Africa to welcome the Americans ashore. In any likelihood,

Churchill said if British soldiers were required for Operation Torch, they should wear American uniforms.

Having had the rug pulled out from under him before, Eisenhower deferred to George Marshall and the British as to where to land in North Africa. George Marshall was concerned about the Spanish. Spain had cannons that could make any North African airstrip or beach a death trap. In addition, the landing force would have to sail through the Straits of Gibraltar under the barrels of those great guns. Marshall announced American troops would land at Casablanca, Oran, and Algiers, and while the British thought this a bit cautious, that Tunis should be included in the operation, FDR quieted them.

Franklin Roosevelt had to wonder if anyone in the European Theater of operations had any idea of what a precarious hold a third-term president had on his office. The American people had only gone along with him because of his previous results. There must be more results, and this time results overseas. FDR had met Eisenhower, had been entranced by him, and had sent him off, evidently to irritate every officer in the British high command. In addition, the Republicans were calling for senate hearings over the conduct of the war. Why couldn't those people in London get moving on something, anything?

When Ike became Supreme Commander, he realized he should have a deputy. His choice was Mark Clark, a soldier who was despised by George Patton and his generation because Mark Clark had leaped ahead of so many senior officers. Now, because Mark Clark could also get along with most anyone and see the big picture, he and Eisenhower would become two of the youngest men leading the American effort in Europe, not older generals who thought seniority should play a larger role.

Upon taking command of II Corps, Clark told the chaplain he thought the minister much too old to go overseas. The chaplain replied that he thought Clark much too young to command II Corps. On the spot, Clark changed his mind and the chaplain remained with II Corps.

Told by Eisenhower there would be no cross-channel attack in 1943, meaning that the field command Clark desperately wanted to keep was useless, he agreed to be Ike's deputy. Still, that wasn't enough action for Mark Clark, and when American Ambassador Robert Murphy came forward and said he could deliver the French resistance force in North Africa to the Allies, Clark leaped at the opportunity to conduct reconnaissance. After all, Clark was the liaison between the Americans and Free French.

Eisenhower had to wonder what his number two was thinking. General Charles De Gaulle, creator of the Free French, had appealed to his countrymen, all forty-five million of them, and only a thousand men had crossed over. The resistance effort under the Nazis was nonexistent, and here was Robert Murphy saying he could deliver the French forces in North Africa to the Allies. Once Clark left the meeting with Ike, he summoned James Stuart to his London office.

With a slight laugh, and a bit heady from surviving yet another raid across the English Channel, Stuart said, "Just as long as you don't have any secret missions, sir."

Clark eyed the young officer. "Would you happen to know something you shouldn't be talking about, Major?"

"Oh, Jesus," said Stuart, shaking his head and staring at the floor.

So Mark Clark went off on the adventure of a lifetime, almost got everyone in his party captured, and returned to thrill Churchill with his daring exploits of hiding in a wine cellar.

And James Stuart? He was on the phone only to learn that McKenzie's father had died. Instantly, he dashed off a letter. That evening a submarine would ferry Stuart and Petrocelli to the invasion force. Finally, James Stuart was to lead a tank unit into combat, and he couldn't wait to get started.

It was Antonio Petrocelli who made sure the letter reached McKenzie as she was boarding a freighter headed for the States. Why McKenzie was taking the most dangerous route home, Petrocelli couldn't understand. Maybe the woman was as foolhardy as her husband. If so, then the world had better watch out for any children that union produced.

Before Operation Torch could begin, the British had some unfinished business with the Germans. No way did the Brits want the Yanks to land in North Africa and seize all the glory. Montgomery had whipped

Rommel once; he could do it again, and if he hurried it would happen at the second battle of El Alamein before the Americans landed. Otherwise, Torch would become a pincer movement with the British on the short end of the pincer. Prime Minister Winston Churchill could read the tea leaves of the future and he could see that the few divisions arriving from the United States were just the tip of the iceberg. From the moment those Americans landed on the beaches of North Africa, the United States would take the leadership role in the victory over the Nazis.

Trouble was, it was difficult to get Bernard Montgomery to do anything in a hurry, and Monty was still studying how to crack the Germans' front lines. Those lines were made up of a German unit next to an Italian unit next to a German unit next to an Italian unit and so on. Since one flank was the Mediterranean, there would be no sneaking around that side. This meant the Germans knew the British would have to flank them to the south, and they were ready for the English when they struck.

Monty feinted in that direction, but then charged straight into the front lines, broke through the Italian units, and routed them. Unknown to the Germans, Montgomery had slipped all the necessary men, stores, and armament, and even had trenches dug and mines swept out of the way in the middle of the night. Everything was on the front lines, camouflaged, so the Germans were taken by surprise not by the suddenness of the attack but by the devastating firepower of the British.

It wasn't easy to wipe out the German infantry and

cause their armor to engage British tanks, but, looking back, it appears a set-piece battle from the days of the First World War was the only way a decisive victory could be gained against someone as wily as Erwin Rommel. In this Montgomery also had a bit of luck. Rommel was in Germany on sick leave.

Upon hearing of the attack, the Desert Fox left his sickbed. Good thing the Desert Fox did. His replacement had died from a heart attack, probably from the sound of British artillery. Nearly a thousand pieces were shelling the narrow Italian and German position in what could only be described as a literal rain of fire. Then, the Desert Fox took the field, hitting the British with lightning attacks—that were hammered by the Royal Air Force. When the Desert Fox fell back, that ended the dream of the *Afrika Korps'* linking up with the German Sixth Army at the Persian Gulf oil fields in the Mideast.

✳   ✳   ✳

Another arrogant bastard was on his way to North Africa. George Patton had returned from his long exile in the western desert of the United States where he had been training tank troops, and now Patton had command of the Western Task Force headed for Casablanca. His task force would put fifty thousand men ashore on the coast of Morocco.

The Center Task Force, set to seize Oran, was led by Major General Lloyd Fredendall, who lacked any combat experience. A lack of combat experience wasn't all that unusual. It had been a long time since Americans had fought a real war. An Eastern Task Force would seize Algiers, near Tunisia. Major General Charles "Doc" Ryder, one of the most highly decorated American soldiers of World War I, led this unit.

Under Lloyd Fredendall's command was a captain of armor, James Stuart, and Pfc. Antonio Petrocelli. Stuart and Petrocelli peered into the darkness ahead of them. Someone said their ship had just passed Gibraltar. Next to Stuart was Rankin Jones, who thought he would command this unit after his superior broke a leg dismounting from a tank. It appeared to Jones that his new boss had ridden a desk at Ike's HQ, then pulled strings and been given command of a unit that should have gone to Rankin Jones.

Eisenhower was to fly to Gibraltar on November 5th, but the British Isles were socked in with fog and rain. After three days of waiting, Ike would delay no more. He and his staff were driven south, where six B-17s waited. The weather didn't look any better there than near London.

Major Paul Tibbets, the leader of this flight and the pilot who would end the war in the Pacific by dropping the atomic bomb on Japan, said there was absolutely no ceiling. Eisenhower couldn't imagine not being there when his men hit the beaches.

"I have to go."

So up they went, but not very high, as Tibbets would not enter those clouds. If he did, he was sure to get lost. Eisenhower sat between the two pilots, the three of them peering through the mist. A piece of two-by-four covered with a brown army blanket became the Supreme Commander's seat. Only a hundred feet below were whitecaps, if you could see them in the dark. Eight hours later, Gibraltar appeared out of the mist. As the plane gained altitude, Tibbets said, "First time I've ever had to climb to get into landing traffic!"

The airstrip was busy, and as they taxied to a hangar, Eisenhower saw an airfield covered with planes, wing-to-wing as if on an aircraft carrier. When he climbed down, he could see even more planes landing and, on the ground, British unpacking crates and assembling British Spitfires.

Ike walked over to the strands of barbed wire separating British Gibraltar from Spain. Even in the rain, anyone with a good pair of binoculars could see something big was being planned.

In the operations center, eighteen hundred feet below solid rock, Ike rubbed together his six "lucky coins." In his pocket the Supreme Commander carried a coin for every country in the Allied Force: US, Britain, Canada, Australia, New Zealand, and South Africa.

Lucky coins notwithstanding, Gibraltar was a creepy place, dark and dank and full of mold and dripping water that formed pools in the tunnels. It did not suit the temperament of someone who had spent his boyhood on the plains of Kansas. Against one of the walls of the operations center hung a huge map with all three objectives of Torch marked: Casablanca, Oran, and Algiers.

When Ike went out at dusk on November 7th, he

could look down on dark shapes gliding across the water. They were the lead ships of the task force leaving the Atlantic and heading for the furthermost object: Target Algiers. Already one ship had been reported sunk by German U-boats. Spain, Germany, and Italy were strangely silent, and all Ike could do was rub his lucky coins and chain smoke his way through his daily ration of four packs of Camel cigarettes. Ike shook his head as he watched the armada pass by. More than once his staff had heard him express frustration at not being in command of one of those units.

Torch came down to this. Could three separate convoys of ninety thousand inexperienced soldiers sail over three thousand miles and land on terrain no one had seen before? Terrain occupied by two hundred thousand enemy soldiers.

Ike rated Torch's chances to be fifty-fifty, as James Stuart had briefed him about the disastrous results of the South Saskatchewans' raid at Dieppe. Still, if successful, Operation Torch would swing the momentum of the war in the other direction.

During the voyage across the Atlantic, the one-hundred-ship task force used zigzag maneuvers, repeatedly performed abandon-ship drills, and practiced alerts. The armada was under continuous air cover from carriers, destroyers, cruisers, and battleships.

Such extensive cover caused Wolfgang Topp's U-boat to be nudged farther north from its usual hunting grounds. None of the U-boats in the three-boat pack got close enough to see or gain a sense of the size of this mighty fleet. All the Germans knew was there had to be easier prey away from all that continuous air cover.

✳   ✳   ✳

Nicky Lamm was tossing down another drink when the two swabbies approached him at the bar on the outskirts of Chicago. Automatically, the bartender reached for the phone.

"We heard that talk you gave this afternoon."

"Yeah," said the other sailor with a smile, "sounds like you made good your escape and got no plans to return to action. Going to hang around and chase skirts."

Nicky pulled his attention from the haggard face staring back at him from the mirror over the bar. His khaki blouse was wrinkled, his tie hung loose around his neck, and his sandy hair hung down in his face. There were smudges under his eyes, and when he faced the sailors, a cigarette dangled from his mouth.

"Couldn't get laid, could you?" he asked. "Even in a whorehouse."

The two sailors glanced at each other, and then one said, "Maybe I was saving my energy for you." The sailor threw a roundhouse blow Nicky saw coming long before it arrived.

Lamm was knocked off the stool and fell into a waiter carrying a tray of drinks. The waiter yelped, the drinks sprayed all over Nicky, and everyone in the room looked in his direction.

"Well, smart mouth," asked the sailor who had slugged Lamm, "you going to get up or what?"

Nicky shook his head. Blood ran down his face from where his nose had been broken. Again. The sailor who'd thrown the punch kicked Nicky in the ribs. Lamm rolled away, into the stools.

"Hey, take it outside," said the bartender from the far end of the bar. He glanced nervously at the door.

"We can't take it outside," said the sailor who had hit Nicky. "The coward won't fight."

The other sailor spat on Nicky. "War hero, my ass. Coward, that's what you are. You're still running, aren't you?"

Hands were put under his arms and Lamm was hauled to his feet and dragged toward the door. People stared, but no one said anything. Just another brawl between the army and the navy. They'd seen it before.

As the three went through the door, they were met by the shore patrol. The two sailors dropped Lamm and ran for the rear of the bar. It didn't do them any good. The shore patrol was there, too. Cuffs were put on the two men and they were led away.

One of the waitresses bent over Lamm. "Ed, you'd better call an ambulance. This one's coughing up blood."

The nurse woke Nicky for another pill. When she did, his face formed a broken smile. "You're not going to try to steal me from my girlfriend, are you?"

Taking his pulse, the nurse said, "I'm a married woman, fella." The woman inclined her head toward the door leading to the hospital corridor. "You've got a visitor, and it ain't your girlfriend."

Of course it wasn't his girlfriend. His girlfriend was risking her life while he was making pitches for war bonds. Nicky didn't think there was a manufacturing plant or training center in the Midwest he'd missed giving his standard oration about escaping from Bataan and Corregidor. Damn, but things had gone downhill fast after that week at home.

A trip out to the barn housing the Lockheed Sirius low-winged monoplane hadn't been enough to make him forget the sacrifice others were making. The Sirius was the first plane he'd ever built, and as Nicky ran his hand over a fuselage made of wooden slats glued together and covered with wrapping paper, bright paper so the girls could see him from the ground, he wondered how long he would last as a "war bond salesman."

Upon reaching the West Coast, Nicky learned the stories in the newspapers and on the radio about the gallant MacArthur thumbing his nose at the Japanese had fired up his fellow countrymen against their own, especially Japanese-Americans living near burgeoning airplane plants and other war factories. Over a hundred thousand Americans of Japanese descent had been rounded up and sent off to concentration camps. Gooks, chinks, or Chinese were America's friends, but the "goddamn Japs" were an entirely different matter.

In St. Louis, near his hometown, Nicky found that his sisters had taken factory jobs to support the war effort. No one could buy new automobiles, toothpaste in tubes, or beer in cans; the military had first call on any and all metal. His sisters worked in Budweiser's plant that made flashlights.

Everyone talked about something called "The Victory Program," but Nicky didn't feel like a participant. His sisters would come home, change out of their work clothes on the screened porch on the back of the house, slip into housecoats, and fight over whose turn it was to bathe first. The whole country was on "war time," meaning year-round daylight savings time. Butter, sugar, coffee, and meat were all being rationed. As was gasoline, not to save gas but to increase the life of your tires. The speed limit nationwide was now thirty-five miles per hour.

At the War Department, Chief of Staff George Marshall had pinned some medal on him. Nicky never wore it unless ordered to do so. Washington had changed, too. It was said more than fifty thousand people had moved to the nation's capital since the bombing of Pearl Harbor. Government employment had doubled and the District of Columbia was issuing more than a thousand building permits each month!

Formal exams for positions had been dropped. If you could type and had a high school diploma, kiss the family good-bye, get on the next train, and head for Union Station—where it would be impossible to find a cab. Or a room to spend the night.

No matter, girls. Sit down, start typing, and remember to keep an eye on your bags. Washington isn't what it used to be—or would be ever again.

The once-beautiful mall was cluttered with hideous-looking buildings, each about half a city block long with wings jutting out. Foundations were of concrete, walls gray, which after a few hard rains became streaked with grime. And this was a project President Roosevelt had taken time from the war effort to design? What was the country coming to?

A major from administrative services was Nicky's visitor. The tall man had a beak for a nose and wore a serious look. "They say everything will mend. You just need a couple of weeks."

"Does this mean I can't make the next stop on the tour?" asked Nicky sarcastically.

"Captain Lamm, it is quite obvious that your presence is a detriment to our mission. No one will go out with you in the evening, even for dinner, because of the number of fights you have picked."

"You got a witness says I threw the first punch?"

"No, but we have had quite enough of your baiting. Since you wish to return to the front, orders are being cut as we speak."

Despite the pain in his chest, Nicky sat up. "When do I leave?"

"Once the hospital releases you, you'll be flown overseas. If you're lucky, you'll arrive in time for the invasion of Europe."

Nicky put his hands behind his head and smiled. "Just what I wanted to hear."

"Captain Lamm. All you had to do was ask."

✳   ✳   ✳

When Churchill had made his trip to Moscow to give Stalin the news there would be no Second Front until at least 1943, the Soviet premier was incensed.

"Why stick your head in the alligator's mouth in France," asked Churchill rather casually, "when you can go to the Mediterranean and rip apart his belly?"

Stalin had to agree. His country needed supplies from the West to survive, and the communist leader informed the prime minister of the progress his country was making in production of weapons. To add emphasis, or shame the West into action, Stalin told Churchill how his army would destroy the Germans.

The Soviets' plan was to wear down the Germans as they attempted to seize Stalingrad. To seize the city, German soldiers would have to climb or crawl through the rubble that had once been apartment buildings, factories, and shops, and would have to struggle over bomb-created craters and piles of concrete, wire, and reinforcement bars which reinforced nothing. This was the deadly mistake the German army had made. They had leveled Stalingrad, and leveled the playing field.

Hundreds were killed on each side as they attempted to seize this pile or that pile of rubble. T-34s smoldered, issuing the smell of the men who had died inside their armored shell. The German army had experienced street fighting before, but this was enough to drive a person mad. On came the Russians using captured German weapons, shouting "Urrah!" or "Kill!"

The German command staff recognized the symptoms and threw five infantry divisions and two tank divisions supported by artillery and the *Luftwaffe* at the damned city. The diary of the German 62nd Army is a classic example of the ebb and flow of the struggle. At eight o'clock in the morning of September 14 wrote the diarist: "Stalingrad train station in enemy hands." At 8:40: "Station recaptured." At 9:40: "Station retaken by enemy." At 13:20: "Station in our hands once again."

With no way to evacuate the wounded, soldiers on both sides had to listen to the screams and pleas of the wounded as they passed them coming and going, or as they thrust forward or were pushed back. Even those ferrying refugees and the wounded across the Volga were not safe. The *Borodino* went down filled with Russian soldiers so injured they could reach neither shore, then a thousand civilians drowned when the steamer *Iosif Stalin* was sunk. Would this hell ever end?

Not as long as Adolf Hitler was obsessed with destroying Joseph Stalin's namesake. Finally, the Fourth Panzer Army reached the Volga at two different points and Stalingrad was completely encircled. That was when the Soviets sprung their trap.

In the west, the Germans had to contend with partisans cutting the Bryansk to Kharkov rail line near Lokot in the western Soviet Union. Now the Germans struck back. In a concentrated effort lasting two weeks, more than two thousand partisans were killed or captured. The Soviets, however, knew the lay of the land much better, and the partisans slipped away, regrouping to the north. In a mocking tone, these same partisans notified the Russian High Command that they were accepting reinforcements and any equipment the High

Command chose to parachute into their location. Reinforcements were parachuted in a few weeks later.

There is a tendency to think resistance fighters are people who are left behind and have finally had enough of the brutality of the occupier and decided to fight back. This wasn't how the Russian High Command did business. After reinforcing the partisans in the north, another hundred partisans were dropped behind German lines north of Novorossisk. This second airdrop was a reaction to the success of a German offensive that had wiped out the partisans in that area. The leader of the second group was said to be a Jew, and the infuriated Germans began sweeps through the area searching for this particularly damnable Bolshevik.

Soviet marines, traveling by ferry, reached Stalingrad under intense bombardment and took up positions in the city's grain elevator. The marines probably wished they hadn't survived the trip. They had to beat off nearly a dozen German attacks before the end of the first day.

A few days later, German troops reached the Stalingrad tractor factory, converted to the production of T-34 tanks, at the center of the city, and for the first time, the Nazi swastika flew over the headquarters of the communist party; still, the Russians refused to surrender. Hitler dismissed General Franz Halder and replaced him with General Kurt Zeitzler. Zeitzler was as nervous as General Halder had been about the German army being locked in a desperate struggle to take a city that had little to do with seizing oil fields in the Caucasus. Did the Fatherland have enough soldiers to push forward along the whole Russian Front?

While Zeitzler was waiting for a reply to his request for more support, the Russians launched a counterattack with two thousand fresh Siberian troops. The fighting became hand-to-hand, and slowly but steadily the Germans were pushed back through the cellars and ruins of the buildings. Ground zero, as Premier Stalin had predicted, was the rubble that had once been the city of Stalingrad.

Seven hundred miles north of the Volga, Soviet troops crossed the river, pushed back the Germans, and made plans to do even further damage—as both German Generals Franz Halder and Kurt Zeitzler had predicted. German soldiers were trying to secure ruins that had once been Stalingrad while their enemy was flanking them and closing its trap.

Still, there were Germans who remained excited about their work. One was Wernher von Braun, who bubbled with enthusiasm after the successful launching of a twelve-ton rocket capable of carrying a one-ton warhead more than two hundred miles. Upon learning of the test results, Hitler didn't have to calculate the distance from occupied France to London. He quickly authorized the rocket's mass production.

The Germans weren't the only ones with secret weapons up their sleeves. Brigadier General Leslie R. Groves was summoned to Washington, where he was ordered to construct an "atomic bomb." General Groves was told that money was no object. George Marshall wrote him a check for a hundred million dollars.

FOURTEEN

On board the merchant ship *Fitzhugh*, McKenzie lay in her bunk. Above her in the other bunk lay Anastasia.

What would she do with the girl? She'd only agreed to adopt the child to get her out of Russia. McKenzie turned on her side and tried to sleep. What a pickle she had gotten herself in.

Thinking of pickles made her remember her other plight. The smell of food had begun to nauseate her, almost as soon as she had stepped aboard the *Fitzhugh*. She couldn't eat anything; worse, accompanying Anastasia to breakfast each morning, she'd have to leave the girl and rush outside. After retching and throwing up her last meal, or suffering the dry heaves, McKenzie would wipe her face covered with sweat. Passing sailors laughed and continued by.

Returning by ship from Russia, she had never once been ill. Others had thrown up; even Antonio Petrocelli had become a bit green around the gills, but not her. And certainly not James. McKenzie sat up on her bunk bed and swung her feet over the side to the floor. She couldn't be pregnant. It wasn't possible.

It was possible. In a bunk bed much like the one where she now slept, she and James had made wild, passionate love—but only once or twice.

Tears ran down her cheeks. And why was she crying? Every once in a while she would feel so low that she would burst into tears. It upset Annie, and she finally told the child that she missed James so much.

McKenzie wiped the tears away. Her life was over. She would spend the rest of her life tending a baby.

She hit the mattress with her fist. "I will not be a patsy like my mother. I will not."

Twenty-six years of age and forced into a marriage and the adoption of a child—how had this happened? She didn't stand a snowball's chance in hell of wrestling control of her father's newspaper from Jacob Nye.

She could hear the chugging of the engines as the *Fitzhugh* made its way across the North Atlantic. Another story wasted. It was as if she'd never been to Russia or run the paper's bureau in London. Once those controlling the board of *The Record* learned of her pregnancy, she'd be relegated to the copy desk.

McKenzie got to her feet and made her way to the wash basin, where she rinsed out her mouth with some tooth powder and spit it out. Then she blotted away the tracks of her tears. Returning to her bunk, she fumbled around for her cigarettes, found them in the pocket of her greatcoat, and lit one.

She was pregnant with James Stuart's child, and not only did the louse not know about it, but she had tried hard to forget those nights when her body had betrayed her and she had given in to James's demands.

James's demands! He hadn't been the only needy person in that bed. No wonder she was pregnant.

McKenzie glanced at the greatcoat, bit her lip, and pulled out the envelope her hand had touched so many times when fishing around for her cigarettes. Why didn't she just put her smokes in the other damn pocket?

She opened the envelope and took out the letter. It was one single page. Right to the point. Just like James Stuart.

> *My dearest McKenzie,*
>
> *I was sorry to hear of the death of your father and more distressed over your leaving for the States. I only wish I had been able to be there to see you and Anastasia off.*
>
> *Though we have been separated ever since returning from the Soviet Union, I want you to know that both you and the child have been on my mind constantly.*
>
> *Please take care in the decision of your next adventure. You have a choice how to lead your life. A soldier does not.*
> *All my love,*
> *James*
> *P.S. If you should have a chance to phone my aunt when you return to the States,*

please inform her that I am doing as well as can be expected under the circumstances.

Eyes wet, McKenzie refolded the letter and stuffed it into the pocket of the greatcoat. She wiped the tears away with the back of her hand. The baby growing inside her was a Stuart. She would be giving birth to a child whose father came from landed gentry and had some very peculiar ideas about women.

Well, thought McKenzie, straightening up, she would brook no interference in her life. She was headed to New York to give Jacob Nye the fight of his life. McKenzie snuffed out the cigarette and turned in for the night. When she got to the States, she would find a nanny for Anastasia. And a proper school. In addition, buy the child some proper clothes. Oh, God, she was crying again.

Wolfgang Topp was one of four seamen on watch, and hiding from the spray behind the superstructure of the U-boat. The moon danced behind clouds, their boat was beyond the normal range of the British air and sea forces, and beneath Wolfgang, the diesels throbbed as the boat made twelve to fourteen knots through a sea that had six- to ten-foot waves.

Wolfgang had a towel wrapped around his neck, but cascades of water lashed the bridge and the towel was soaked. Water ran down his back and chest. With the binoculars held to his eyes, his sleeves became another easy entry for water to reach his chest despite his heavy oil clothing. From there, the water ran down his trousers and into his boots. Every once in a while someone would try to stomp some feeling back into his feet, and water would spray the boots of everyone on deck.

"Check direction two-eight-oh," said the 1st officer.

Ever since the foul-up that had caused the boat to become stuck on the bottom, the 1st officer had pulled extra watches, determined to make up for his error. Still, the crew noticed the young man no longer trusted his judgment. He always asked for a second opinion, and there were jokes made that the exec probably queried for opinions before moving his bowels.

"Shadow bearing at two-eight-oh," confirmed the petty officer in charge of the watch.

Through his glasses Wolfgang could see that seven to eight thousand meters ahead of the boat appeared a faint shape, followed by another, then another.

"It's a convoy!" shouted Wolfgang, pulling the glasses from his eyes.

The 1st officer nodded. "Yes, I believe it is."

Two more sets of binoculars had spotted the shadows moving west. The icy chill of the spray was forgotten as the submariners turned their backs on the shapes and scanned the North Atlantic for more than this convoy. Rumor had it that their commander was taking them to a point where neither the American nor the British air cover—a hole in the Allied coverage—could reach them. Destroyers, however, could. Were there any British destroyers out there?

"Captain to the bridge!" shouted the petty officer.

The 1st officer beamed at his companions. His subordinates beamed back with excitement, anticipation, and dread. They were about to go hunting.

Below deck, the order passed through the ship, and moments later the captain appeared. Once his eyes adjusted to the darkness, he was able to make out the line of ships. The commander did a three-hundred-sixty rotation with his glasses, scanning the waters surrounding his small craft in this very large ocean, then the dark sky.

"Not a destroyer on this side of the formation and that is the last freighter," confirmed the captain.

As orders were given for the 2nd officer to plot the attack, the destroyer veered off and headed toward them.

"My God!" exclaimed the exec. "They have spotted us."

Through the voice tube on the tower the captain ordered the radioman to tune to the six-hundred-meter wavelength used for international traffic and see if their boat had been detected. In short order, the reply came back in the negative.

"Ah," said the captain. "Not enough firepower so they are sailing in a weave pattern."

To Wolfgang, the exec explained. "Sailing back and forth among the convoy."

Through the hatch, the captain shouted, "Battle stations. Left full rudder. Steer two-eight-oh. Both engines full ahead together. And," he added through the voice tube, "have someone continue to monitor the six-hundred-meter wavelength."

There were two other U-boats in their pack, and as the strong night binoculars were fastened atop the target-bearing transmitter, Wolfgang heard the coordinates of the convoy flashed to the other two U-boats.

The extra seaman was ordered below but not Topp. Wolfgang continued to peer through his binoculars and ignore the freezing water spraying across his front. The 1st officer was adjusting the Siemens-Schukert torpedo computer, linked to the master sight, gyro compass, and fire interval calculator. Below them the torpedo gang had rushed to their tubes. Wolfgang could hardly contain his excitement.

Information from the other members of the pack told them they were on their own. One boat was having difficulties with its engine; the other was so far south it would have to cut off the convoy several hundred kilometers from its current position.

"Well," replied the captain, "I have one ship in my sights and another bearing down on me. I am going into action."

Water sprayed Wolfgang as the commander demanded more and more power from his engine room. The boat was into the wind now, waves crashing over the bow and lashing the tower.

"Sir," offered the exec, "perhaps we should wait until the destroyer passes."

"And why is that?" asked the older man without taking his eyes from his binoculars. "These are the last two ships in the convoy and the destroyer is about to take away my angle of attack. I want them both and I am determined to have them."

Steve Brown

Binoculars trained on the British destroyer, Wolfgang realized it would be close. Actually, Wolfgang failed to see how their boat could miss a collision with the larger ship if the captain was intent on firing on both the merchant ship and the destroyer.

The 2nd officer took fresh readings and relayed them to the conning tower. "What's the target's course and speed?" he asked.

From the tower came: "Target speed twenty knots, course two-six-oh."

Wolfgang gulped. Seconds after they emptied their tubes, the destroyer would cross their path. Wolfgang looked at the captain. The commander did not appear overly concerned about the destroyer's bearing down on their position.

After checking and double-checking the numbers, and less than a thousand meters from the freighter, the captain gave the order to fire both tubes and quickly reload. Once the torpedoes were away, immediate orders were given for their boat to swing around hard, lining up its bow with the destroyer crossing *their* course. A bearing was given to the captain and he shouted it to those below deck.

This was followed by orders to make ready to dive, and Wolfgang and the other members of the topside crew were ordered below. As Wolfgang slid down the ladder, their craft's nose was brought around and he heard the captain shout, "Fire! Fire!" Two more torpedoes splashed ahead of the sub, now on a collision course with the destroyer.

As Wolfgang's feet slammed into the deck of the control room, the torpedoes hit both ships almost simultaneously.

"Dive! Dive!" shouted the captain, the last man down the ladder. He closed the hatch behind him.

The exec faced the captain. The younger man still had the strong night binoculars in his hands.

"Full speed on the dive," demanded the captain, ignoring the exec's look. "All seamen not at essential stations move to the bow."

With that Wolfgang started forward, following his mates, once again, practically into the torpedo tubes, which had already been reloaded.

"Everyone forward," came the order from several of the petty officers moving the laggards along.

"What are we doing?" asked members of the crew as they stumbled through hatches toward the bow.

"Trying to slip under a destroyer," Wolfgang informed them.

"But what of the depth charges?" asked another.

"The least of our worries."

On the *Fitzhugh* the thud of the torpedo's impact rocked McKenzie out of her bunk. Annie was thrown out, too, and landed on top of her mother.

"Mama! Mama! What's happening?"

The girl clutched McKenzie as they staggered to their feet. The deck was uneven under them.

Someone was at the door. "Mrs. Stuart! Mrs. Stuart!"

McKenzie grabbed her coat and slipped into it. She wasn't fast enough and the hatch opened in her face.

"Oh," said the sailor, a man McKenzie recognized as

the ship's first mate. "Sorry, ma'am, but we've taken a hit and the ship's going down. The captain assigned me to make sure you and the girl get off."

"How much time do we have, Mr. Hawthorne?"

"Ten minutes at the most."

"I would think you have important gear to move into the boats?"

"Yes, ma'am, but—"

"Then Annie and I will meet you topside."

"Er—yes, ma'am, but I'm sure that the captain will ask me to return to check on you."

When the sailor closed the hatch, McKenzie turned to the girl. "Annie, do you need to use the bathroom?"

The girl nodded. "Yes, Mama." She glanced at the deck. "I almost wet my pants."

"Then let's take care of that before we get into a boat with a bunch of sailors."

On the German submarine, a voice from the control room reached those of the crew huddled in the bow: "Two hundred meters to target. Depth two meters."

Someone cursed, others prayed, many held their breath.

Moments later, the voice said, "One hundred meters to target. Depth five meters."

The sub shuddered and rocked as the destroyer ripped itself apart above them. Wolfgang's hand was jerked from a handle and he hit someone on the head. Before he could apologize, the same had been done to him. Sweat ran partly because of the close quarters, partly because of the next call from the control room, where everyone could imagine the officers, several of the petty officers, and the essential personnel staring, not at the gauges, but overhead.

"Fifty meters to target. Depth eight meters."

"What if the ship breaks up and sinks on top of us?"

A petty officer laughed. "You have watched too many movies. Ships take a long time to die, and if you are lucky, we will resurface on the far side of the convoy and be able to watch the end of the show."

Wolfgang finally understood. That was why the captain had taken both shots. Not only did he have the kills, but now he planned to make it to the safety of the far side of the convoy where there were no destroyers.

"Twenty meters to target."

Quickly followed by, "Fourteen meters to target."

Then: "Target directly overhead."

When Hawthorne returned to McKenzie's cabin, he tapped on the hatch before opening it. The woman's musette bag sat on the bunk and the bulkheads tilted, but not too severely. The woman and child were dressed warmly, but not in those greatcoats they had worn aboard. The greatcoats lay on the upper bunk with other items they would not be taking along. They were now wearing slickers with sweaters underneath.

"We're ready to go," she said to the first mate. Around McKenzie's neck hung a camera; her Jimmy Olsen had been left behind in London. The camera was a gift from her husband, though where he had located it in wartime England McKenzie had no idea.

My God, thought McKenzie, gripping Annie's hand

so hard that the child yelped, at moments like this it becomes clear what's important and what's not. James Stuart had had one of those moments in Moscow and he had married her to smuggle Anastasia out of the country. Not that James had the time, but no solicitor had served divorce papers on her.

How did that stack up to what she had done since arriving in England? James was off on another mission for his country while she was cheating on him. Not once had she thought of her first husband while reporting from the English Channel where Jeremy Rivers had officially been declared missing in action.

And the child she carried. It was James's and hers. She had to take care of it. She had to protect this baby. Still, there was one last story to report. McKenzie smiled inwardly. The old McKenzie Rivers died hard.

The first mate was surprised to see both woman and child were wearing the new life jackets, called life vests, and had their helmets on their heads. A field cap was crammed in the woman's pocket. Moreover, when she raised her hand so her slicker slipped back from her cuff, Hawthorne saw the luminous dial worn inside her wrist.

"Er—let me take that for you, ma'am." The first mate reached for the bags, and the two of them preceded Hawthorne out the door. "I don't think the captain will believe you're packed and ready to go."

"My husband taught me to always keep everything in my bag while we were at sea, no matter how inconvenient that might be." In the muster bag was an extra set of clothing, another camera, film, and four of McKenzie's favorite lenses.

"Smart man, your husband. Is he with the army or the navy?"

"I'm not sure. He appears to be able to change branches at will."

Hawthorne grinned. "No doubt the attraction."

On the submarine, there was a collective holding of breath as the men contemplated the height of their conning tower versus the displacement of the enemy vessel.

"Sixteen meters," came the voice from the conning tower.

"Return to your stations," ordered the chief.

The crew did, letting out sighs of relief, then whoops of joy. Ten minutes later, the captain ordered the boat to surface.

"Come along, Wolfgang," said the exec with a grin. "Let's see what we have."

Topside on the *Fitzhugh*, McKenzie saw lifeboats being swung over the side and a line forming at each station. The wind kicked up as she stepped back and snapped off a shot. Dawn had broken over the horizon, and opening the lens for maximum exposure, McKenzie snapped photographs as Annie stood by her side, gripping her mother's slicker.

"Ma'am, we need to get you into the boat."

"Mr. Hawthorne," said McKenzie, lowering her camera but looking at the sea instead of at the sailor, "I know which lifeboat is ours. We attended the drills. Now, if you would be so kind as to put my bag in the boat. My daughter, too."

"Mama, I want to stay with you."

McKenzie looked at her daughter for the first time. She was responsible for this child as well. "But only if you'll keep a hand on my slicker at all times."

"Yes, Mama."

"Er—Mrs. Stuart," said the first mate, "I'm not so sure about this."

Taking a picture of the destroyer that had been hit, McKenzie said, "Mr. Hawthorne, I know you have a tradition of women and children first, but I have a job to do and my daughter wishes to remain at my side while I do that job. Please honor her wishes."

"But the captain says—"

"Mr. Hawthorne, if you don't mind." McKenzie used a hand to guide him out of her line of sight. "Please stand aside. I want to shoot in the other direction."

Sailors ran past them as the first mate said, "I'd best check with the captain."

"If you're not going to place our bag in the lifeboat, please leave it here. Something my husband taught me: never leave your gear under combat conditions."

"Er—yes, ma'am."

When the Germans rushed topside, binoculars were swung around to check the ocean, then the dawn sky. There were fires on the surface of the ocean, but they were of little interest to those on the conning tower. German eyes were searching for danger, such as other destroyers steaming their way.

The damaged destroyer was half in and half out of

the water, smoke pouring from her as the water doused her flames. The radio crackled with news of the attack on the international frequency, and as calls of Mayday went out, the British destroyer fought back. Depth charges sprayed the sea around the dying ship even as lifeboats were lowered away.

As Wolfgang eyed the freighter, he saw the ship was dead in the water. Wolfgang wondered why those people would risk crossing the Atlantic when they knew this ocean belonged to the German people. A woman in a yellow slicker stood on one side of the ship calmly snapping photographs. When she pointed the camera in his direction, he waved. His commander saw this and spoke to him sharply.

"I rather doubt she sees this in the same light as you do, Topp."

Wolfgang lowered his hand, turned in the opposite direction, and, using his glasses, searched the ocean for other dangers.

Anastasia said, "That man is returning, Mama."

"Why thank you, Annie." McKenzie snapped a long-range shot of what she thought was the superstructure of a German U-boat, then pulled down the camera. She smiled at her daughter when she knelt in front of her. "We work well together, don't you think?"

Surprise showed on the girl's face. "Yes, Mama."

McKenzie noticed Anastasia wasn't holding onto her but gripping a railing on the bulkhead. The tilt of the deck wasn't all that bad, but water had soaked the deck from the torpedo splash.

"Time to go, Mrs. Stuart."

McKenzie smiled as she stood. "Thanks for your patience, Mr. Hawthorne."

"I don't make the rules, but they are to be followed. I only say that because you'll be under my command once we board the boat. Step this way, please." He showed McKenzie and Annie over to the Number Six lifeboat where their shipmates were already seated.

No one was smiling and it had nothing to do with the Stuarts' tardiness. When McKenzie stepped into the boat, she went into water to her hips, another present from Jerry's torpedo splash. Annie stood on a seat out of the water while everyone held onto a line to be lowered away.

Once Hawthorne was aboard, he moved about the boat, pulling plugs as they were lowered away. The water quickly ran out of the holes, the plugs were replaced, and Hawthorne gave the all-clear signal for the lifeboat to make its final descent to the sea.

The boat hit the water, the lines were let loose, and everyone sat down. Seated beside Hawthorne was a Baptist minister who had been caught smuggling bibles into the Soviet Union; at home he would tell the world about godless communism. There was a very hardy and fat merchant returning to the States with orders for any and everything; whether he would be able to fill those orders he didn't know. He had left the States before rationing had been put into effect.

An American soldier said he was quite ill, actually on his way home to die. McKenzie, however, noticed the soldier always cleaned his plate at meals and could be seen lying in the sun on the deck. Probably AWOL, but his money was as good as anyone else's on a ship where papers might not be so closely inspected.

The AWOL soldier sat next to a bureaucrat who worked for some secret agency of the government, at least that is what he had told everyone. The bureaucrat constantly glanced around, especially to see who was approaching him from behind. On the seat in front of him sat the O'Learys, an Irish-American couple who had taught English in Moscow for the past ten years. Mrs. O'Leary welcomed Anastasia into her arms.

"This is quite an adventure, isn't it, my dear?"

The little girl grinned. "Mama says she and I work well together."

"Make a good team," interjected Mr. O'Leary.

Annie was puzzled at the different phraseology but dutifully repeated the phrase "make a team" several times. Mr. O'Leary was determined that Annie would know the proper American slang before reaching the States. O'Leary even knew some words McKenzie didn't recognize, and she wondered if they were in common usage stateside. McKenzie got to her feet, taking a last shot of the dying ship.

Hawthorne announced there would be plenty of time for photographs, but this boat wasn't going anywhere without its passengers taking out their oars and putting their backs to it. Everyone but the sick soldier dragged the oars out of storage and fitted them into their oarlocks. Around them the seas had calmed.

A general directive followed regarding who would sit where so the lifeboat would be rowed straight ahead and not in circles. Once Hawthorne was satisfied, he moved the wounded soldier where he could handle the tiller, and they rowed away from the starboard side of the *Fitzhugh*, where she had taken the hit.

As Hawthorne rowed, he leaned back to McKenzie. "Wouldn't mind having a copy of that picture you took for me mom, Mrs. Stuart."

"And you will if you can get me and my daughter on one of those ships over there."

An explosion more than a mile away punctuated her remark. The U-boat had torpedoed another ship. Across the surface came the sound of a klaxon.

"I'll surely do that. If there are any ships left."

In Washington, D.C., the War Department, at last housed in what was called the "Pentagon," where guides became lost and virgins emerged as mothers after days of wandering its corridors, generals waited for word from the beaches of North Africa.

Katherine Marshall had tickets to a night game played by the Washington Redskins football club, and she left the Pentagon in a huff when her husband, the chief of staff of the army, would not accede to her demands to accompany her to the game. Instead, Hap Arnold and his wife took Katherine Marshall to the game.

During the game, loudspeakers blared: "The President of the United States announces the successful landing of American soldiers on the African coast."

Katherine Marshall couldn't contain her excitement. Eleven months after Pearl Harbor, America had finally struck back.

Several of the lifeboats from the *Fitzhugh* had lashed themselves together and formed a floating city in which one of the boats had been set aside for the women and Annie. It was chilly, so a ration of rum was passed out, along with slices of canned meat and cheese. The American bureaucrat said he should have a more liberal ration, that he carried information valuable to the war effort. Mr. Hawthorne told him to shut up or he'd throw him over the side, and they'd all share his ration.

Anastasia said, "I read in a book that there are sharks in the ocean."

"Too cold for sharks, I would think," replied her mother, knowing nothing of the habits of sharks.

"I bet we'll get to see a whale or two." Mrs. O'Leary glanced in the direction of the orange sun breaking the surface to the east.

"I'd rather see another ship," said her husband from the adjoining boat.

Anastasia clutched her mother. "I want Papa!"

"We all want your papa," said her mother, hugging the girl and thinking how safe she always felt when James Stuart was around. Wherever James Stuart was, McKenzie wished she was with him now.

Dawn arrived in North Africa and men splashed ashore. Behind them came the tanks. In one of them rode James Stuart and his driver, Antonio Petrocelli. Only twenty yards inland, a mine blew off the right track and their tank sat helpless, other members of the unit moving ahead of them. Stuart turned his command over to Rankin Jones.

"What now, boss?" asked Petrocelli from the driver's seat. Next to him, the loader's eyes were wide with fear.

Stuart already had the hatch open. "Well, Tony, unless you can repair that track, we walk to Oran."

On the other side of the world, which was still in darkness, a hospital ship was hit by friendly fire. Only by turning on its lights could the ship identify itself. The American destroyer apologized for scaring the hell out of wounded soldiers and sailors who thought they had put the war behind them.

Chief nurse Ann Anderson asked for a head count. The only member missing was Katie O'Kelly.

"I think she went down to the supply room," volunteered one of the nurses.

"The supply room—wasn't that the side that was hit?"

Anderson rushed out of the ward, down the corridor, and slid down the stairs like an experienced sailor. Entering the corridor, her hand came to her mouth. The hatch to the supply room had been blown open.

Rushing to the opening, Anderson found a hole in the side of the ship above the waterline large enough to drive a truck through.

"Katie?"

No answer.

"Katie," called Anderson again, stepping among the shambles that had once been the medical supplies. "Katie O'Kelly, are you there?"

EPILOGUE

On the afternoon of November 7, 1942, Adolf Hitler left the Eastern Front for Munich. In the early hours of the morning, his train was signaled to a halt at a railway station. There was an urgent message for *Der Führer* from Berlin. Allied invasion forces were disembarking at Algiers, Oran, and Casablanca.

About the Author

After graduating from the University of North Alabama
with a degree in history and political science,
Steve Brown served as a combat platoon leader
with the 25th Infantry Division in South Vietnam.
A member of Mystery Writers of America,
Brown is the author of the popular
Susan Chase™ mysteries. He is also the author of
Fallen Stars, which deals with the long-range
recon patrols (Lurps) that operated during the
Vietnam War. He lives with his family in
South Carolina. You can contact Steve through
www.chicksprings.com.

Bibliography

These are just some of the books that have kept alive my interest in the Second World War:

A Soldier's Story, by Omar N. Bradley
Above & Beyond, by Charles Patrick Weiland
Andrew Jackson Higgins and the Boats That Won World War Two, by Jerry E. Strahan
A Genius for War, by Carlo D'Este
American Caesar, by William Manchester
Barbarossa, by Alan Clark
Crusade in Europe, by Dwight D. Eisenhower
Churchill: A Life, by Martin Gilbert
Delivered from Evil, by Robert Leckie
DeShazer, by C. Hoyt Watson
Doolittle, by Lowell Thomas and Edward Jablonski
Douglas MacArthur, by Michael Schaller
Eisenhower, by Stephen E. Ambrose
Eisenhower, by Geoffrey Perret
F.D.R., by Nathan Miller
General of the Army, by Ed Cray
George C. Marshall, by Forrest C. Pogue
God's Samurai, by Gordon W. Prange with Donald M.Goldstein and Katherine V. Dillon
Guadalcanal Diary, by Richard Tregaskis
Guadalcanal Remembered, by Herbert Christian Merillat
Harry Hopkins, by Henry H. Adams
Her War Story, edited by Sayre P. Sheldon
I Could Never Be So Lucky, by General James H. "Jimmy" Doolittle with Carroll V. Glines
In and Out of Harm's Way, by Doris M. Sterner
Iron Coffins, by Herbert A. Werner
Japan's War, by Edwin P. Hoyt

Mark Clark: The Last of the Great World War II Commanders, by Martin Blumenson

Marshall: A Hero for Our Times, by Leonard Mosley

Midway: The Battle That Doomed Japan, by Mitsuo Fuchida and Masatake Okumiya of the Imperial Japanese Navy

Montgomery as Military Commander, by Ronald Lewin

No Ordinary Time, by Doris Kearns Goodwin

No Time for Fear, by Diane Burke Fessler

The Pacific Campaign, by Dan van der Vat

The Pacific War, by John Costello

Their Finest Hour, by Philip Kaplan

Reporting World War Two, American Journalism 1938–1944

Rommel, by Charles Douglas-Home

Roosevelt, by James MacGregor Burns

Roosevelt and Hopkins, by Robert E. Sherwood

Soldier and Statesman: George Marshall, by Harold Faber

The Amphibians Came to Conquer, by Vice Admiral George Carroll Dyer, USN (Retired)

Stalingrad, by Antony Beevor

The First Team and the Guadalcanal Campaign, by John B. Lundstrom

The First Team, by John B. Lundstrom

The Second World War, by John Keegan

The Second World War, by Martin Gilbert

The Two-Ocean War, by Samuel Eliot Morison

The War Journal of Major Damon "Rocky" Gause, by Major Damon "Rocky" Gause

The Women Who Wrote the War, by Nancy Caldwell Sorel

Twentieth Century Caesar: Benito Mussolini, by Jules Archer

Washington Goes to War, by David Brinkley

We Band of Angels, by Elizabeth M. Norman

Women Recall the War Years, edited by George L. McDermott

World War Two, by Norman Polmar and Thomas Allen

Wolfpack, by Philip Kaplan and Jack Currie

NOTES